POLITICAL POSTMODERNISMS

Political Postmodernisms shows how sites outside of Western Europe and North America undermine an established narrative of architecture theory and history. It focuses specifically on postmodern architecture, which is traditionally understood as embodying the flippant and apolitical aesthetics of capitalist affluence. By investigating postmodern architecture's manifestations in the unlikely settings of Chile during the neoliberal dictatorship of Augusto Pinochet and Poland during the late socialist Polish People's Republic, the book argues for a new account that incorporates the political roles it plays when seen in a global perspective. *Political Postmodernisms* has three goals. First, it challenges the familiar narrative regarding postmodern architecture as following the "cultural logic of late capitalism" (Fredric Jameson) or as a socially conservative project (Jürgen Habermas). Second, it fills in portions of Chilean and Polish architectural history that have been neglected by Chilean and Polish architectural historians themselves. Third, *Political Postmodernisms* shows how architecture can work as a political form – serving propagandistic purposes and functioning as part of oppositional projects. The book is projected to be of use to students and scholars in global modern and contemporary architecture history, history of urban planning, East European Studies, and Latin American Studies.

Lidia Klein is an Assistant Professor in Architectural History at the School of Architecture, University of North Carolina – Charlotte, specializing in global contemporary architecture. She earned her first Ph.D. from the University of Warsaw in Poland in 2013 and her second from Duke University in 2018. Prior to joining UNCC in 2018, Klein was awarded a Fulbright Junior Advanced Research Grant to the AAHVS Department at Duke (2010–2011) and was a Visiting Assistant in Research at the Yale School of Architecture (2016). Her book projects include the single-author study, *Living Architectures: Biological Analogies in Architecture of the End of the 20th Century* (Warsaw: Fundacja Kultury Miejsca, 2014, in Polish) and the edited books *Transformation: Polish Art, Design and Architecture after 1989* (Warsaw: Fundacja Kultury Miejsca, 2017, in Polish) and *Polish Postmodernism: Architecture and Urbanism* (Warsaw: 40000 Malarzy, 2013, in Polish).

The Archi*text* Series

Edited by Thomas A. Markus and Anthony D. King

Architectural discourse has traditionally represented buildings as art objects or technical objects. Yet buildings are also social objects in that they are invested with social meaning and shape social relations. Recognizing these assumptions, the Archi*text* series aims to bring together recent debates in social and cultural theory and the study and practice of architecture and urban design. Critical, comparative and interdisciplinary, the books in the series, by theorizing architecture, bring the space of the built environment centrally into the social sciences and humanities, as well as bringing the theoretical insights of the latter into the discourses of architecture and urban design. Particular attention is paid to issues of gender, race, sexuality and the body, to questions of identity and place, to the cultural politics of representation and language, and to the global and postcolonial contexts in which these are addressed.

Postmodern Architecture in Socialist Poland
Transformation, Symbolic Form and National Identity
Florian Urban

Architecture, State Modernism and Cultural Nationalism in the Apartheid Capital
Hilton Judin

Building Practice in the Dutch East Indies
Epistemic Imposition at the Beginning of the 20th Century
David Hutama Setiadi

Political Postmodernisms
Architecture in Chile and Poland, 1970–1990
Lidia Klein

For more information about this series, please visit: https://www.routledge.com/Architext/book-series/SE0397

POLITICAL POSTMODERNISMS

Architecture in Chile and Poland, 1970–1990

Lidia Klein

LONDON AND NEW YORK

Designed cover image: Model of the Congreso de Chile in Valparaiso (1988–1990, Juan Cárdenas, José Covacevic, and Raúl Farrú), published in "Primer Premio," CA 60 (1990), 31 (Fondo Revista CA, courtesy of Archivo de Originales, FADEU-PUC).

First published 2023
by Routledge
4 Park Square, Milton Park, Abingdon, Oxon OX14 4RN

and by Routledge
605 Third Avenue, New York, NY 10158

Routledge is an imprint of the Taylor & Francis Group, an informa business

© 2023 Lidia Klein

The right of Lidia Klein to be identified as author of this work has been asserted in accordance with sections 77 and 78 of the Copyright, Designs and Patents Act 1988.

All rights reserved. No part of this book may be reprinted or reproduced or utilised in any form or by any electronic, mechanical, or other means, now known or hereafter invented, including photocopying and recording, or in any information storage or retrieval system, without permission in writing from the publishers.

Trademark notice: Product or corporate names may be trademarks or registered trademarks, and are used only for identification and explanation without intent to infringe.

British Library Cataloguing-in-Publication Data
Names: Klein, Lidia, 1983- author.
Title: Political postmodernisms : architecture in Chile and Poland, 1970–1990 / Lidia Klein.
Description: Abingdon, Oxon : Routledge, 2023. | Includes bibliographical references and index. |
Identifiers: LCCN 2022047351 (print) | LCCN 2022047352 (ebook) | ISBN 9781032016542 (hardback) | ISBN 9781032016573 (paperback) | ISBN 9781003179467 (ebook)
Subjects: LCSH: Architecture, Postmodern—Chile. | Architecture, Postmodern—Poland. | Architecture—Political aspects—Chile—History—20th century. | Architecture—Political aspects—Poland—History—20th century.
Classification: LCC NA865.5.P67 K59 2023 (print) | LCC NA865.5.P67 (ebook) | DDC 724/.6—dc23/eng/20230126
LC record available at https://lccn.loc.gov/2022047351
LC ebook record available at https://lccn.loc.gov/2022047352

ISBN: 9781032016542 (hbk)
ISBN: 9781032016573 (pbk)
ISBN: 9781003179467 (ebk)

DOI: 10.4324/9781003179467

Typeset in Bembo
by codeMantra

To Bowie, Salem, and Thomas

CONTENTS

Acknowledgments   *ix*

Introduction   1

    I.1 The "Rise" and "Fall" of Postmodern Architecture and Urbanism 4

    I.2 The Apolitical Legacy as Culminating in Postmodern Revivalism 12

    I.3 Chilean and Polish Postmodernism 16

    I.4 Recent Scholarship on Postmodernism 20

    I.5 Outline 23

1   Postmodernism and the State in Pinochet's Chile   29

    1.1 From Eduardo Frei Montalva and Salvador Allende to Augusto Pinochet: Transformations in Urban Space 30

    1.2 Postmodern Architecture as Propaganda: The Plaza de la Constitución and the Congreso Nacional de Chile 38

2   Postmodernism against the State under Pinochet's Dictatorship   48

    2.1 The Origins of CEDLA and Its Emergence in Santiago 49

    2.2 CEDLA's Project for Santiago Poniente 56

    2.3 Social Housing 62

    2.4 Dissent and Compliance 69

    2.5 Chile's Distinctive Postmodernism 69

viii Contents

3   Socialist Postmodernism in the Polish People's Republic   72

   3.1 Postmodern Architecture and Propaganda in the Polish People's Republic 72

   3.2 Architektura 74

   3.3 Na Skarpie Estate (Centrum E) 79

4   Postmodernism and Dissent in Socialist Poland   90

   4.1 Oppositional Postmodernism: Czesław Bielecki and the DiM Group 90

   4.2 Reforming the System from within: Marek Budzyński and the Legacy of Socialist Realism 96

   4.3 North Ursynów: City, Church, and Continuity 100

   4.4 Poland's Distinctive Postmodernism 114

Conclusion: Postmodernism as a Political Form   *119*
Appendix: Interviews   *123*

   Interview with Humberto Eliash, August 23, 2016 123

   Interview with Pedro Murtinho, August 30, 2016 127

   Interview with Pedro Murtinho, September 1, 2016 128

   Interview with Pilar Garcia, September 1, 2016 129

   Interview with Cristián Boza, September 5, 2016 130

   Interview with Fernando Pérez Oyarzún, September 6, 2016 132

   Interview with Humberto Eliash, September 7, 2016 133

   Interview with Fernando Pérez Oyarzún, September 12, 2016 134

   Interview with Marta Leśniakowska, June 5, 2017 136

   Interview with Czesław Bielecki, June 9, 2017 137

   Interview with Romuald Loegler, July 1, 2017 138

   Interview with Wojciech Szymborski (WS) and Ludwika Borawska Szymborska (LBS), July 26, 2021 140

Bibliography   *143*
Index   *149*

ACKNOWLEDGMENTS

This book would not have been possible without the Chilean and Polish architects and scholars who agreed to devote their time and expertise to conduct interviews with me: Czesław Bielecki, Cristián Boza, Humberto Eliash, Pilar Garcia, Marta Leśniakowska, Romuald Loegler, Pedro Murtinho, and Fernando Pérez Oyarzún. I am also immensely grateful to the scholars in Poland and Chile who have been more than generous in sharing their knowledge with me, particularly Fernando Carvajal, Błażej Ciarkowski, Francisco Díaz, and Alicja Gzowska.

Political Postmodernisms started as a dissertation, defended in 2018 at the Department of Art, Art History, and Visual Studies at Duke University. I am deeply and sincerely thankful to my graduate adviser and dissertation director, Annabel Wharton, who urged me to undergo this Ph.D., has steadily guided me with her rigorous approach to research and writing, and has generously offered me her support in many ways that go beyond this project. I am also especially grateful to my dissertation committee, each member of which provided essential feedback as reader of my dissertation: Profs. Esther Gabara, Fredric Jameson, Neil McWilliam, and Alan Plattus who generously agreed to participate from Yale. Many other faculty and staff members helped me in my years at Duke and I would like to thank in particular Profs. Sara Galletti and Rebecca Stein for their continuous support of my research and invaluable professional advice. I would like to thank the AAHVS department for the special assistance and flexibility offered to me in times of need, which allowed me to continue my graduate studies despite tough circumstances. Relatedly, I thank my fellow graduate students not only for their support during that time but also for being great friends in general – above all, Karim Wissa, John Stadler, Adra Raine, Mimi Luse, and Max Symuleski. I am also immensely grateful to Lee Sorensen and all the Lilly Library Staff at Duke for their help and resources over the years.

This book would not be possible without my Visiting Assistant in Research opportunity at the Yale School of Architecture, and I would like to thank the faculty and staff of the school for their generous support, especially Alan Plattus, Robert Stern (Dean of the School at the time), and Keller Easterling. The early research for this book dates back to my first doctoral program at the Art History Department at the University of Warsaw, and

x Acknowledgments

I would like to thank my professors there who are my ongoing inspirations in scholarship and teaching, especially Profs. Waldemar Baraniewski, Maria Poprzęcka, Gabriela Świtek, and Antoni Ziemba.

The task of writing a book requiring research in two continents during subsequent COVID waves was challenging and ultimately made possible thanks to the tremendous help from friends in Poland (Alicja Gzowska) and Chile (Pilar Pinchart, Daphne Agostin) and from family members (specifically, Lisa Salem). Additionally, Diego Vilches and Carlos Silva Cáceres helped tremendously with images for this book when I couldn't get them myself during numerous lockdowns. I am very grateful to Robby Sachs who saved the day with some last-minute photo editing. I also want to thank architecture scholars and friends for their help and support (with this book and beyond): Vladimir Kulić, Michał Murawski, Grzegorz Piątek, Łukasz Stanek, and Kuba Snopek.

I am aware of my great luck to be working in the generous and supportive School of Architecture at UNCC. For their kindness and readiness to help since 2018 while I worked toward turning the dissertation into a book (while also having my second child during COVID), I thank my colleagues and supportive leadership for working tirelessly on my behalf. Many thanks especially to Associate Director Emily Makaš, Directors Chris Jarrett and Blaine Brownell, and Deans Ken Lambla and Brook Muller. The complete list of colleagues to thank for their support would be very long but I need to single out Kathy Bywaletz and Greer Friedrich who helped to organize research trips leading to this book.

Portions of this book have been published with other venues, and I am grateful that the presses have permitted me to reprint versions of them here. Parts of Chapters 2 and 3 can be found in special issue "The Geopolitical Aesthetic of Postmodernism," edited by Maroš Krivý and Léa-Catherine Szacka, in the EAHN (European Architectural History Network) journal *Architectural Histories*, published with the Open Library of Humanities, forthcoming as of the time of writing these acknowledgements. Portions of the introduction were originally published in the anthology *The Contested Territory of Architectural Theory*, edited by Elie Haddad (Routledge Press, 2022). Several paragraphs from Chapter 4 were originally published in an essay coauthored with Alicja Gzowska in the anthology *Second World Postmodernisms: Architecture and Society under Late Socialism*, edited by Vladimir Kulić (Bloomsbury Visual Arts, 2019). I also would like to thank the Association of Polish Architects SARP, the Facultad de Arquitectura y Urbanismo Universidad de Chile and Archivo de Originales, Facultad de Arquitectura, Diseño y Estudios Urbanos at Pontificia Universidad Católica de Chile for giving me permissions to use archival material.

Many thanks are owed to everyone at Routledge who put in their time and skills turning my manuscript into a physical book. I especially want to thank Fran Ford for her interest in the project, her support, and her patience in working with me between 2019 and 2022. I also thank editorial assistant Jake Millicheap for answering countless questions and his overall help in preparing the manuscript.

Finally, I would like to thank my parents – Artur and Monika – and my partner, Thomas. I thank him not only for taking my share of diaper changing and waking up at 3 a.m. for almost two years while we were both writing and struggling to keep our two children alive and not too neglected but also for being the first reader, providing especially useful feedback to my manuscript.

INTRODUCTION

After a period of neglect lasting roughly two decades, architectural postmodernism is on the way back. Renewed interest in postmodern aesthetics and theory can be seen in a proliferation of postmodern buildings and projects worldwide in designs by MVRDV, the New London Fabulous group, and WAM Architecten, to take a few examples, as well as in the academic world of exhibitions, publications, conferences, and symposia. "Postmodernism is no longer a dirty word – or the style that must not be named," Owen Hopkins writes, "as a new generation of architects and designers have begun to reassess and reinterpret its ideals, tactics and aesthetics."[1] Recently, this postmodern revivalism has prompted heated critical discussions on its suitability for today's social, political, and economic environment. In a 2017 article for *Dezeen*, Sean Griffiths writes:

> There is one big reason why now is absolutely not the time to be indulging in postmodern revivalism. Its name is President Donald Trump. And while Donald Trump means that golden Baroque remains transgressive, it is now transgressive in a bad way. Bigly so, to coin a phrase. … As all good postmodernists know, signifiers – the vessels that convey meanings – have a tendency to become untethered from their moorings. In less dangerous times we can delight in their floating free, reveling in the magical manufacture of meaning that the detachment of the signifier from its signified permits. But the artful twisting of meaning through the gentle massaging of signifier is less appealing when the gaps between truth and representation provide a petri dish for the fake news of the alt-right.[2]

For Griffiths, to find inspiration from a current based on playfulness, irony, and formalist aestheticism is to play a dangerous game in the time of fake news and increasingly fragile democracy. The aesthetics of free-floating signifiers was liberating in the wake of structuralism, but that uncoupling from the signified comes with its dangers in a time when the assault against "truth" has especially dire implications. More concretely, the postmodern obsessions with image, superficiality, language, and architectural jokes are misguided in a

DOI: 10.4324/9781003179467-1

2 Introduction

time when architecture needs to address issues like inequality, urban poverty, or climate emergency – issues of material significance that no postmodern sense of play could plausibly address.

This critique joins a broader chorus of anti-postmodern sentiment that understands postmodernism as a style of Western European or North American late capitalist affluent societies that confirms the neoliberal status quo without consideration of the social problems and inequalities inherent to it. Indeed, in both architectural scholarship and the popular discourse on architecture, postmodernism is often regarded as the epitome of bad taste and kitsch at a time when architects have lost their sense of good aesthetic judgment. It is also seen as architecture that affirms the reality of late capitalism and abandons the progressive social ideals of the modern movement. Recently, concerns similar to those voiced by Griffiths were raised during the 2018 Dean's Roundtable, the annual meeting of deans of architectural schools in the Northeast organized by the Center for Architecture in New York. The main thread of the meeting was the discussion of the possibilities of activism in architecture two years into Donald Trump's presidency, which resulted in a resurgence of racism, homophobia, and sexism. Some deans expressed their concerns with the revival of postmodernism in this political and social reality, seeing it as a dangerous distraction from urgent social matters that need to be addressed by architects. Julio Fernandez (CCNY's Spitzer School of Architecture) expressed a worry that "many schools here have moved to a re-evaluation of Postmodernism" and stated that "we have better things to do."[3] The University of Virginia's Ila Berman, who was moderating the gathering, recalled the architectural discourse of the 1970s and 1980s, when "all of the environmental and social issues fell off the table, and architects were operating within a different sphere" and added "I'm concerned when I see it happening again. … Is this just another, 'Make Architecture Great Again' moment, that's aligning with what's happening politically?" Similarly, in "Design for the One Percent," a recent article in *Jacobin* magazine, Alex Cocotas paints a grim picture of the contemporary architecture of "radical free market urbanism" – one that is fixated on iconic buildings and star-architects, and focused solely on "aesthetics to the detriment of social context."[4] Not surprisingly, the author sees postmodern architecture as the beginning of this condition and as the time when pro-social and progressive ideals of the modern movement were abandoned in the name of economic profit. For this reason, Cocotas writes, postmodernism should be blamed for the "partly aesthetic, partly political favoring of leaving things as they are," and thus that "postmodernism will not be forgiven lightly for what it did to architectural culture from the 1970s onwards."[5]

It is not this book's aim to join or critique this postmodern revivalism, but rather to situate postmodernism in a different light. What has gone largely neglected in historical and political treatments of postmodernism, and indeed what its enthusiasts and its critics alike miss, is its history in areas outside of Western Europe or North America, which reveal not an apolitical flippant postmodernism of free-floating signifiers, but a more overtly political postmodernism, one intricately involved in state power and resistance to state power. We can see this side to the history of postmodern architecture if we choose to examine South America and Eastern Europe, sites usually neglected by the dominant discourse of architectural history. Specifically, by considering postmodern architecture in Chile under Augusto Pinochet's dictatorship and in Poland during late socialism, this book examines cases in which postmodernism is deeply implicated in political and social projects, not so untethered from material struggle or flippant with regards to social movements. This book complicates the assumed link between postmodern architecture and late capitalism by examining postmodernism's involvement in State politics in late socialist Poland and as a part of the anti-neoliberal agenda of Chilean architects oppositional toward Pinochet's regime in Chile. Across four chapters, I argue that Chilean and Polish architecture between 1970 and 1990 complicate the prevalent view of postmodern architecture as politically disengaged and as an exclusively neoliberal phenomenon, disinterested in any progressive social agenda. In both countries, postmodern currents were appropriated by the regimes for propagandistic purposes and in their efforts to build a positive image of the State. At the same time, they were also used by architects who were oppositional toward the regimes and urban politics promoted by them.

Chile and Poland represent very different geopolitical realities, yet they allow for a productive juxtaposition. Postmodern architecture in these two countries had a similar trajectory in terms of the ways it was used as a politically and socially engaged project across roughly the same period of years. In Chile, postmodern ideas infiltrate architectural discourse around 1977, following the founding of CEDLA, or the Centro de Estudios de la Arquitectura (Center for Architectural Studies), an independent collective of Chilean architects based in Santiago de Chile. In Poland, although the term is first used in 1979, the first widespread discussions around postmodern ideas can be noted in the architectural press in 1978.

In both countries, postmodern architecture was used both by governments as a form of propaganda and by architects for whom postmodern spaces brought the promise of architecture that could actively challenge the politics of their respective governments. These separate developments cannot be said to produce a unified narrative of global postmodern architecture, but they do demonstrate that politically and socially engaged postmodern architecture was a global phenomenon.

The choice of time-frame 1970–1990 indicated in the book's title is motivated by architectural discourses and political realities in Chile and Poland. While the majority of the projects discussed were designed in the second half of the 1970s or in the 1980s, the discourse of the 1970s is important for multiple reasons. Within Poland, postmodern currents in architecture emerged as a continuation of criticism of modernist mass housing estates, which appeared in Polish architectural discourse beginning roughly in 1971. Additionally, 1970 is when Edward Gierek became as the First Secretary of the Polish Worker's Party. Gierek's government brought about liberalizing changes that influenced many architectural realizations, including the North Ursynów housing estate, one of the case studies discussed in Chapter 3. Political changes shape "the 1970s" even more clearly in Chile. September 11, 1973, marks the coup d'etat that finishes Salvador Allende's era and begins Pinochet's. On the other end, 1990 does not designate the end of postmodern architecture in these countries but political realities shifted in clear ways that affected postmodern architecture's political potential: on March 11, 1990, Pinochet's presidency ends while December 29, 1989, marks the official end of the socialist Polish People's Republic. Over the course of the rest of this introduction, I discuss a history of theorizations of postmodernism and some examples of postmodern revivalism in order to distinguish the importance of Chilean and Polish postmodernism and to show how their examples use some of the standard tropes associated with postmodernism while also departing from some of their most familiar connotations and functions. In the first section, I provide an overview of theorizations of postmodern architecture through its "rise" in prominence (in Jane Jacobs, Robert Venturi, Aldo Rossi,

4 Introduction

Christopher Alexander, Charles Jencks, and Paolo Portoghesi) and "fall" with its identification with late capitalism and the apolitical or post-political (in Jürgen Habermas, Fredric Jameson, and Mary McLeod). Second, I turn to some examples of postmodern revivalism in order to bring out some of the apolitical legacies of postmodernism through its focus on image and historical referentiality. These discussions will help prepare a fuller presentation of this book's argument in a third section that addresses the distinctive features of Chilean and Polish postmodernism, its dependence on some of the above critics and architects and its differences from the examples of postmodern revivalism. In a fourth section, I discuss recent scholarship on postmodernism and the body of work on both Chilean and Polish postmodernism. Finally, I turn to a fuller outline of this book, providing more detailed descriptions and rationales for the chapters that follow.

I.1 The "Rise" and "Fall" of Postmodern Architecture and Urbanism

There is no comprehensive definition of postmodern architecture that can be applicable to every realization considered postmodern. Even key postmodern architects (like Robert Venturi) often avoid labeling their work as "postmodern" or outright deny its appropriateness to a description of their works. Perhaps this might be attributed to the "bad press" postmodernism has had.[6] Rather than tracing the appearance of a word, it seems more useful to study postmodernism as, following Jameson, "a conception which allows for the presence and coexistence of a range of very different, yet subordinate features."[7] Rather than a specific "style," it should be described as a current or tendency distinguished by the presence of certain theoretical and formal qualities, which can be used selectively. Above all, it can be understood through its criticism of dogmas associated with modern architecture and urban planning – for instance, modern architecture's pursuit of universal comprehensive solutions with the pretense of objectivity, its emphasis on the primacy of expert architectural knowledge over the actual needs of the inhabitants, its foregrounding of technocracy and standardization, and its disregard for history in the name of the affirmation of the present.

The first sustained critiques of modernism pointing out these fallacies appeared in the early 1960s. A work foundational for this criticism was Jane Jacobs' *The Death and Life of the Great American Cities*, published in 1961. Even though it was written before postmodernism became a prominent term in architectural discourse, it "marked a transition from modernity to postmodernity in thinking about urban planning."[8] *Death and Life* rejects the city planning dogmas based on the theories of Le Corbusier and CIAM.[9] As a journalist and activist without academic architectural background, Jacobs proposed a bottom-up approach based on specific case studies and a theory constructed from the perspective of an average user. For Jacobs, it is the real cities, not theoretical models, from which "city planning should have been learning and forming and testing its theories."[10] Rejecting the modernist obsession with the separation of functions, Jacobs argues for diversity, intricacy, and complexity: the "intricate minglings of different uses in cities are not a form of chaos," she writes; rather, "they represent a complex and highly developed form of order."[11] A well-functioning city offers the "most intricate and close-grained diversity of uses that give each other constant mutual support, both economically and socially."[12] It should be stressed that the need for economic and social diversity, crucial for Jacobs, was rarely (if at all) taken up by future postmodern theoreticians who focused more exclusively on the formal diversity of urban textures, architectural layers, and the mélange of aesthetics effects they produce. According to Jacobs, a well-functioning healthy city is a palimpsest of people of different backgrounds (social, cultural, economic, ethnic), functions, historical layers, and spatial complexity.

The urban qualities praised by Jacobs formed the foundation for canonical postmodern theories developed in the late 1960s and 1970s. One such work is *Collage City* by Fred Koetter and Colin Rowe, published in 1978. *Collage City* is a reaction to the totalizing, rationalized city planning of modernism. Instead of using the technocratic language of modernist urban planning, Koetter and Rowe borrow terminology from art discourse (such as collage or *objet trouvés*) to describe their vision of the city. *Collage City* postulates urban forms based on fragmentation, strategies of bricolage, and juxtaposition of various layers of historical tissue, allowing for multiple interpretations by its users. Koetter and Rowe think of a city as a palimpsest and an open-ended form defined by its users rather than a finished and definite plan outlined on the urbanist's drafting table.

The poetics of fragmentation is central to many canonical documents of postmodernism, including the writings of Robert Venturi. In *Complexity and Contradiction in Architecture* published in 1966, Robert Venturi stresses the importance of tradition and criticizes modernism for rejecting complexity in urban planning, which leads to an alienating, unaccommodating architecture. Instead of grand totalizing planning visions of modernism, Venturi promotes visual, symbolic, spatial, and functional complexities embraced by architecture and urban planning of the past. In place of Mies van der Rohe's famous dictum that *less is more*, Venturi proposes to recognize that *less is a bore*, and turns toward historical examples such as the architecture of Francesco Borromini or John Soane to illustrate his claims. He calls for architecture and urban forms based on the concept of "the difficult whole" – "an architecture that can simultaneously recognize contradictory levels" and is "able to admit the paradox of the whole fragment: the building which is a whole at one level and a fragment of a greater whole at another level."[13] For Venturi, the "difficult whole in an architecture of complexity and contradiction includes multiplicity and diversity of elements in relationships that are inconsistent or among the weaker kinds perceptually."[14] In *Complexity and Contradiction*, as is typical for postmodern documents, visual material is not reduced to a mere illustration of the text, but is used to develop the author's argument. As Joan Ockman notes, Venturi's book was instantly criticized by the reviewers for "his skirting of social issues" and for a formalistic approach to architecture.[15]

The lack of social consideration was a subject of criticism also for the second seminal book by Venturi, *Learning from Las Vegas* (co-authored with Denise Scott Brown and Robert Izenour), published in 1972. The authors apply a bottom-up approach based on a case study of Las Vegas, from which broader conclusions are drawn ("learning from the existing landscape").[16] Such an approach is radically different from the "grand narratives" of modernism, which are based on large theoretical claims to which examples are secondary and serve as illustrations supporting general theories (as can be seen, for example, in the writings of Le Corbusier). The case study selected – a vernacular, popular site universally scolded as an epitome of bad design – is an ideological manifestation itself. Judged by the standards set by high modernism, Las Vegas disregards the cardinal rules of good taste (such as simplicity, clarity, and specificity of medium), functionalism (the principle of *form following function*) or spatial organization (the disregard of the principles of CIAM and the *Athens Charter*, such as zoning).[17] Las Vegas ignores not only the formal but also the ethical values of modernism, represented especially by the early heroic phase of Peter Behrens or Le Corbusier. Yet, as the authors want to persuade the readers, Las Vegas can be a valuable lesson. First of all,

6 Introduction

it answers the real existing needs of a specific time and place (not as determined by "the experts") and responds to them, leaving out ethical considerations, since "Las Vegas values are not questioned here."[18] Secondly, Las Vegas is an example of how architecture can operate as an effective semiotic system. The authors treat architecture as a signifying device, not limited to the aspects of function and form. To analyze architecture in such terms, they develop a methodology based on images (drawings, photos, charts) and witty, intentionally simplified classifications (such as their most famous juxtaposition: duck and decorated shed, which explains the relation between form and function in architecture, illustrated with cartoon-like drawings).[19] They show that the "ugly and ordinary in architecture" should be appreciated because of their rhetorical and symbolic potential.[20] Las Vegas is analyzed as an interdependent system, not a mere set of buildings. The modernist view on architecture as the "masterly, correct and magnificent play of masses brought together in light"[21] is replaced by the city "as a pattern of activities."[22]

The seductive narrative of *Learning from Las Vegas* obfuscates its omissions. Questions on the social and environmental sustainability of an utterly commercial city in the middle of a desert are absent. Moreover, the vernacular and popular in architecture are assumed to be equal with the commercial, reducing architecture to a commodity. As we will see, in Chile's and Poland's respective postmodernisms, these aspects of postmodern design, including complexity, historical references, and bottom-up approach will play socially and politically engaged roles.

Another work fundamental for the postmodern movement in architecture was Aldo Rossi's *The Architecture of the City*, first published in 1966. Rossi shares Venturi's interest in the history of architecture and in the symbolic aspects of buildings and cities, but without the commercialism and populism so eagerly explored by Venturi and other North American architects of his time. Divided clearly into four parts ("The Structure of Urban Artifacts"; "Primary Elements and the Concept of Area"; "The Individuality of Urban Artifacts"; and "The Evolution of Urban Artifacts"), with subchapters unfolding and explaining each problem, the structure of Rossi's book resembles a classical architectural treatise known from Italian or French traditions. The main idea in Rossi's theory is the concept of the "analogous city," which he defines as "a system of relating the city to established elements" constituted by architectural types.[23] The core tool for the analysis of urban structure is, therefore, typology ("I have given typology the preeminent place, viewing it as the essential basis of design," writes Rossi).[24] It is defined as "the study of types of elements that cannot be further reduced, elements of a city as well as of an architecture."[25] In Rossi's book, the notion of type replaces the modernist focus on function. He rejects the belief "that functions bring forms together and in themselves constitute urban artifacts and architecture"[26] and dismisses "naïve functionalist classifications" of modernist architecture, which presuppose that "all urban artifacts are created to serve particular functions in a static way."[27] While functionalism falsely assumes that the functions of the building should be petrified in their forms (*form follows function*), the history of European cities shows clearly "the multiplicity of functions that a building … can contain over time and how these functions are entirely independent of the form."[28] Rossi's interest in typology should not be seen as a return to the Durandian formalistic approach to architecture. He goes beyond the formal, material dimensions of urban elements and considers them as cultural forms, close to the concept of archetypes (as when he discusses the relation between monuments, myths and rituals).[29] As Rossi writes, "I would define the concept of type as something that is permanent and complex, a logical principle that is prior to form and that constitutes it."[30] "Architecture," Rossi says, "is deeply rooted in the formation of civilization and is a permanent, universal, and necessary artifact"[31] while the city is a "great, comprehensive representation of the human condition."[32] His focus on typology can be seen as an architectural version of structuralism, a quest for finding a universal language of architecture, an attempt of decoding urban syntax and revealing urban meaning – a "type is the very idea of architecture, that which is closest to its essence."[33]

Rossi's interest in language is very different from Venturi's fascination with the *pop-parole* of casino neons and road signs, for Rossi's approach attempts to reach the level of *langue* – the abstract preexisting structure helping to understand the true nature of things. The approach to language is not the only aspect marking the difference of Rossi's attitude from American postmodernism. The second major difference lies in its treatment of history. Rather than a subject of blithe pastiche or a source of forms ready to be arbitrarily recombined and assembled, history is treated seriously. In *The Architecture of the City*, there is little place for trivialities or architectural jokes. "The study of history seems to offer the best verification of certain hypotheses about the city, for the city is in itself a repository of history," writes Rossi.[34] Within his project typology and history are complementary: "typology and history come to be measures of the mutations of reality, together defining a system of architecture…. Thus, they are opposed theoretically to the disorder of contemporary architecture."[35] Rossi's reliance on typologies sourced from architectural and urban history is one of the fundamental tropes in postmodernism.

Rossi's work helped to generate increased interest in typologies and spatial patterns in architectural discourse in the 1970s and 1980s, a trend best exemplified by two books by Christopher Alexander: *The Timeless Way of Building* (1977) and *A Pattern Language* (1979). Alexander (who did not consider himself as postmodernist) advocated against standardized mass-produced architectural solutions and, as a remedy, proposed a method of designing based on spatial patterns present in towns, buildings, and construction over centuries. According to Alexander, "each pattern describes a problem which occurs over and over again in our environment, and then describes the core of the solution to that problem, in such a way that you can use this solution a million times over."[36] Rossi's typologies and Alexander's patterns have informed the renewed interest in traditional, historical urban forms essential for postmodernism.

Many of the designs investigated in this book from both the Chilean and Polish contexts draw upon the ideas of Jacobs, Venturi, Rossi, and Alexander. More specifically, as the following chapters discuss in more detail, the examples of Chilean and Polish postmodernism take up Jacobs's, Denise Scott Brown's, and Venturi's emphasis on the specific case studies, perspective of the average user, and a bottom-up approach, Venturi's focus on architectural tradition, as well as Rossi's and Alexander's attention to traditional typologies and patterns. Following these authors, they also understand architecture as a meaningful act that goes beyond the technocratic approach of modernism and that can and should engage other discourses and disciplines such as visual arts or anthropology. However, what is characteristic to the Chilean and Polish architects influenced by these concepts is that they interpreted postmodern forms and theories in political ways: as powerful tools to either defend or oppose agendas of the regimes in power and considered them as having a real potential to influence (affirm or contest) the social and political realities under which they practiced.

Since these initial theorizations, postmodern architecture has been taken up and explored by critics, including, most prominently, Charles Jencks, Paolo Portoghesi, and Heinrich Klotz.

8 Introduction

Despite their differences, their definitions coincide regarding the crucial architectural features that they identify as postmodern as well as in the genealogies they ascribe to postmodern architecture. Additionally, to a large degree they discuss the same body of texts, realizations, authors, and architects as significant to the postmodern turn in architecture. In architectural discourse, the term "postmodernism" was greatly popularized by Jencks, whose first work on this notion in architecture appeared in print in 1975.[37] Jencks traces the beginnings of postmodernism to the crisis of modern ideals which began in the late 1960s and 1970s; he sets 1972 as a symbolic date of the end of modernist architecture. In his book *The New Paradigm in Architecture: The Language of Post-Modernism*, Jencks writes that "Modern Architecture died in St. Louis, Missouri on July 15, 1972 at 3.32 pm (or thereabouts) when the infamous Pruitt Igoe scheme, or rather several of its slab blocks, were given the final coup de grâce by dynamite."[38] Since Pruitt Igoe – a late modern mass housing complex designed by Minoru Yamasaki (completed in 1956) – was "a widely recognized symbol of ... the failure of modern architecture," its demolition was a suggestive metaphor for a final collapse of modernist ideas, which gave space for postmodernism in architecture.[39] He frames postmodernism as a critical answer to the failures of modernism, such as "cheap prefabrication, lack of personal 'defensible' space and the alienating housing estate,"[40] and states that "the main motive for Post-Modern architecture is obviously the social failure of Modern architecture."[41]

For Jencks, postmodernism retains some of the elements characteristic for modernism, but what distinguishes it is its distinctive mode of communication, which he calls *double-coding*: "the combination of Modern techniques with something else (usually traditional building) in order for architecture to communicate with the public and a concerned minority, usually other architects."[42] He continues,

> Modern architecture had failed to remain a credible party because it didn't communicate effectively with its ultimate users – the main argument of my book *The Language of Post-Modern Architecture* – and partly because it didn't make effective links with the city and history. Thus the solution I perceived and defined as Post-Modern: an architecture that was professionally based *and* popular as well as one that was based on new techniques *and* old patterns. Double coding to simplify means both elite/popular and new/old and there are compelling reasons for these opposite pairings. ... All the creators who should be called Post-Modern keep something of a modern sensibility, some intention which distinguishes their work from that of revivalists – whether it is irony, parody, displacement, complexity, eclecticism, realism or any number of contemporary tactics and goals.[43]

Postmodern architecture rejects the values of modern architecture such as "'truth to materials', 'logical consistency', 'straightforwardness', 'simplicity'" in the name of playful deceptions, linguistic games, and complexity of meanings, historical references, forms, and materials.[44] According to Jencks, the characteristics distinguishing modern from postmodern architecture:

> concern differences over symbolism, ornament, humour, technology and the relation of the architect to existing and past cultures. Modernists and Late-Modernists tend to emphasize technical and economic solutions to problems, whereas Post-Modernists tend to emphasize contextual and cultural additions to their inventions.[45]

An important idea fundamental for postmodernism then is pluralism: "the idea that the architect must design for different 'taste cultures' ... and for differing views of the good life."[46]

Some examples of postmodern architecture frequently analyzed by Jencks include Robert Venturi's Vanna Venturi House in Philadelphia (1962–1964), Charles Moore's Piazza d'Italia in New Orleans (1978), Michael Graves's Dolphin and Swan hotels in Orlando (1989), and James Stirling's Neue Staatsgalerie (1979–1984) in Stuttgart.[47] In *What Is Post-Modernism?*, Jencks analyzes Neue Staatsgalerie as an illustration of double-coding. On the one hand, the building hides endless references legible for specialists: its plan, composed of a series of connected galleries around three sides of a central rotunda, is a quote from Karl Friedrich Schinkel's Altes Museum in Berlin, its façade with stone slabs "fallen out" from the building evokes the eighteenth-century tradition of artificial ruins. On the other hand, the aesthetics of Neue Staatsgalerie is accessible and inviting, and not just for experts:

> Virtually every Post-Modern architect – Robert Venturi, Hans Hollein, Charles Moore, Robert Stern, Michael Graves, Arata Isozaki are the notable examples – use popular *and* elitist signs in their work to achieve quite different ends, and their styles are essentially a hybrid. To simplify, at Stuttgart the blue and red handrails and vibrant polychromy fit in with the youth that uses the museum – they literally resemble they dayglo hair and anoraks – while the Classicism appeals more to the lovers of Schinkel. ... The pluralism which is so often called on to justify Post-Modernism is here a tangible reality.[48]

While Jencks's influence in promoting postmodernism came through his emphasis on communication, double-coding, and pluralism, Paolo Portoghesi's influence in his exhibitions and writings lies more in his embrace of superficiality, theatricality, and image. In 1980, the first edition of the Architecture Biennale in Venice was opened under the name *The Presence of The Past*. The 1980 Biennale was dominated by postmodern proposals, the most crucial of which was *La Strada Novissima* exhibition curated by Portoghesi. The *Strada Novissima* was a hypothetical street composed of twenty façades designed by leading postmodern architects. The façades "were in a Free-Style Classicism, a style which used the full repertoire of mouldings, keystones and columnar orders, but usually in an ironic fashion again indicating their place in history after Modernism."[49] In his book *Postmodern: The Architecture of The Post-Industrial Society* published in 1983, Portoghesi describes *La Strada Novissima* as architecture which "returns to the condition of the theater, of the stage" and is "a machine for thought."[50] In its very concept, the exhibition was symptomatic of postmodernism with its emphasis on artificiality and irony. Stripped of function entirely, the façades are playful quotations of the buildings, embracing their superficiality and focus on the aesthetic dimension.

In *Postmodern*, Portoghesi defines the postmodern movement in architecture and provides short analyses of key postmodern architects. In a vein similar to Fredric Jameson (to be discussed below), but without his critical thrust, Portoghesi characterizes postmodernism as a "product of 'postindustrial' society"[51] and a heterogeneous, diverse notion based on the rejection of modernism and its

> natural product: the modern city, the suburbs without quality, the urban environment devoid of collective values that has become an asphalt jungle and a dormitory; the loss

10 Introduction

> of local character, of the connection with the place: the terrible homologation that has made the outskirts of the cities of the whole world similar to one another and whose inhabitants have a hard time recognizing and identity of their own.[52]

Portoghesi describes the postmodern movement as "a kind of new renaissance," which refutes modernist values such as the "perpetual invention of and search for the new at all costs ..., perspective decomposition" and "abstract volumetric play," and instead discovers the importance of "the imitation of types" and "the knowledge of rules and canons produced over centuries" and acknowledges the fact that "the character of a place is a patrimony to use and not to mindlessly squander."[53] Unlike critics of postmodernism, Portoghesi embraces rather than vilifies this superficiality, stating that it is "an architecture of the image for a civilization of the image."[54] Echoing Jencks, Portoghesi puts emphasis on the communicative role for postmodernism in this use of traditional typologies (or "archetypes"). This he sees as a remedy for the decontextualized, homogeneous, and alienating architecture produced by modernism: "The Postmodern in architecture can therefore be read overall as a reemergence of archetypes, or as a reintegration of architectonic conventions, and thus as a premise to the creation of an *architecture of communication*," he writes.[55]

The accounts of Jencks and Portoghesi present different views on whether postmodernism should be framed more as a continuation of modernism or a radical break with it, and the authors put emphasis on different aspects of postmodern architecture when describing the movement. For example, Portoghesi accentuates the return to tradition and history, while Jencks accentuates playfulness and irony. Nevertheless, the core of their argument is the same. They analyze postmodernism as a heterogeneous movement held together by two elements: a critique against modernism and functionalism initiated in the 1960s and a return to historical ideals, forms, and typologies interrupted by the modern approach to architecture and the city. Postmodern architecture, as outlined by Jencks and Portoghesi, is playful, singular, and unique (rather than anonymous and homogenous), ironic, textual (as it provides an abundance of metaphors and references possible to "read" by audiences of different levels of cultural literacy and coming from various backgrounds), and popular (as it acknowledges the *vox populi* rather than solely the opinions of architectural experts), and respects the context and *genius loci* of the place it occupies. It is a form of art rather than a technical discipline focused solely on functionality or a technocratic scientific means for solving spatial problems.

As we will see, many of these ideas will be taken up in Chilean and Polish forays into postmodernism as well. Jencksian double-coding becomes an especially instructive way of understanding some of these postmodern designs, although the multiple communicative aims function directly for dual (sometimes conflicting) political and artistic purposes, such that a single design may present as one way in order to uphold a state-held ideology while also speak more subversively to architects seeking to transcend official ideology. Additionally, the theatricality of postmodern designs in government-sanctioned buildings in Chile serves straightforwardly propagandistic aims, not just using historicizing forms but also performing fashionable cutting-edge artistic sensibilities associated with the West. In these ways, core elements considered synonymous with postmodernism play complicated political roles.

The turn against postmodern architecture and design began to solidify in the Reagan and Thatcher era of the 1980s with the writings of Habermas, Jameson, and McLeod. This decade provided a different vantage to the playful and so-called populist or user-centered response to Modern architecture. Habermas develops his defense of modernism and critique of postmodern architecture in two essays: "Modernity – An Incomplete Project," written in 1980, and "Modernism versus Postmodernism in Architecture," published in 1981. For Habermas, modernism is an "unfinished project" of social, emancipatory character, which should be continued. "Modernity" was written in the context of the first architectural Biennale in Venice in 1980, titled *The Presence of the Past*, which was dominated by post-modern proposals, and uses architecture as a point of departure to diagnose the current situation. For Habermas, postmodernism negates and rejects modernist values in the name of relativist language games and the superficial, aesthetic tricks of transforming "depart-ment stores into Medieval rows of houses, and underground ventilation into pocket-book size Palladian villas,"[56] and is based on "the cult of the vernacular and reverence for the banal."[57] Postmodern architects, instead of working in and for the community, are "surre-alist stage designers" who take part, deliberately or not, in a socially and politically conser-vative project.[58]

Fredric Jameson presents postmodernism as a product of late capitalism in "Post-modernism, or, The Cultural Logic of Late Capitalism," published a few years later in 1984 (and in his expanded book-length study published in 1991). Jameson's discussion of postmodernism is in part conducted through architectural examples, since "of all the arts, architecture is the closest constitutively to the economic, with which, in the form of commissions and land values, it has a virtually unmediated relationship." Jameson continues, "it will therefore not be surprising to find the extraordinary flowering of the new postmodern architecture grounded in the patronage of multinational business, whose expansion and development is strictly contemporaneous with it."[59] Even though Jameson uses buildings (along with films and art objects) to illustrate his point, he stresses that postmodernism should not be framed as a "style," but rather as "a dominant cul-tural logic" characterized by the economic deregulation and globalization of the Ron-ald Reagan and Margaret Thatcher era. Jameson describes "postmodernist positions in architecture" as

> inseparable from an implacable critique of architectural high modernism … where formal criticism and analysis (of the high-modernist transformation of the building into a virtual sculpture, or monumental "duck," as Robert Venturi puts it), are at one with reconsiderations on the level of urbanism and of the aesthetic institution. High modernism is thus credited with the destruction of the fabric of the traditional city and its older neighbourhood culture (by way of the radical disjunction of the new Utopian high-modernist building from its surrounding context), while the prophetic elitism and authoritarianism of the modern movement are remorselessly identified in the imperious gesture of the charismatic Master.[60]

Postmodernism, as evidenced in architecture, is "a kind of aesthetic populism," fascinated by the "landscape of schlock and kitsch, of TV series and *Reader's Digest* culture, of adver-tising and motels, of the late show and the grade-B Hollywood film" and characterized by "depthlessness, which finds its prolongation both in contemporary 'theory' and in a whole new culture of the image or the simulacrum; a consequent weakening of historicity."[61] Jameson's book solidified the recognition of postmodern architecture as an inherent product

12 Introduction

of late capitalism and as a telling diagnosis of late twentieth-century economy. As critic Justin McGuirk recently wrote,

> with its deceptive surfaces and furniture that doesn't do what it's supposed to, postmodernism is not just the backdrop to but a metaphor for unbridled capitalism, where a plump balance sheet conceals all manner of sins and where marble-effect plastic laminate hides chipboard.[62]

Another influential diagnosis of postmodern architecture was presented in Mary McLeod's article, "Architecture and Politics in the Reagan Era: From Postmodernism to Deconstructivism," published in *Assemblage* in 1989. McLeod analyzes postmodernism as a manifestation of the neoliberal politics of Thatcher and Reagan, and as "the new corporate style": commercial architecture devoid of the revolutionary spirit and social vision embedded in modern architecture in its heroic phase. Postmodern architecture takes part in the neoliberal project not in the form of active engagement but rather in its passive acceptance of the status quo.[63]

Habermas', Jameson's, and McLeod's analyses have been decisive in defining postmodernism in architectural scholarship since the 1980s. Their claims provide wide-ranging diagnoses of Western European and North American examples, on which the authors base their theoretical discussions. However, as we will see, these critiques are not so easily suited to the case studies in Chile and Poland, in which postmodern designs cannot be simply equated with free-market capitalism and neoliberalism.

I.2 The Apolitical Legacy as Culminating in Postmodern Revivalism

Examining postmodern architecture in Chile and Poland will mean reinterpreting the implications of some of the defining features of this architecture within political and economic contexts quite different than those of North America or Western Europe. In order to perceive of the distinctive qualities of the examples from Chile and Poland, it will be useful to set up by contrast examples of postmodern design in current postmodern revivalism. As we will see, Chilean and Polish postmodernism take up interest in postmodern uses of "image" and "historical referentiality"; however, they do so quite differently than the practitioners of postmodern revivalism. Designers of this latter trend exuberantly take up "image" and "historical referentiality" in ways that are unabashedly apolitical or politically complacent with capitalist forces, in this sense opening themselves up to the same critiques brought out by Habermas, Jameson, and McLeod in the 1980s.

In the article discussed briefly at the beginning of this introduction, Sean Griffiths describes postmodern revivalism in this way:

> In recent weeks, I have found myself writing references for young American academics who wear bow ties and Bertie Wooster jumpers, and who write about architecture's relationship to literature on the internet in the style of David Foster Wallace. The Chicago Architecture Biennial is full of a renewed and apparently confident postmodernism, of a sort that seems just a little too respectable. The artist, Pablo Bronstein is plastering neo-Georgian all over the RIBA. And who today can switch on the television, read the newspaper or go online without the chirpy visage of Adam Nathaniel Furman staring back from inside the 24-hour news cycle?[64]

Griffiths here refers to Adam Nathaniel Furman, one of the most consistent figures in cultivating a postmodern aesthetic and a leading figure in the movement represented by designers including Yinka Ilori, Camille Walala, Morag Mysercough, and himself, for which he coined the term "New London Fabulous." Furman characterizes it as "design and architecture as a visual and cultural pursuit, which is highly aesthetic, sensual and celebratory of mixed cultures" and which "picks and chooses and mixes from different periods and it does look back."[65]

The "New London Fabulous" architects and designers are best known for ornamental urban and architectural installations saturated with bright colors and bold patterns offering visually hypnotic spatial experiences. Walala, for instance, whose website describes her work as using the "man-made landscape as a platform for disseminating positivity," specializes in murals transforming buildings into two-dimensional, cartoon-like drawings (such as the façade of the Industry City building in Brooklyn, NY, 2018) and urban interventions (such as the Adams Plaza Bridge in London's Canary Wharf, 2020 or a mural on a pedestrian crossing and building façade in London's White City, 2020).[66] With the Adams Plaza Bridge, Walala changed the tunnel-like structure of the bridge into a three-dimensional op-art installation by installing bright colorful panels in its window and on the ceiling. In the murals in White City, Walala used a similar set of primary colors and geometric patterns referencing the aesthetics of the 1980s and 1990s to bring a joyful pop of color into a rather uniform and uncompelling environment. Walala's visually pleasing designs indeed also make them desirable to private real estate companies who eagerly use art and architecture in their efforts of placemaking. White City was commissioned by a consortium of Stanhope, Mitsui Fudosan UK, and Alberta Investment Management Corporation, while Adams Plaza Bridge was commissioned by Canary Wharf Group. In both cases, Walala's urban interventions are part of branding strategies targeted to market these locations as centers of businesses, creative industries, and commerce, inevitably subjecting them to the forces of gentrification. Indeed, Walala's optimistic architecture as a "platform for disseminating positivity" is also a platform for fostering socio-spatial inequalities, inevitable in projects turning neighborhoods into enclaves scripted by developers according to a strictly profit-driven business plan.

These projects are broadly characterized by their prioritizations of play and pleasure as conveyed through an obsession with image. One of Walala's most recent gallery projects is *Walala x Play* in Now Gallery (2017): a colorful, Memphis-inspired labyrinth constructed of patterns and reflective surfaces that resembles mirror mazes and playground equipment in order to encourage the visitors to "unleash their inner child."[67] Yinka Ilori's designs use similar playful aesthetics and intends to evoke analogical associations. His *Happy Street* for London Festival of Architecture (2019) was aimed to "overhaul a gloomy underpass in south London, with a proposal featuring vibrant colours and bold patterns."[68] In the same year, Ilori realized *Playland*, an installation commissioned by Pinterest as part of the Cannes festival. *Playland* features movable chairs, a see-saw, and a roundabout, covered in colorful patterns corresponding with Pinterest's "most pinned colours from around the world" and, like Walala's installation, was intended to "create a play space that gave adults the opportunity to play and tap into their inner child."[69] Ilori's *Playland* not only represents data retrieved from this online platform, but it also has the same palatable aesthetic characteristic as a Pinterest board and, like its digital counterpart, its main goal is to visually please.

Postmodernists of the 1970s and 1980s had realized this focus on image through their fascination with architectural drawing understood as a form of art and with their exploration

14 Introduction

of the connections between architecture, the visual arts, and the popular ionosphere. This twenty-first-century interest in postmodernism takes up different forms of visualities as it revolves around digital images shared on social media, taking lessons from Pinterest and Instagram rather than Las Vegas. Whether turning a three-dimensional object into a flat schematic sketch (Walala's Industry City building) or reducing space to an Instagrammable background (Ilori's *Playland*), these designs persistently treat architecture as a visually satisfying background, deprived of depth both in the physical and the ideological senses. As such, they are symptomatic of a much broader tendency defining contemporary architecture – its fixation on image and representation.

Some qualities found in Walala and Ilori's projects – lack of depth, emphasis on playfulness and optimism, the use of bold colors and patterns – are also characteristic of Furman's designs, though Furman's work also magnifies the importance of historical references. Furman is best known for his design objects (wallpapers, household objects) and small-scale architectural interventions. His most recent works include an installation for the 2017 edition of the London Design Festival, a gate composed of a sequence of colorful arches with openings of different shapes creating a mesmerizing kaleidoscope-like effect. The arches are clad with ceramic tile, as the installation was commissioned by *Turkishceramic*, an association promoting the Turkish ceramic industry. Furman freely juxtaposes tiles of different patterns and traditions, evoking a range of historical references, from patterns used in London Underground stations in the 1970s to traditional Islamic motives used in mosques. Visually attractive, aesthetically and intellectually accessible (while at the same time offering artistic and cultural references ready to be decoded by more culturally literate audiences), Furman's installation provides a perfect example of commercial, populist, egalitarian, and witty postmodern design. His second famous project, *The Democratic Monument*, designed in the same year, is based on similar qualities. *The Democratic Monument* was commissioned by the 2017 Scottish Architectural Fringe as part of a *New Typologies* exhibition, showcasing visions for future civic architecture. The entrance to *The Democratic Monument* is placed in an elaborate front façade composed of an inlay of overlapping segments of contrasting colors, textures, and materials combined with classical architectural elements such as columns and arches. The entrance leads to a spacious public hall and an office tower. Like the front façade, interior spaces offer a contemporary version of mannerist *horror vacui* compositions with a myriad of historical references, bold patterns, and bright colors. As they fill ceilings, walls, and floors, they result in surreal, dream-like, fragmented, and disorienting spaces, similar to John Portman's postmodern hyperspaces.[70] *The Democratic Monument* offers an updated, revamped, and amplified version of postmodernism for the new generation. Furman generously draws from the classics – ironic projects such as Michael Graves' Disney Hotels, Charles Moore's Piazza d'Italia, and Memphis group furniture design – and combines those elements with more recent references, such as 1990s rave culture aesthetics with its acid-neon colors and eye-confusing visual effects. Furman sees his proposal as "an expression of urban pride, chromatic joy, and architectural complexity" and "a monumental embodiment of our evolving Liberal democracy as it moves into another new phase of energetic activity and robust intervention."[71] According to Furman, *The Democratic Monument* sends a message of "architectural plurality in compositional unity" as "architectural language and expression can both embody, and reconcile, the perpetual tensions between market & state, and minority and majority,"[72] and embodies "the perpetual dialogue in our Liberal democracy between the need for consensus and shared values, and the vital fostering and celebration of minority needs and interests."[73]

Furman's referential image-based architecture capable of reconciling tensions recalls Chantal Mouffe's diagnosis of the *post-political*, which she calls the predominant "view which informs the 'common sense' in a majority of western societies."[74] Mouffe characterizes this condition as a situation in which the

> "free world" has triumphed over communism and, with the weakening of collective identities, a world 'without enemies' is now possible. Partisan conflicts are a thing of the past and consensus can now be obtained through dialogue. Thanks to globalization and the universalization of liberal democracy, we can expect a cosmopolitan future bringing peace, prosperity and the implementation of human rights worldwide.[75]

Further, Mouffe characterizes the post-political era as based on "optimistic view of globalization," and "consensual form of democracy," and describes it as an "anti-political vision which refuses to acknowledge the antagonistic dimension constitutive of 'the political.'"[76] *The Democratic Monument* provides a perfect illustration of a building for post-political times. Furman mentions tensions between the market and the state, the minority and the majority, but instead of engaging them in his project, the architect offers a false vision of reconciliation which – as the contemporary crisis of democracy, marked by Brexit, the refugee crisis, and a surge of nationalist politics worldwide has shown – is an optimistic and unrealistic view. *The Democratic Monument* affirms the status quo by providing an illusion of unity and harmony and avoids to mention real irreconcilable tensions and divisions. In this sense, paradoxically to its function, it is an example of apolitical architecture deceptively using the rhetoric of pluralism without any serious engagement in its essence. In interviews, Furman often raises the need for diversity – especially by rejecting heteronormativity – in architecture and presents postmodern aesthetics as well-suited for this endeavor due to its unlimited openness to different ideas and forms. His vision, however, refuses to seriously address or acknowledge tensions, conflicts, and negotiations that are inevitable parts of any project founded on the idea of true involvement of different groups and fostering a dialogue between them. The optimistic inclusivity of *The Democratic Monument* then appears indifferent to the mounting pressure to acknowledge diversity in architecture in recent years as voiced by the #MeToo movement or Black Lives Matter activists, which ask architects to engage in uncomfortable conversations and to challenge the status quo. Furman's vision of democracy in architecture doesn't seem to be truly invested in acknowledging different voices but effectively silences them by offering an architectural illusion of "unity and reconciliation."

As such, the shallow optimism of *The Democratic Monument* embodies the dangers embedded in the new wave of postmodernism, as seen by its critics. The architectural postmodernism as used by Furman and "New London Fabulous" is populist, commercial, and formalist, focused on aesthetics, superficially pluralistic, and disengaged from urban problems closely connected to the current crises in our economic and political systems. As the vast majority of architects and designers today use postmodern aesthetic in ways similar to "New London Fabulous," postmodern revivalism is broadly criticized by socially aware practitioners and theoreticians. But if a focus on image and playful historical reference is apolitical or "post-political" in a North American or Western European context, it is not necessarily so in cases of postmodernism elsewhere, as will be discussed in the chapters that follow.

1.3 Chilean and Polish Postmodernism

Robert Venturi's populism, the significance of historical typologies in Aldo Rossi or Christopher Alexander, Jane Jacobs's notion of the ordinary citizen, the understanding of double-coding in Jencks, and the emphasis on image, historical referentiality, and the communicative role of architecture throughout the theorizations of these writers and culminating in postmodern revivalism – all of these resurface in familiar yet different ways in Chilean and Polish postmodernism. The differences can be largely attributed to the fact that, under these countries' nondemocratic regimes, postmodern architecture brought stakes higher than the generation of profit. As Chapters 1 and 3 show, postmodernism was used as a platform for propaganda by, respectively, the authoritarian government of Pinochet in Chile and the socialist regime in Poland. In buildings such as the Congreso Nacional de Chile (1988–1990), then, the postmodern strategies of free juxtapositions of different historical references, textures, and patterns do not result in the same playful, frivolous architecture we recognize from Graves' hotels or Moore's Piazza d'Italia, which use analogical stylistic effects. Instead, they are used to create a building that is "austere, dignified and transcendent" and thus in line with Pinochet's propaganda.[77] Similarly, in late socialist Poland, the function of postmodern architecture as used by the government was to, as architect Romuald Loegler described it, "appease dangerous social unrest"[78] with the use of inviting popular postmodern forms applied in State-funded housing estates. For the architects analyzed in this book postmodernism was a serious high-stakes project, as it was driven by political and social goals. As explained in Chapter 1, this does not necessarily mean that Chilean and Polish postmodernism is devoid of irony, but rather that its ironic dimension itself reflects the complicated, if sometimes contradictory, intentions of architects and the State.

Chilean and Polish architects who used postmodernism as a means to contest their government's agendas (discussed in Chapters 2 and 4) also source their postmodern inspirations selectively and/or redefine well-known postmodern tropes in their practice. Their interest in postmodernism can be described in three ways. The first can be seen in their methodology. These architects utilized, for instance, bottom-up approaches through case studies of local architecture and targeted solutions instead of general abstract claims to solve very different spatial problems (following Jacobs or Venturi). Secondly, these architects drew from postmodernism in their departures from the rationalized technocratic treatment of architecture prevalent in modernism in favor of the understanding of architecture as a symbolic, meaningful form. In a Western context, this aspect of postmodernism is often explored in a way that turns buildings into playful and surprising forms referring to various sources, from pop culture to quotes from architectural history. In the locations explored in this book, postmodern architecture's symbolism can play multiple political and social communicative and performative roles. Thirdly, these architects revived historical forms and spatial solutions – specifically, traditional typologies like urban squares, piazzas, and streets – understood as elements vital for social life and not merely utilitarian. The postmodern influence is especially visible in their emphasis on the importance of streets as social forms, irreducible to "simple connectors,"[79] as had been understood in modernist urban planning. Therefore, their main theoretical references are authors such as Rossi (especially in the Chilean cases, due to personal contacts between Rossi and the CEDLA group) and Jacobs, who – although her main works were published in the peak of modernism in architecture – set the directions taken up by postmodern authors.

In this sense, Chilean and Polish postmodern architects are populist, but in a fundamentally different way than the commercialized populism of Western architects evident in *Learning from Las Vegas*, for example. In accordance with the postulates of Western postmodernists (such as Jencksian "double-coding"), Chilean and Polish architects reject the reliance on expert culture and turn to the average, non-specialist user by using historical and traditional forms rather than the refined abstract forms of modernism praised by critics but often rejected by users. In some cases (like Budzyński's North Ursynów), they also engage future users in the design process. Unlike in Venturi et al., the deployment of architectural populism by Chilean and Polish architects is founded on the philosophical commitment that architecture needs to be connected to the community – a politically vital position in the context of Chile and Poland in the 1970s and 1980s. Both the Chilean and Polish governments (despite their official rhetoric) sought to bring about the atomization and alienation of individuals within society. In these charged political atmospheres, as the 1970s and 1980s were times of increasingly widespread dissent and social unrest, social organizing and community building through urban designs were dangerous to the regimes.

Both Chilean and Polish architects often underline these differences between Western postmodernism and their practices. Marta Leśniakowska, a Polish architectural historian engaged in oppositional architectural circles, sums up this difference in this way:

> for us, in Poland, the interest in postmodernism was different than in the West. It was a chance to revive the traditions of Polish architecture instead of the universalist international language of modernism. Postmodernism wasn't for us a matter of form, a matter of façade, we were interested in how the city works, we wanted to return to traditional urban forms such as streets, quarters or squares. ... For us, the form was an expression of ideological and political attitudes. We understood postmodernism as a chance for the renewal of architectural vocabulary. We believed that the return to detail, to human and urban scales ..., to traditional thinking about urban fabric – very different from the oppressive character of late socialist architecture – would shape new kinds of social relations.[80]

Very similar statements are made by architects engaged in the Chilean group CEDLA (Centro de Estudios de la Arquitectura). Pedro Murtinho says that, for CEDLA, postmodernism was primarily an exploration "of our roots, and of how the city functions."[81] Likewise, Cristián Boza clarifies that CEDLA did not understand postmodernism in a formalist, stylistic way within the group: "postmodernism was not only about columns and friezes. It was about regaining our identity. ... We did not agree with the military government. We were talking about liberation, about bringing our country and its respective architecture back."[82] The degree and character of political engagement of architects discussed in this book varies from overt and direct (as in the case of Czesław Bielecki, whose career in architecture is parallel to his underground oppositional activity) to more subtle attempts to "make politics through architecture,"[83] as Chilean architect Humberto Eliash described his engagement in CEDLA.

The professional trajectories of Chilean and Polish architects discussed in the following four chapters offer an opportunity to address broader questions regarding architecture and the State: Can architectural practice be a form of dissent? If so, under what circumstances? Chilean and Polish postmodernism allow the productive investigation of what

18 Introduction

"oppositional" means for an architect who wishes to remain practicing her profession. Some of the architects, like Polish architect Romuald Loegler, decided to engage in projects endorsed and funded by the State, the politics of which these architects opposed. While taking part in the governments' propagandistic efforts, in their designs they included spatial solutions which were part of an oppositional agenda (as in the Na Skarpie Estate, discussed in Chapter 3). These complexities are even more visible in Chilean architecture, as in the practice of Cristián Boza. While he was one of the founders of CEDLA – a group with a program focused on urban solutions intended to counter Pinochet's neoliberal policies – Boza was one of the architects who took part in the national competition for the Chilean Congress in Valparaiso. Moreover, Boza's studio was also one of the most prosperous during Pinochet's regime and realized numerous commissions for thoroughly neoliberal spatial formats.

Poland and Chile are not the only examples of Eastern European or South American countries in which postmodern designs play complicated political and social roles. Many architects in the former Eastern Bloc united their interests in postmodernism with a critique of socialism. One example of such a practice can be seen in what Inez Weizman has called "kitchen architects": architects who, after going to work in their day jobs at state design offices or design schools, would meet in private houses "to produce drawings that were meant to challenge the stifling, standardized language of Soviet architecture."[84] This after-hours design activity usually took place in kitchens, which, in socialist countries at the time, played a crucial social and cultural role as centers of unofficial meetings and hotbeds of dissident ideas. As Weizman writes, these drawings, produced mainly in the 1970s and 1980s,

> sought to introduce 'culture' … into architectural articulations of allegories, legends, and postmodern contextualization. Such kitchens, private and intimate, were seen as subversive micro-sites where some form of autonomy from state power was articulated, where fantasy would be unrestricted by reality, and where smuggled journals from the West could be safely gleaned.[85]

Another example of Eastern European architecture outside of Poland that displays political (although in this case propagandistic) uses of postmodernism can be found in the Romanian Palace of the Parliament (Casa Republicii) in Bucharest, commissioned by Nicolae Ceaușescu and designed by Anca Petrescu in 1984 (completed in 1997).

Clearly inspired by Ricardo Boffill, the gargantuan Palace of Parliament was, as Augustin Ioan writes, expected to "produce the amplest urban post-modern project in Europe" compared to Francois Mitterand's grand architectural realizations in Paris.[86] Indeed, with its stylistic features and the broader intention behind its commission to build the image of the dictatorship, the Romanian Palace can be instructively compared to the Congreso Nacional de Chile analyzed in Chapter 1. Like the Congreso, the Palace forces us to rethink categories usually identified with postmodernism. Ioan notes that

> the composition types and ornaments, the assemblages of classical/eclectic elements discharging an evocative/aesthetic function, the use of identities, a praise to the urban façade – are, undoubtedly, comparable to those celebrated by postmodern architecture. However, several essential ingredients are missing, e.g. irony, double encoding, cues to indicate the concessions meant to flatter kitsch mass culture. The complex is

FIGURE 0.1 Romanian Palace of the Parliament in Bucharest (1984–1997, Anca Petrescu) (George Groutas, distributed under CC BY-SA 2.0 license).

a stark set of buildings, designed to be taken quite seriously, although they are hilariously kitsch, just like the former Securitate secret agents, dressed in black suits, with dandruff specking their collars, and wearing white cotton socks in black laquer shoes. This is an instance of unintentional humor, and the laughs come from the critics, not the authors; from interpretation, not creation.[87]

Even if we assume that the humor of the Palace (and the Congreso) is unintentional we could ask if that itself is a disqualifying factor in categorizing these building as postmodern. After all, one of the fundamental concepts in the postmodern methodology of analyzing culture was based on the assumption that, contrary to common belief, the author's intentions do not determine the interpretation.[88] Perhaps it is possible to both acknowledge the fact that they were undoubtedly "designed to be taken quite seriously" and that, at the same time, they have ironic and humorous dimension (intended or not), thus realizing the postmodern principle of double-coding in a subversive and unexpected way. This is one question that will be taken up more fully in Chapter 1.

In South American countries outside of Chile, clear-cut cases of propagandistic uses of postmodern architecture are harder to find, though there are cases in which postmodernism overlaps with anti-government sentiments. One example can be found in Argentina, with La Escuelita, an independent research institute established by Tony Díaz, Ernesto Katzenstein, Justo Solsona, and Rafael Viñoly, operating from 1976 to 1983 during the dictatorship of Jorge Rafael Videla. Banned from the university, these architects pursued their independent educational endeavors through studio exercises, seminars, and lectures

20 Introduction

of invited architects – most importantly, those of Aldo Rossi, whose studies on typologies and the city were crucial for La Escuelita's philosophy. While La Escuelita's members do not frame their involvement in the school as oppositional, given that the school operated during the dictatorship with a strong anti-communist agenda, even the mere invitation of Rossi, known for his Marxist beliefs, could be seen as a meaningful gesture. In projects such as the study for Avenida de Mayo (1978), La Escuelita used postmodern forms and ideas to create public democratic spaces, which, in the charged political context of a dictatorship, are hard to interpret as completely neutral and disengaged.[89]

While instances of politically and socially engaged postmodern architecture can be found in many locations, Chile and Poland stand out as cases in which postmodern architecture is utilized both by governments and architects with oppositional agendas. The regimes in power in Chile and Poland in the 1970s and 1980s represented contrasting political and economic philosophies – of neoliberalism and socialism, respectively. Therefore, this juxtaposition reveals that the political and social engagement of postmodernism is not limited to any particular economic reality. Contrary to common belief, postmodernism was not only a manifestation of the "logic of late capitalism" but, as the example of Poland shows, also suited to the needs of a late socialist state. Likewise, in Chile, as discussed in Chapter 3, architects utilized postmodern theories and forms in ways that they believed could counter Pinochet's neoliberal agenda.

I.4 Recent Scholarship on Postmodernism

The last decade has brought a surge of interest in the historicization and theorization of postmodern architecture. The vast majority of these efforts are limited to Western architecture, as is visible in the most widely discussed books – most significantly, K. Michael Hays' *Architecture's Desire: Reading the Late Avant-Garde* (2009), Reinhold Martin's *Utopia's Ghost: Architecture and Postmodernism, Again* (2010), Aaron Vinegar's *I Am a Monument: On Learning from Las Vegas* (2012), Emmanuel Petit's *Irony; or, The Self-Critical Opacity of Postmodern Architecture* (2013), Martino Strieli's *Las Vegas in Rear View Mirror* (2013), Léa-Catherine Szacka's, *Exhibiting the Postmodern: The 1980 Venice Architecture Biennale* (2016), and *The Klotz Tapes*, edited by Oliver Elser (2018). Many of these scholars voice the need to correct false assumptions that shape the dominant discourse on postmodernism. Petit's analysis is especially relevant, as he argues that, contrary to the most influential theorizations of postmodern architecture, it cannot be reduced to a careless, formalist, and solely market-driven project. Petit argues that, thanks to its use of irony as a critical tool, postmodern architecture was far from "an embarrassing episode of arbitrary aesthetic, nostalgic ethic, and compliant politics," but rather deserves to be taken seriously as engaged in "self-critique."[90]

The topic of postmodern architecture and design has also occupied a central place in many popular publications, coffee table books, and exhibitions.[91] Several exhibitions have paid particular attention to the works of the Memphis group members (*Nathalie Du Pasquier: Big Objects Not Always Silent* at Kunsthalle Wien in 2016, *Ettore Sottsass: Design Radical at the Met Breuer* in 2017); others have offered comprehensive retrospective examinations of postmodernism, like *Postmodernism: Style and Subversion, 1970–1990* in the Victoria and Albert Museum of Art (2011–2012); while others have offered radical critical reassessments like Sylvia Lavin's *Architecture Itself and Other Postmodernist Myths* at the Canadian Center for Architecture (2018–2019), which offers a "counter-reading of postmodern procedures, replacing the myth of the autonomous architect with accounts of empirically describable architectural activity," focusing on the relations between architecture, the art market, bureaucracy, and institutions.[92]

Still, the publications and exhibitions mentioned above continue the practice of treating Northern American and Western European architecture almost exclusively. Petit's argument on irony and Lavin's attention to the bureaucracy and art market behind postmodernism, for example, are supported exclusively by case studies designed by "the usual suspects": Peter Eisenman, Michael Graves, Arata Isozaki, Rem Koolhas, James Stirling, Stanley Tigerman, Venturi Scott Brown Associates, etc. At the same time, the lack of attention to non-western regions in architectural knowledge on postmodernism has been recognized by scholars of architecture and urban studies. The need to fill this gap in architectural knowledge can be observed in a range of conferences and symposia such as "Intersections: Late Socialism and Postmodernism" (MIT, 2012), "Socialist Postmodernism: Architecture and Society under Late Socialism" (EAHN Turin, 2014), "Re-framing Identities: Architecture's Turn to History, 1970–1990" (ETH Zurich, 2015) (focused on the relations between Eastern and Western European architecture between 1970 and 1990), "Publicly Postmodern" (SAH Glasgow, 2017) (focused on postmodern architecture beyond its most well-known settings of North America and Britain), and "For Lack of a Better Word: Postmodernism across the Three Worlds" (EAHN Edinburgh, 2021). This current of research is also represented by book publications (*Second World Postmodernisms: Architecture and Society under Late Socialism* ed. Vladimir Kulić, published by Bloomsbury in 2019) and academic journals (special issue "The Geopolitical Aesthetic of Postmodernism" in *Architectural Histories*, forthcoming). In addition to casting light on marginalized locations ignored by existing accounts on the period, these academic endeavors unfold the complexity of relations between architecture and the State that complicate existing accounts on postmodernism.

The specific literature on Chilean and Polish postmodern architecture is limited. Chilean and Polish scholars rarely view postmodern architecture in their countries as a field worthy of scholarly investigation. It has been common to marginalize its importance or even deny its presence, for postmodern architecture in these countries has come to represent a repressed past. Polish critics and architects tend to characterize postmodern architecture as the epitome of bad taste and as imperfect copies of Western designs. As postmodern architecture was especially visible in the first ten years after the systemic transition from socialism to capitalism in 1989, critics deride it as architectural evidence of the clumsiness and awkwardness of provincial early capitalism. Similarly, as Chilean architect Smiljan Radić has said, postmodernism was "associated with the neo-liberal economic policies of Augusto Pinochet" and thus "imposed on Chile."[93] In an interview following his appointment as the curator of the Architecture Biennale in Venice in 2016, Alejandro Aravena goes further and says that Chile was "protected from postmodernism,"[94] disavowing its role in the country's architectural history completely. The conception of postmodern architecture in both countries revealed in such scattered remarks is based on misunderstandings, suppressions, inaccuracies, and conflicting accounts.

Only very recently has postmodern architecture in Chile and Poland begun to be taken up as matters for serious scholarly attention. The first broader attempt to investigate Chilean postmodern architecture was undertaken in 2008, when a group of architecture students at Pontificia Universidad Católica de Chile created "Docoposmo" – a website (in Spanish, currently inactive, not archived) with the goal of documenting postmodern architecture

22 Introduction

in Santiago de Chile. The group printed an abbreviated guide in the form of a leaflet with a map and short descriptions of postmodern buildings in Santiago. Despite its popular nonacademic character, "Docoposmo" deserves mention as a pioneering effort of recognizing Chilean architecture of the 1970s and 1980s. One of the "Docoposmo" founding members, Francisco Díaz, is the author of two other significant publications: an essay on Chilean architecture and memory, "Los arquitectos y la falta de memoria," a large portion of which is devoted to the Congreso Nacional de Chile in Valparaíso (covered in Chapter 1), and a second essay recently published on Chilean postmodern architecture and neoliberalism, "Complejidad y contradicción en la dictadura" (both in Spanish).[95] The broader edited collection in which the latter essay can be found, *Santiago de Chile 1977–1990: Arquitectura, Ciudad y Política*, edited by Daniel Talesnik, promises to be a significant addition to this scholarship as several of the essays discuss postmodernism and CEDLA.[96] There are no books focused on Chilean postmodernism, although two recent publications, *Portales del Laberinto. Arquitectura y ciudad en Chile, 1977–2009* (an anthology of essays edited by Jorge Francisco Liernur, in Spanish) and *Editar para transformar* (a collection of interviews about architectural Chilean magazines in 1960s and 1970s), discuss the postmodern group CEDLA briefly. Additionally, CEDLA is discussed in the context of Chilean architectural culture in the 1970s and 1980s by Fernando Carvajal in his doctoral dissertation, "Modernización autoritaria y cultura arquitectónica, Chile 1975–1992: una lectura crítica a partir del CEDLA," defended at Pontificia Universidad Católica de Chile in 2021 (in Spanish).[97]

Polish postmodern architecture is somewhat better represented in existing scholarship, though efforts to analyze it have only appeared in recent years. Previously, analyses of Polish postmodern architecture had been rare and, in the case of studying the late socialist period, nonexistent. It had been commonly believed that postmodern architecture started with the systemic change of 1989 when the newly adapted capitalist system enabled unlimited absorption of Western (especially American) culture.[98] One of the first scholarly works concerned with Polish postmodern architecture under late socialism was Piotr Bujas and Łukasz Stanek's exhibition, *Postmodernizm jest prawie w porządku: polska architektura po socjalistycznej globalizacji* (translated *Postmodernism Is Almost Alright: Polish Architecture after Socialist Globalization*). Bujas and Stanek's exhibition traced the activity of Polish architects who spent time working in North Africa and the Middle East in the 1970s and 1980s. In these countries, the architects had a chance to experiment with postmodern forms, which they then used in their realizations in Poland, upon returning to the country. This exhibition was accompanied by a catalogue (in Polish and English) and followed with a comprehensive scholarly article authored by Stanek.[99] Another effort to document and analyze postmodern architecture in Poland was an anthology of commissioned essays, *Postmodernizm polski – architektura i urbanistyka* (translated *Polish Postmodernism: Architecture and Urbanism*), edited by myself. This book was complemented with an anthology of interviews with key Polish postmodern architects, *Postmodernizm polski – wywiady* [translated *Polish Postmodernism: Interviews*], edited by Alicja Gzowska and myself. These books covered the period between 1970 and 2000, though they did not discuss late socialist architecture in detail. The two most recent research projects devoted to postmodern architecture are *Architecture of the 7th Day*, an exhibition and catalogue authored by Kuba Snopek, Iza Cichońska, and Karolina Popera and Florian Urban's book *Postmodern Architecture in Socialist Poland: Transformation, Symbolic Form and National Identity* (Routledge, 2021). The first project documents Polish churches built in the 1970s and 1980s and analyzes them as expressions of anti-government resistance.

The latter book introduces some of the main threads of Polish postmodernism to international readers, focusing specifically on church architecture, mass housing, and approaches to conservation and urban space.

Since the 2000s, architectural scholarship has been particularly invested in redefining the canon of architectural knowledge from the position of non-Western locations. In the field of twentieth-century architecture, these efforts are focused on modern architecture. Postmodernism outside North America and Western Europe has been subject to a double exclusion from architectural discourse, both because of the continued marginalization of the South and the East and because of a more general lack of interest in postmodernism among architecture historians from the early 1990s until recently. This book is a part of larger efforts to fill gaps in knowledge regarding locations that are under-represented in architectural scholarship and while doing so, change familiar assumptions about postmodernism. Chilean and Polish architecture reveals how postmodern architecture does not necessarily need to be focused solely "on aesthetics to the detriment of social content"[100] (Cocotas) and that postmodern architects cannot be described as merely "surrealist stage designers"[101] (Habermas) taking part in a socially and politically conservative project. In Chile and Poland, postmodernism wasn't "the new corporate style" or a "movement … that affirms a status quo" characterized by "passivity vis-a-vis economic and political power" (McLeod).[102] In these locations, as well as in many more countries outside Western democracies, postmodernism was used as a means to challenge the status quo and to produce social and political change through spatial and architectural solutions. Chilean and Polish postmodernism shows that less prominent locations have the potential to challenge established truths based on Western architectural canon of texts and buildings. This book then analyzes Chilean and Polish architecture not only to add their histories to existing scholarship on architecture but also to challenge the dominant narrative of postmodern architecture from the position of these locations.

I.5 Outline

What follows are four chapters and a conclusion. The first two chapters focus on Chile and Chapters 3 and 4 center on Poland. The two sets of chapters parallel each other in their alternating focus on, first, postmodernism as a tool for the State and, second, postmodernism as involved in oppositional tactics.

The first chapter, "Postmodernism and the State in Pinochet's Chile," discusses propagandistic uses of postmodern architecture by Pinochet's regime in Chile, using two case studies: the Plaza de la Constitución in Santiago de Chile (Cristián Undurraga and Ana Luisa Devés, 1980–1982) and the Congreso Nacional de Chile (1988–1990, Juan Cárdenas, José Covacevic, and Raúl Farrú) in Valparaíso. Both were the results of prominent public architecture competitions organized during Pinochet's reign. The postmodern forms of the Plaza de la Constitución and the Congreso Nacional de Chile were used to present a desired image of the State, signaling a new direction in the politics of the country.

The second chapter, "Postmodernism Against the State Under Pinochet's Dictatorship," examines how postmodern ideas were used by Chilean architects who opposed Pinochet's policies. It analyzes the practice of architects who were members of CEDLA (Centro de Estudios de Arquitectura, Center for Architectural Studies), an independent collective of Chilean architects established in 1977 in Santiago de Chile. The members of CEDLA – most importantly, Humberto Eliash, Cristián Boza, and Pedro Murtinho – through their

24 Introduction

projects, magazine, organized conferences, and symposia promoted a version of politically and socially engaged postmodernism that could counter the neoliberal agenda of the regime.

Chapter 3, "Socialist Postmodernism in the Polish People's Republic," analyzes how the Polish Socialist Party, the governing body in the Polish People's Republic, first appropriated postmodernism as a Soviet invention and then used it as a means to appease social tensions in times of increasing unrest. In addition to discussing state-sanctioned architectural discourse, this chapter analyzes the Na Skarpie housing estate in Kraków (Romuald Loegler, Wojciech Dobrzański, Michał Szymanowski, 1987–1995), which reveals how postmodernism was used as a means of propaganda by the State and at the same time by the architect as an opportunity to implement socially progressive spatial solutions.[103] This coexistence of opposing ideological interpretations and contrasting uses of postmodern architecture within a single realization is typical in Polish architecture and is further analyzed in the following chapter.

Chapter 4, "Postmodernism and Dissent in Socialist Poland," elaborates on architects who used postmodern forms and ideas as tools to oppose the vision of society and urban space imposed by the politics of the Polish People's Republic – most importantly, Czesław Bielecki and Marek Budzyński. It analyzes documents issued by Bielecki's architectural group DiM (Dom i Miasto, existing between 1980 and 1984), which united postmodern inspirations with oppositional agendas and Budzyński's practice. The chapter centers specifically on Budzyński's flagship realization – the North Ursynów housing estate in Warsaw (1972–1977) – and the Church of the Ascension of Christ (1980–1985 by Budzyński, Zbigniew Badowski and Piotr Wicha), which was realized as a part of the North Ursynów estate. Like Loegler's Na Skarpie, North Ursynów offers an example of how postmodernism was interpreted not only as radically anti-government (as in Bielecki's case) but also as a tool to achieve social change by slowly transforming the oppressive system from within. In analyzing North Ursynów, this chapter puts emphasis on the legacy of socialist realism, which Budzyński saw as anticipating key ideas brought by postmodernism decades later.

In the conclusion, I step back and discuss the distinctive qualities of postmodernism in these countries and the implications of creating a narrative of postmodernism that takes into account its political histories in traditionally marginalized locations.

Notes

1 Hopkins, *Postmodern Architecture*, 224.
2 Griffiths, "Now is not the time." A founding member of FAT Architecture studio, Griffiths built his own career on postmodern revivalism himself. However, he claims that his own uses of postmodernism as an architect were critical and ironic, while the current interest in postmodernism is affirmative and lacks critical distance.
3 Fernandez, "2018 Dean's Roundtable."
4 Cocotas, "Design for the One Percent."
5 Hatherley, "Postmodernism will not be forgiven lightly."
6 For example, Robert Venturi claims that "I first heard the word 'postmodernism' when I was in college. I occasionally used it. But we [Venturi and Denise Scott-Brown] are not postmodernists." Paperny, "An Interview with Denise Scott Brown and Robert Venturi."
7 Jameson, *Postmodernism*, 4.
8 Irving, "The Modern/Postmodern Divide and Urban Planning," 479.
9 CIAM (The Congrès internationaux d'architecture moderne, or International Congresses of Modern Architecture) was an organization existing from 1928 to 1959, which promoted the principles of modern architecture through a series of events and congresses across Europe.

10 Jacobs, *The Death and Life of Great American Cities*, 6.
11 Jacobs, 222.
12 Jacobs, 14.
13 Venturi, *Complexity and Contradiction in Architecture*, 104.
14 Venturi, 88.
15 Ockman, "Review," 490.
16 Venturi et al., *Learning from Las Vegas*, 3.
17 Venturi et al., 7, 9, and 52, respectively.
18 Venturi et al., 6.
19 Venturi et al., 87. *Learning from Las Vegas* is symptomatic of a broader change in the status of drawing within architectural discourse brought about by postmodernism. Instead of a mere tool for representation and visualization of designs, drawing became a field of architectural experimentation and research. Moreover, for many postmodern architects, the attention to drawing confirmed architecture's position as a fine art rather than a mere technical, pragmatic discipline.
20 Venturi et al., 90.
21 Le Corbusier, *Towards an Architecture*, 157.
22 Venturi et al., 76.
23 Rossi, *The Architecture of the City*, 176.
24 Rossi, 170.
25 Rossi, 41.
26 Rossi, 46.
27 Rossi, 55.
28 Rossi, 29.
29 Rossi, 24.
30 Rossi, 40.
31 Rossi, 21.
32 Rossi, 34.
33 Rossi, 41.
34 Rossi, 127.
35 Rossi, 179.
36 Alexander, *A Pattern Language*, x.
37 Jencks, *What Is Post-Modernism?*, 14.
38 Jencks, *The New Paradigm in Architecture*, 9.
39 Bristol, "The Pruitt–Igoe Myth," 163.
40 Jencks, *The New Paradigm in Architecture*, 15–18.
41 Jencks, *The New Paradigm in Architecture*, 15.
42 Jencks, *What Is Post-Modernism?*, 14.
43 Jencks, *What Is Post-Modernism?*, 14–15.
44 Jencks, *What Is Post-Modernism?*, 19.
45 Jencks, *What Is Post-Modernism?*, 23.
46 Jencks, *What Is Post-Modernism?*, 22.
47 Jencks identifies also "borderline cases" of architects such as Leon Krier, who is "traditional and straightforward in a manner that Post-Modernism is not." Jencks, *What Is Post-Modernism?*, 22.
48 Jencks, *What Is Post-Modernism?*, 19.
49 Jencks, *What Is Post-Modernism?*, 47.
50 Portoghesi, *Postmodern*, 31.
51 Portoghesi, 7.
52 Portoghesi, 7.
53 Portoghesi, 8.
54 Portoghesi, 11.
55 Portoghesi, 11. Though not taken up by the Chilean or Polish architects to be discussed, another protagonist in the promotion of the theory of postmodernism along with Jencks and Portoghesi was Heinrich Klotz. Klotz started his work on postmodernism in late 1970s, when the term was already established and widely circulating. His contributions to this field include books, most importantly *The History of Postmodern Architecture* published in 1988, and curatorial activity. Klotz frames postmodernism in architecture as a continuation of modernism, aimed to fix its failures rather than make a radical break with it: "postmodern architecture should be seen as a revision of

modernism," he writes (Klotz, *The History of Postmodern Architecture*, xiv.). The main amendments introduced by postmodernism are "the rich scope of meaning and the fictional content of the message from which the form of the building derives its directive" rather than the "functional aptness alone." Klotz formulates the chief postulate of postmodernism as "not only function but fiction as well." For Klotz, postmodern architecture, although diverse, is guided by a "common goal: to again conceive architecture as a form that conveys meaning and to view it as a species of art." "The final goal" for postmodern architecture is for Klotz

> to liberate architecture from the muteness of 'pure forms' and from the clamor of ostentatious constructions in order that a building might again become an occasion for a creative effort, attuned not only to facts and utilization programs but also to poetic ideas.
>
> (5)

56 Habermas, "Modern and Postmodern Architecture," 328.
57 Habermas, 328.
58 Habermas, 328.
59 Jameson, *Postmodernism*, 5. Further, Jameson stresses that:

> It is in the realm of architecture, however, that modifications in aesthetic production are most dramatically visible, and that their theoretical problems have been most centrally raised and articulated; it was indeed from architectural debates that my own conception of postmodernism – as it will be outlined in the following pages – initially began to emerge.
>
> (2)

60 Jameson, *Postmodernism*, 2.
61 Jameson, *Postmodernism*, 6. As mentioned above, the link between late capitalism and postmodern architecture was also made in Portoghesi's *Postmodern*. More in: Margaret A. Rose, *The Post-Modern and the Post-Industrial: A Critical Analysis* (Cambridge: Cambridge University Press, 1991).
62 McGurik, "Has postmodernist design eaten itself."
63 As Robert Stern, one of the most prolific American postmodern architects put it: "Postmodernism is not revolutionary in either the political or artistic sense; in fact, it reinforces the effect of the technocratic and bureaucratic society in which we live." See Robert Stern, "The Doubles of Post-Modern," *Harvard Architecture Review* 1 (1980), quoted in McLeod, "Architecture and Politics in the Reagan Era," 54. McLeod uses this quote from Stern as symptomatic of postmodernism in architecture.
64 Griffiths, "Now is not the time."
65 Furman, "Live interview." Despite clear references to postmodernism present in the projects by "New London Fabulous," Furman stresses that the movement shouldn't be seen as restricted to stylistics. See Marcus Fairs, "Colourful New London Fabulous design movement is challenging minimalism, says Adam Nathaniel Furman," *Dezeen* (May 26, 2020). https://www.dezeen.com/2020/05/26/new-london-fabulous-design-movement-adam-nathaniel-furman/.
66 Walala, "Profile."
67 Walala, "Walala Play."
68 Ilori, "Happy Street."
69 Ravenscroft, "Yinka Ilori covers adult playground."
70 On hyperspaces as characteristic to postmodernism and John Portman, see Jameson, *Postmodernism*, 38–39.
71 Furman, "The Democratic Monument."
72 Furman, "The Democratic Monument."
73 Furman, "The Democratic Monument."
74 Mouffe, *On the Political*, 1.
75 Mouffe, 1.
76 Mouffe, 1–2.
77 "Bases y Fallo," 29. Quoted in Díaz, "Los arquitectos y la falta de memoria," 11. Translation by Díaz.
78 Loegler, "Rozmowa z Romualdem Loeglerem," 154. Translation mine.
79 Boza et al. "Tema II La ciudad de Santiago proposición para Santiago Metropolitano," 74. Translation mine.

80 Leśniakowska, interview by Lidia Klein.
81 Murtinho, interview by Lidia Klein (August 30).
82 Boza, interview by Joaquín Serrano, 165.
83 Eliash, interview by Lidia Klein (August 23).
84 Weizman, "Citizenship," 113.
85 Weizman, 113–114. The most famous "kitchen architects" are Alexander Brodsky and Ilya Utkin, Moscow-based "paper architects" producing fantastic drawings as a way to escape from and criticize late socialist reality of Soviet Union.
86 Ioan, "The History of Nothing."
87 Ioan.
88 This idea was proposed, most importantly, by Roland Barthes in "The Death of the Author" (1967).
89 The status of La Escuelita is described by Luis E. Carranza and Fernando Luiz Lara in their book *Modern Architecture in Latin America*: "given the highly intimidating political situation following the coup, the possibility of snitches, and the known issue of the desaparecidos (disappeared), [La Escuelita's] gatherings remained apolitical (not depoliticized, as in with politics removed)" (p. 275). The nature of the relationship between La Escuelita and the broader political context in which it worked has been discussed by many scholars, most recently by Jonas Delecave de Amorim in his unpublished dissertation, "Uma disciplina em crise: disputas pela arquitetura na Escuelita de Buenos Aires (1976–1983)," defended in 2020 at São Paulo University.
90 The passage in its entirety reads:

> it is not useful to rehearse what has turned into a historiographic cliché, according to which postmodern architecture is seen as synonymous with a certain type of "easy" aesthetic and a parochial imagery assembled from an uncritical pillage of history, and both effortlessly and uncritically assimilated by the market. The 1970s and early 1980s have heard the critical voices which formulated (Marxist) resistance against postmodern architects' alleged easy acceptance of the rules of the consumerist world. Hal Foster, Kenneth Frampton, Andreas Huyssen, Fredric Jameson, Mary McLeod, and Manfredo Tafuri are only some of the detractors of the ideology of complacency they identified at the core of architecture during these years. The more they condemned Philip Johnson's AT&T building as historical nostalgia, Michael Graves' Portland Public Services Buildings as lowbrow populism, Hans Hollein's Austrian Travel Agency as commercial pastiche, Peter Eisenman's Wexner Center as disillusioned iconoclastic diversion, and Charles Moore's Piazza d'Italia as eclectic kitsch, the more these projects were codified as the icons of postmodernism which had written off any ambition of "resistance" in favor of architects' subjective and private diversion with form. Part of the critical assessments in those years was still geared toward convincing the world that there was indeed such a cultural phenomenon as postmodernism in architecture, and that it was to be evaluated as a creative and intellectual impasse because it let go of any resistance and no longer coincided with the activist program of the modern avant-garde; at worst, all postmodernism was degraded into either commodified kitsch or camp…Postmodern architecture could then be relegated to historical space as an embarrassing episode of arbitrary aesthetic, nostalgic ethic, and compliant politics.
>
> (18–19)

91 Recently published visually attractive titles addressed to broad audiences include Judith Gura's *Postmodern Design Complete Design, Furniture, Graphics, Architecture, Interiors* (2017) and Terry Farrels' and Adam Nathaniel Furman's *Revisiting Postmodernism* (2017). For the sake of brevity, this list excludes monographs of selected locations or buildings such as Elain Harwood and Geraint Franklin's *Post-Modern Buildings in Britain* (London: Batsford, 2017).
92 Lavin, "Architecture Itself." See also *The Return of the Past: Postmodernism in British Architecture* at Sir John Soane's Museum, London (2018) and *Postmodernism 1980–1995* at Helsinki's Design Museum (2015).
93 Miranda, "Rough, yet poetic."
94 Hawthorne, "Pritzer winner Alejandro Aravena on Pinochet."
95 The latter analyzes the relation between architecture and history during the dictatorship and generally understands Chilean postmodernism as complicit in Pinochet's neoliberal project. Díaz discusses CEDLA though does not analyze the particular projects covered in this book.

28 Introduction

96 With the exception of Díaz's and Talesnik's entries, which were shared with me privately, the collection was published too late to be consulted for this book. Talesnik's and Díaz's essays focus specifically on postmodernism: see Talesnik, "Fue el posmodernismo la arquitectura del pinochetismo? Arquitecturas en el centro de Santiago en la década de 1980" and Díaz, "Complejidad y contradicción en la dictadura: Arquitectura e historia en el Chile de Pinochet." Fernando Carvajal's essay on CEDLA, based on his dissertation mentioned below, is entitled "La contrapropuesta del CEDLA: Cambios en la cultura arquitectónica a fines de los setenta."

97 The dissertation was defended after the completion of this book so could not be consulted in time for the purposes of my discussions.

98 For example. Adam Nadolny in his essay on postmodern architecture in Poznań published in 2012 notes that "postmodern architecture appeared in Poland only at the end of the 1980s and at the beginning of the 1990s. That delay was caused by the communist system that prevailed in Poland." Nadolny, "Postmodern architecture in the historical quarters." Nadolny, "Postmodern architecture in the historical quarters of Poznan," 49.

99 Stanek, "Mobilities of Architecture in the Global Cold War."

100 Cocotas, "Design for the One Percent."

101 Habermas, 328.

102 McLeod, 29, 38.

103 By "propaganda" I mean messaging designed deliberately to gain support among a target audience and to persuade this audience to act and think in a desired way.

1

POSTMODERNISM AND THE STATE IN PINOCHET'S CHILE

With the coup d'état that put Augusto Pinochet in power on September 11, 1973, Chile's political system shifted from democratic to authoritarian and its economic system shifted from socialist to neoliberal. Following the coup, a military junta composed of Pinochet, Air Force General Gustavo Leigh, Navy Admiral José Toribio Merino, and Carabinero Chief General César Mendoza was established as the country's supreme authority. The junta maintained legislative authority in the country after suspending the constitution and the Chilean Congress in 1973, and while in power, banned political parties and trade unions, imposed a curfew and restrictions on gatherings, and assumed control over the media. A month after the coup, the government established Dirección de Inteligencia Nacional (DINA, National Intelligence Directorate), a secret police force authorized to detain, torture, and murder individuals suspected of any activity against the regime. The militarization of the government and its apparatuses was combined with a strong agenda of privatization and deregulation such that the social and economic efforts of Pinochet's administration were focused on reversing the pro-social policies of the previous governments of Eduardo Frei Montalva (1964–1970) and Salvador Allende (1970–1973).

Pinochet's shift toward a radical free market economy and the dismantling of social welfare institutions built by previous administrations had significant impacts on Chilean urban space and architecture. The privatization-oriented policies of the new government led to the emergence of architectural formats new (or at least not previously popular) to urban space in Chile. While the eras of Frei and Allende were represented by late modern social housing and public buildings, the architecture of Pinochet's era was defined by banks, hotels, headquarters of private (or newly privatized) companies, and shopping centers. As these buildings, burgeoning in the 1970s and 1980s, were mostly designed according to the newest, postmodern trends, for Chilean architects and architectural critics, postmodernism became widely interpreted as a style of Pinochet's time.[1]

As many critics point out, Chilean architecture of the 1970s and 1980s not only reflected economic and social changes implemented by Pinochet but also (whether intended by the architects or not) actively contributed to these transformations. Writing about postmodern

DOI: 10.4324/9781003179467-2

30 Postmodernism and the State in Pinochet's Chile

corporate buildings in Santiago, Daniel Talesnik analyzes them as instrumental in creating a new, neoliberal image of Chilean capital.[2] Similarly, Liliana de Simone, architectural critic writing on new types of commercial centers in Pinochet's Chile describes them as signs of "awaited and expected progress, imbued with the discourses of modernization advocated by the military regime."[3] Postmodern forms in banks, hotels, and other commercial buildings and spaces populating Chilean cities in the 1970s and 1980s aided the government's political agenda as they helped to normalize painful neoliberal reforms and create an image of prosperity and progress.

In this sense, we can understand Chilean postmodern commercial architecture as an active agent responsible for normalizing and validating dramatic social, economic, and political changes.

At the same time, Pinochet's government did not formulate any direct program regarding architecture. Just as in other domains, architecture was supposed to be regulated by the market forces exclusively, and freed from any influence or control from the government. Despite the lack of any straight-forward guidelines regarding architecture, Pinochet's government had a clear preference for postmodern forms. This is apparent in the results of public architectural competitions organized during Pinochet's regime. The two most important of these concerned symbolically and politically charged sites of high significance: the Plaza de la Constitución in Santiago de Chile (1980, organized by the Municipality of Santiago) and the Congreso Nacional de Chile (1988) in Valparaíso. Together, the competitions marked the two most significant political events in the post-coup history of Chile – the establishment of the constitution and the Chilean national plebiscite, respectively – and the winning designs were based on postmodern forms and ideas.

This chapter examines the relation between postmodern architecture in Chile and Pinochet's State, discussing urban policies with direct impact on architecture, as well as these two commissions resulting in postmodern realizations. As we will see, postmodernism is connected not just to the turn to a neoliberal (Milton Friedman-inspired) economic system, but also to the image of an authoritarian regime: postmodernism in Pinochet's Chile is simultaneously a style of late capitalism and a part of the State's political propaganda.

1.1 From Eduardo Frei Montalva and Salvador Allende to Augusto Pinochet: Transformations in Urban Space

Beginning in the mid-nineteenth century and into the twentieth, Chile experienced intensified migration from rural areas to cities, which resulted in a deficit of urban housing. The first major effort to alleviate the lack of housing was passing the Ley de Habitaciones Obreras (Law for Worker's Housing) in 1906 under the presidency of Germán Riesco (1901–1906). After that, Chile created various institutions and organizations devoted to the challenges of urban renovation caused by increasing metropolitization. These had a special focus on government-supported housing, which was supposed to replace growing *campamentos* (shanty towns). The most significant effort in this respect was undertaken during Frei's presidency. In 1965, the government created the Ministry of Housing and Urban Development (MINVU, Ministerio de Vivienda y Urbanismo). Along with MINVU emerged four affiliated organizations: COU (Corporación de Obras Urbanas, Urban Works Corporation) responsible for urban infrastructure, CORHABIT (Corporación de Servicios Habitacionales, Corporation for Housing Services), CORVI (Corporación de

Vivienda, Housing Corporation) dedicated to social housing, and CORMU (Corporación de Mejoramiento Urbano, Corporation of Urban Improvement), focused on urban renewal. Among these newly established organizations, CORMU played an especially crucial role in shaping the architecture and urban planning of Chile, and became a symbol of the government's efforts to modernize the country and reduce its housing shortage. CORMU's mission, the long-term improvement of cities, was characterized by a holistic approach to integrating interventions in architecture, infrastructure, and social vision. CORMU operated by acquiring deteriorating sites in strategic locations (such as downtown Santiago) with the goal of transforming them into sustainable urban environments, in which people from different socioeconomic statuses could intermingle.

Its two showcase realizations were the San Louis housing project (1970–1973) designed by Miguel Lawner – converting rural terrain in Las Condes in Santiago into an urban space – and, most importantly, the Remodelación San Borja mass housing complex (1966–1973) by Sergio Miranda Rodriguez, Carlos Buchholtz Galigniana, and Eugenio Salvi Rosende.

Remodelación San Borja is located in the center of Santiago de Chile and includes twenty housing towers accommodating ten thousand people, distributed loosely in an urban park. These buildings are connected with a network of elevated walkways (realized only partially) and surrounded by vast area of greenery. San Borja constitutes a homogenous "superblock" uninterrupted by traditional typologies, such as streets. As each tower follows the same

FIGURE 1.1 San Borja housing complex in Santiago de Chile (1966–1973, Sergio Miranda Rodriguez, Carlos Buchholtz Galigniana, and Eugenio Salvi Rosende) (Felipe Restrepo Acosta, distributed under CC BY-SA 4.0 license).

format – a twenty-story tall building, with six apartments per floor – San Borja is subject to the repetitive rational geometry that defines many orthodox modernist housing projects across the globe.

Remodelación San Borja offers a representative example of the urban philosophy of CORMU, which was based on the postulates of Le Corbusier and the *Charter of Athens*, published in Chile in 1946. Like other urban interventions realized by CORMU, San Borja was based on the idea of separation of functions within the city, the isolation of pedestrians from vehicular traffic, and the typology of towers. As Rodrigo Pérez de Arce writes in his study on CORMU's working method and San Borja as its example,

> at CORMU, the tower was defined as an a priori element. … The tower was valued as an instrument to liberate the ground, making the city permeable and generating large green areas. … CORMU kept to the canons of modern urbanism by adopting spatial fluidity and the prevalence of green spaces as generic objects.[4]

This "unitary, formal, totalizing intention of modern urbanism and its heroic period, leaning on geometry and formal relationships" visible in San Borja corresponded with the design methods of CORMU's studio.[5] As de Arce describes,

> the very mechanisms used to represent the city corresponded to those urban aspects privileged in the project: volumes were more important than any other concern. Furthermore, the presence of large urban models would give the studio a character similar to the strategy room of a high military command: a stock of towers was always available.[6]

Another project representative of the urban philosophy of CORMU was the proposed revitalization of the Western area of central Santiago, Santiago Poniente, which was expected to begin at the end of 1973, but which was permanently halted by the coup d'état in September of 1973. In 1972, CORMU announced an international competition for the revitalization of Santiago Poniente, which is located between the Mapocho River and the Bernardo O'Higgins promenade, and composed by predominantly nineteenth-century architecture.

In the second half of the twentieth century, Santiago Poniente had experienced a gradual disappearance of its population, and the deterioration of the neighborhood was worsened by the construction of La Avenida Norte-Sur (completed in 1975) highway, which cut it off from the city center.[7] The area to be developed included roughly sixteen blocks of Santiago Poniente, stretching between Santo Domingo street as its Northern limit, Agustinas street as Southern border, Amunátegui containing it from the East and Almirante Barroso from the West. The winning proposal, designed by a group of Argentinean architects associated with la Universidad Nacional de La Plata (Emilio Sessa, Enrique Bares, Santiago F. Bó, Tomas García, and Roberto Germani) was a rational modernist plan laid out on a clear grid imposed on the intricate existing urban fabric of Santiago Poniente. The architects reorganized the neighborhood into four larger blocks, separated car and pedestrian traffic by adding two elevated pedestrian circuits, and added underground parking spaces. The existing historic urban tissue was made more dense by adding high rise housing. Like Remodelación San Borja, Santiago Poniente became a symbol of urban planning and architecture under Frei and Salvador Allende, both in terms of the social

FIGURE 1.2 Street view of Barrio Brasil (Santiago Poniente) in Santiago de Chile (Diego Antonio Vilches).

FIGURE 1.3 Courtyard at Barrio Brasil (Santiago Poniente) in Santiago de Chile (Diego Antonio Vilches).

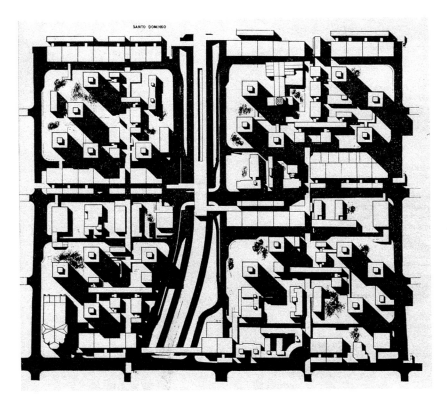

FIGURE 1.4 First-prize-winning proposal for Santiago Poniente neighborhood in Santiago de Chile, plan (1972, Emilio Sessa, Enrique Bares, Santiago F. Bó, Tomas García, and Roberto Germani), reprinted in Barés, et al., "Internacional Área de Remodelación en el Centro de Santiago," AUCA 24–25 (1973), 26.

ideologies underlying the project and the late modern forms in which it was designed. In both of these cases, the late modern forms promoted a rationalized vision of the city that was organized and efficient, attentive to the social good if also alienating in its social effects.

After the coup, the radical political and economic transformations enabled and encouraged by the administration of Pinochet would bring about significant ideological and formal changes to architecture. Pinochet's vision for the country's development was based on the neoliberal paradigms associated with Milton Friedman's economic doctrine. A group of Chilean economists who trained at the Department of Economics at the University of Chicago, known as the "Chicago Boys," brought these principles to Chile as they returned to their home country and assumed prominent positions in Pinochet's government. Since 1960s, the Chicago Boys had been working on an economic program for Chile, which they had hoped to pursue if Jorge Alessandri Rodríguez, the candidate of the Chilean right-wing party, were to become president in the elections of 1970. After Alessandri lost to Salvador Allende, the Chicago Boys continued working on their economic plan for Chile. This plan became known as "The Brick (El Ladrillo)," due to the size of the document in which it would be presented.[8] Because the Chilean economy was in a state of deep crisis during the time of Allende's government, marked with hyperinflation and significant shortages of basic consumer goods, the Chicago Boys pushed "The Brick" as a plan to recover the country's economy, promoting it among Allende's political opponents. In 1973, they presented their plan to the Navy Admiral José Toribio Merino, who would later be a part of the junta which overthrew Allende. After the coup, Pinochet, who had been initially undecided regarding an economic plan for Chile, endorsed the ideas of the Chicago Boys and ultimately put the principles of "The Brick" into practice. The Pinochet administration undertook efforts of economic liberalization, including removing tariff protections for local industry and banning trade unions, as well as privatizing social security and state-owned enterprises. These policies resulted in a period of economic boom described by Friedman as the "Chilean miracle."[9] Economic growth did not benefit all Chilean citizens equally, however, and resulted in high social costs paid for by the most vulnerable members of society. While neoliberal reforms protected and benefited the interests of private enterprises and newly privatized national companies, at the same time they significantly worsened the conditions of the working class, and contributed to deepening social inequality and poverty among those who were already the least affluent.[10]

The welfare state model that existed under the governments of Frei and Allende – which held the objectives of universal access to state-provided health care, education, as well as housing – was replaced by a radically different model. Pinochet sought to sharply limit state assistance in providing these services, resulting in moves toward deregulation, privatization, and the gradual destruction of state institutions. Education, health care, and housing ceased to be considered as rights, and instead were treated as commodities which individuals should purchase using their own resources. Radical reforms were combined with strategies of political terror initiated by the military coup, involving kidnappings, torture and the murders of citizens accused of socialist sympathies. Using the term coined by Naomi Klein, Pinochet's politics was an example of the "shock doctrine": the "brutal tactic of using the public's disorientation following a collective shock – wars, coups, terrorist attacks, market crashes or natural disasters – to push through radical pro-corporate measures."[11]

This new laissez-faire direction of Chilean politics resulted in radical changes in approach to urban space and a new set of institutions devoted to its development. As part of a broader effort to dismantle the state organizations created under Frei and Allende, in 1976 Pinochet's administration restructured and regionalized MINVU (Ministerio de Vivienda y Urbanismo; Ministry of Housing and Urban Development).[12] CORHABIT, CORMU, CORVI, and COU were terminated and replaced by a new single institution – SERVIU (Servicios Regionales de Vivienda y Urbanización, Regional Service of Housing and Urbanization) – which took over the responsibilities of these bodies, but in a reduced and decentralized way. SERVIU embodied the philosophy that the provision of public services should operate like a private market, on a cost-effective basis, and that the role of regional municipal governments should be to deliver only necessary services; it was not involved in decision-making. The SERVIU branches were created in each region of Chile to undertake housing construction and urban maintenance services, but the organization did not have the capacity to develop comprehensive master plans or housing plans.

Another change introduced by Pinochet's administration crucial for urban space was the National Urban Development Policy (Política Nacional de Desarrollo Urbano) announced in 1979.[13] The basic principle of this document was that "urban land is a resource which can be traded freely."[14] According to the new policy, zoning laws should be shaped by the

36 Postmodernism and the State in Pinochet's Chile

demands of the market, "caused by economic and social activities of the population" and should be guided by "observation and rigorous study of market behavior."[15] This shift toward radical privatization was solidified with the new Chilean constitution introduced in 1980. This document, replacing the earlier constitution effective from 1925, was approved by Chilean voters in the government-controlled plebiscite of September 11, 1980. The constitution of 1980 was subjected to the principles promoted by the Chicago Boys' school of economic thought. One of the most distinctive elements of the new constitution was a strong focus on the protection of private property, which had serious consequences for urban space. The new constitution, unlike the previous, did not impose limitations on private interventions in urban spaces that were harmful to the public interest. Likewise, urban regulation plans at the local level were subject to easy repeal if shown to be too restrictive and harmful to the interests of private owners.[16]

Another crucial aspect of the privatization of architecture and the city under Pinochet's dictatorship was its post-1973 approach to housing, which contributed greatly to the increasing segregation of Chilean society. Housing ceased to be considered as a universal human right protected by the State. It was, instead, ruled by the principles of supply and demand. Following the National Urban Development Policy announced in 1979, the role of the State in providing housing was limited to people living in extreme poverty. The government's solution for the housing crisis was characterized by the displacement of the urban poor to the peripheries. Moreover, as government agencies such as CORMU and CORVI were terminated, the construction of housing was awarded to private companies. The main criteria of obtaining a commission for new housing were price and realization time, not quality. As a result, Pinochet's responses to the housing crisis were oriented toward immediate makeshift solutions instead of creating holistic urban environments contributing to a healthy balanced society in the long term.[17]

As a consequence of these new policies, between 1979 and 1985, around 30,000 families living in *campamentos* located in the otherwise wealthy North-East area of Santiago were displaced and the land was sold to private owners. They were moved to the South and North-West areas of the city, creating neighborhoods consisting solely of inhabitants living in poverty. As many researchers have shown, the urban policies implemented under Pinochet had severe and long-lasting repercussions. The large-scale displacement undertaken by Pinochet's government created "homogeneous communities, thereby accentuating the already extreme level of residential segregation in the city."[18] In this way, the free market approach to urban space resulted in displacements that had disastrous social consequences. As historians Cristián Palacios and César Leyton have argued, these consequences can be seen as spatial manifestations of Pinochet's biopolitics.[19] Pinochet's approach to housing quickly led to a situation in which citizens with the lowest income were able to afford only housing in the peripheries, mostly without adequate infrastructure and lacking access to resources and opportunities available in more desirable locations, populated only by those from the middle and upper middle classes.

In addition to transforming housing policies according to the principles of the free market, Pinochet's administration introduced changes that affected the ways that architects worked and exchanged ideas. Pinochet's regime oversaw the liquidation of professional associations (Colegios Profesionales) – organizations whose goal was to ensure standards of ethics and integrity among active professionals. Colegios Profesionales had the power of granting (and revoking) professional titles in professions such as law, medicine, journalism, and architecture. Membership in these associations was mandatory for each professional working in Chile. One such entity was the Colegio de Arquitectos de Chile (Chilean College of Architects), established in 1942.[20] For Pinochet's advisors, such organizations operated against the principles of the free market – they created monopolies by benefiting their members only and by disallowing individuals with more competitive services to enter the market. In 1981, as a result of a new regulation (Ley 3.163) introduced by Pinochet's government, professional associations were transformed into Asociaciones Gremiales (professional unions). Like Colegios Profesionales, these organizations also grouped individuals of the same profession, but they were no longer authorized by law to grant and revoke professional titles. The Colegio de Arquitectos de Chile was turned into an Asociación Gremial. Although still operating under the same name as before the reform, it ceased to have any actual legal power to ensure that Chilean architecture would benefit society rather than simply generate profit for developers and designers. The Colegio's power and independence were also crippled by the government's intervention in its structure. Before the coup, the management of the organization (including its president) was elected by members of the Colegio. After the coup and before the regulation in 1981, Pinochet's Ministry of the Interior and Public Security replaced the democratically-elected vice president and president with their own nominations (Adela Celis and Cristián Fernandez). This form of governmental direct influence on Colegio's structure would remain in place until 1982 when the Colegio turned into an Asociación Gremial and lost its legal power to control the architectural market in Chile, and at which point direct intervention became unnecessary.[21]

Despite these interventions, architectural circles under Pinochet's rule were not entirely controlled. Architects were still able to hold professional meetings of a formal and informal character. More generally, the question of censorship was complicated during Pinochet's rule and changed over the course of the 1970s. Initially, with the coup in 1973, the government established La Dirección Nacional de Comunicación Social (DINACOS, National Directorate of Social Communication), which was in charge of supervision and censorship of all media, as well as of managing official government messages sent to the press and television. Radio, television, as well as newspapers and magazines published in Chile were screened and revised by DINACOS, and if the content was considered inappropriate, the publication needed to be corrected and sent back for revision. However, as historian Steve J. Stern describes, with time, "direct censorship of all media had begun to give way to a more subtle and layered pattern of control."[22] Thus, outlets such as magazines or minor radio stations "would evolve through self-censorship and an inconsistent, unpredictable government vigilance. The result, by 1976–1977, was the appearance of a limited media pluralism."[23] Despite continual arrests and repressions (such as harassment and threats) of journalists, the waning intensity of censorship made it possible to publish even harsh critiques of the government – a phenomenon that often baffled international observers. In 1986, New York Times correspondent Shirley Christian reported that, to her surprise, "the kiosks of Santiago were selling a variety of newsmagazines whose splashy covers accused the Government of terrorism and torture and showed a caricature of President Augusto Pinochet sprouting horns."[24]

In this context, it is possible to understand how the content published in architectural magazines or presented during exhibitions could be critical of the government, while also self-regulating. Indeed, architectural magazines and exhibitions were not directly censored by the government. Neither of the two major architectural magazines in Chile during this period – CA (Revista Oficial del Colegio de Arquitectos de Chile), published semiannually from 1968 by the Colegio, nor AUCA (Arquitectura, Urbanismo, Construcción, Arte), a

38 Postmodernism and the State in Pinochet's Chile

particularly left-leaning independent magazine existing from 1965 to 1986 – was subjected to direct censorship.[25] For one thing, it is important to realize that despite the fact that the government used architecture for propagandistic purposes (as we will consider in the cases of Plaza de la Constitución and the Chilean Congress) and imposed restrictions on Chilean architects (visible in the control over Colegio's management), architecture was not in fact seen as a particularly dangerous discipline. As a technical and pragmatic profession, architecture was considered generally as a politically innocuous field and the government's interventions in it were concerned mainly with minimizing the role of state support in architectural enterprises, and in ensuring that the field operates under the principles of the free market.

At the same time, the broader context of censorship and persecution of members of the opposition affected architectural discourse in subtler ways. Just as Stern described a shift from "direct censorship of all media … to a more subtle and layered pattern of control," magazines like *CA* and *AUCA* became to a certain extent regulated by architects themselves. As architect Humberto Eliash recalls,

> There wasn't explicit censorship of architectural publications or debates. But, for example, I remember that during a lot of the discussions during the Bienial de Arquitectura [an architectural event in Santiago, organized from 1977 by the Colegio], the public, especially the students, was voicing critical opinions against the government. Discussions which were part of the Bienial were then published in the *CA*, but excluding these voices. So there was a form of internal censorship within Colegio, and people were careful about what they were publishing.[26]

Thus with its radically different economic and political agendas, Pinochet's regime brought about a range of changes to architecture and urban design in Chile. Restructuring the Ministry of Housing and Urban Development (dissolving organizations like CORMU) and replacing it with SERVIU left behind the uniform model of late modernist housing and prioritized the protection of private property and the privatization of housing. Additionally, the changes to professional organizations and to censorship drastically changed the nature of architectural discourse, which, while not directly censored, adopted modes of self-censorship. As mentioned previously, Pinochet did not declare any official interest in architecture. Nonetheless, this approach (which was consistent with the newly adopted philosophy of *laissez-faire* that replaced government interference with regulating powers of the market) itself determined the nature of architecture in Pinochet's Chile and the boom in commercial architecture of the 1970s and 1980s provided tangible evidence of the country's growth. Moreover, two of the most significant political events in the post-coup history of Chile were marked with new architectural realizations – the Plaza de la Constitución and the Congreso Nacional de Chile. Both of them were postmodern designs.

1.2 Postmodern Architecture as Propaganda: The Plaza de la Constitución and the Congreso Nacional de Chile

The Plaza de la Constitución (Constitution Square) occupies one hectare north of the entrance façade of the neoclassical presidential palace Palacio de la Moneda in the heart of Santiago de Chile. It is surrounded by other government and state buildings, such as the Chilean Central Bank and the ministries of Justice, Finance, and Foreign Affairs. Due to its prominent location, Plaza de la Constitución had also been used as a space for social and political demonstrations, but on a day-to-day basis served as a large parking lot for cars. From 1973 on, Plaza de la Constitución increasingly took on new meanings. On September 11, La Moneda, attacked with tanks and bombed, became the main site of the coup. After the coup and for the following eight years, La Moneda ceased to serve as a presidential seat, and for a time the regime used its basements as a secret torture chamber for political opponents known as "El Hoyo" ("The Hole").[27]

In 1980, the Municipality of Santiago announced a public competition for the renovation of Plaza de la Constitución. The timing of the renovation was closely connected to the announcement of the new constitution from September 11, 1980, mentioned above. The constitution, in addition to containing temporary articles ensuring that Pinochet would remain in power for at least eight more years, also introduced a model of "protected democracy" ("democracia protegida"), a neoliberal vision of democracy in which economic progress is seen as the main goal and in which political pluralism and the citizen's influence over decision-making are heavily restricted. The competition was won by the office of Cristián Undurraga and Ana Luisa Devés, architects known for their postmodern preferences. Their project was based on a simple layout with a clear reference to traditional urban typologies. According to the new design, the square is divided into four parts by two diagonal lines constituting pedestrian paths. As a result, the Plaza de la Constitución was divided into four triangles. The triangle before the entrance to La Moneda is paved, and the remaining three are covered with grass. An additional pedestrian path runs perpendicularly toward the façade, which emphasizes the bilateral symmetry of the design. The paths are connected in the middle with a circular, paved plaza. The utterly traditional form of the Plaza de la Constitución – bringing to mind an array of historical associations, from idealized Italian

FIGURE 1.5A Plaza de la Constitución (1980–1982, Cristián Undurraga, Ana Luisa Devés) (Chad Ehlers, Alamy Stock Photo).

40 Postmodernism and the State in Pinochet's Chile

renaissance urban designs to the regularity of French baroque formal gardens – corresponds with the neoclassical form of the palace. Because of the simplicity of the design, traditional typologies – path, plaza and court – are exposed and presented in a distilled, purified form. For these reasons, the Plaza de la Constitución is often described as one of the most consequently postmodern realizations in Chile.[28]

The new design effectively erased the democratic character of the previous space as well as the violent history of the site. Unruly and unregulated, the pre-1973 Plaza de la Constitución had responded to citizens' needs – from manifesting dissent and opinions on current political events to performing the mundane and ordinary function of providing parking spaces. The new design did not maintain any connection with the people, its ceremonial and official character resembling more of a baroque *cour d'honneur* than a civic space. More importantly, the historicizing design of Undurraga and Devés erases memory, covering up the darkest history of the space with clean, elegant forms. In this sense, the Plaza de la Constitución subverts key postmodern tropes of history, memory, and genius loci. It erases the existing memory of this space and its character and replaces them with an idealized and purified vision of history. While postmodernists usually advocated for using historicizing forms as a way to make architecture more relatable and familiar, Undurraga and Devés' design reversed this logic. In the Plaza de la Constitución, historical references are employed to replace real and living memories with forms that are abstract and distant to detract attention from trauma by bringing up a vague and innocuous vision of history and tradition, one that fits into the image that Pinochet's government intended to project.[29]

Stern interprets Plaza de la Constitución in the context of the introduction of the new Chilean constitution and describes this new urban realization as a "part of the military regime's institutionalization project and celebration of a new Constitution," which deliberately silenced the collective memory of this space.[30] The significance of the new design for the Plaza de la Constitución was well captured by a representative of the Human Rights Watch who in 1988 was delegated to report on the human rights situation in Chile:

> I looked down on Santiago's famous Plaza de la Constitución, where citizens historically gathered to praise or protest the actions of their government. At first the expanse of grass in the plaza was pleasing, it was so green and neat. Then I remembered that it was Pinochet's poorly paid minimum-work program for Chile's large unemployed population that kept the parks so clean, indeed among the cleanest in the world. Pinochet had changed the layout of the plaza. More than two thirds of the traditional cobblestone public space was now subdivided into a series of well-kept elevated grassy sections. Citizens could walk along the guarded pathways but not congregate in the plaza – discouraging to protest.[31]

Crucially, the classical references used in the Plaza de la Constitución are far from being lighthearted or cheery, as we might expect from postmodern designs. Instead of performing erudite games and being subject to playful recontextualizations, here the quotes from the Italian renaissance and the French baroque are used to boost a specifically political image of grandiosity, authority, order, and power. Indeed, in some ways, the Plaza de la Constitución opens itself up to the same sorts of critiques we found in Griffiths and Hatherley as to the damaging potential of "free-floating signifiers." However, whereas the postmodern revivalism criticized by Griffiths or Hatherley was guilty of overlooking or ignoring social and political matters, with the Plaza de la Constitución, the postmodern forms are, for the government, convenient tools to distract from the terrors of Pinochet's dictatorship. Here, the postmodern strategy of "free-floating signifiers" does not merely speak to complacency but can be understood as overtly political. Unlike the works of architects such as Furman or Walala, the postmodern design of Plaza de la Constitución is not merely a symptom of and subservient to laissez-faire capitalism, but it is explicitly produced in order to silence an immediate past through new evocations of grandiosity.

Here we will need to distinguish the uses of historical referentiality and traditional typologies more precisely from those theorized by Alexander, Portoghesi, Rossi, or Venturi. While for Portoghesi the postmodern use of historical references was founded upon the belief that "the character of a place is a patrimony to use and not to mindlessly squander,"[32] the Plaza de la Constitución does the opposite, specifically producing a non-local past – a past more evocative of the Italian renaissance or the French baroque period. This also plays into a different use of image than that theorized by Portoghesi: here the image is a propagandistic image of grandiosity, meant to signal to a population a new era that is also continuous with older respectable civilizations.

If the establishment of the new constitution in 1980 was one significant political event that Pinochet's administration symbolically signaled through a work of postmodern architecture, then the Chilean national plebiscite held on October 5, 1988, was another, as it would be accompanied by the new building for the Chilean Congress. The constitution had established eight years in advance the 1988 plebiscite, which could result in two scenarios. If Pinochet were to be approved for another eight years, parliamentary elections would take place nine months after he is sworn into office. Alternatively, if Pinochet were to lose, both presidential and parliamentary elections would follow. In the years following the new constitution, Pinochet's administration introduced legislative changes in preparation for future democratic elections. Most importantly, two laws, one which allowed the creation of (non-leftist) political parties, and another, which opened national registers to voters, both passed in 1987. The return of democracy assumed reinstating the Chilean National Congress, which had been dissolved by Pinochet in 1973.

As the old nineteenth-century Congress Building located in Santiago needed renovation, planned elections sparked discussions regarding the space the congress would occupy in the future. In 1987, Pinochet's administration announced the decision to erect a new building instead of renovating the old one. Moreover, it was decided that the new building would be located in Valparaíso, the decaying port city located 77 miles from Santiago.[33] The official reasons for the move were the intention to decentralize power in Chile and to initiate the urban renewal of Valparaíso. As Francisco Díaz mentions in an article about the new congress building, both stated reasons are ultimately unconvincing: the constitution ratified by the military government in fact reinforces the centralization of power, and the government did not plan to undertake any efforts to stimulate Valparaíso's development besides the Congress. Additionally, it was clear that the congresspeople would commute to Valparaíso from Santiago (especially since the highway between Santiago and Valparaíso had been recently improved), rather than move there permanently, thereby potentially stimulate the process of revitalization of the city. Since Pinochet hoped to still hold power after the elections, both the declaration of decentralization of power and the implied message that the president cares about the forgotten parts of the country were intended to improve Pinochet's image among voters. Following Díaz, we can then understand the motives behind the decision to build a new edifice for the Congress in Valparaíso as primarily politically strategic. Further, Díaz argues that an additional factor behind the decision to move the Congress was the rise of anti-government riots in the Chilean capital city (which had intensified especially in 1987), making "Santiago seem like a city under the constant threat of social upheavals."[34] If Pinochet were to win the plebiscite, the Congress would likely be a place that would attract the opposition's riots in the next eight years of his term. Valparaíso, as a more peripheral location, would be less likely to face protests or to attract public attention. Another explanation provided by Díaz: in a de facto "centralized state, the idea of sending the only institution able to monitor the actions of the government as far away as possible, might have seduced more than one within the Regime." As the Congress was one institution capable of monitoring Pinochet's regime, the physical distance could minimize the capacity for such oversight.[35] The reinstatement of the National Congress was both a real legislative move and a symbolic gesture to open up a new chapter in Chilean history. Erecting a new building in a new location rather than renovating the old one was a way to signal a new beginning for a disgraced dictatorship. Therefore, the propagandistic image-building potential of the future seat of Congress was crucial to its design.

The results of the national competition for the Congress building were announced on June 30, 1988, three months before the plebiscite's results. The organizers (Dirección de Arquitectura de Ministerio de Obras Públicas [Architecture Department at the Ministry of Public Works] and Colegio de Arquitectos de Chile) received 539 projects. The winning entry was a design of the team of Juan Cárdenas, José Covacevic, and Raúl Farrú.[36] In

FIGURE 1.5B   Model of the Congreso Nacional de Chile in Valparaiso (1988–1990, Juan Cárdenas, José Covacevic, and Raúl Farrú), published in "Primer Premio," CA 60 (1990), 31 (Fondo Revista CA, courtesy of Archivo de Originales, FADEU-PUC).

Postmodernism and the State in Pinochet's Chile 43

FIGURE 1.6 South view of the Congreso Nacional de Chile in Valparaiso (1988–1990, Juan Cárdenas, José Covacevic, and Raúl Farrú) (unknown author, under CC BY-SA 2.0 license).

FIGURE 1.7 Congreso Nacional de Chile in Valparaiso (1988–1990, Juan Cárdenas, José Covacevic, and Raúl Farrú), portico (Carlos Adolfo Silva Cáceres).

the statement discussing the results, the organizers stated that Cárdenas', Covacevic's, and Farrú's "project fully fulfilled the requirements asked in the commission: to project over Valparaíso's plan a building of national and monumental character, and also austere, dignified and transcendent, able to house the Chilean National Congress."[37]

The massive 60,000 square meter building of the Chilean National Congress is divided into two main parts. The first part, which makes up the northern portion of the building, is a four-story edifice housing the chamber of deputies, the chamber of senate, and the plenary room. The entrance to the building is located in the center of the northern part and is emphasized by a large portico. The portico is covered with a massive grid-like roof supported on twelve columns with plain shafts recalling Doric order and stylized terracotta-red capitals loosely evoking Egyptian temples or art deco architecture with its geometricized forms. An additional four oversized columns with shafts clad with charcoal tiles and red cuboid-shaped capitals flank the entrance, two on each side. The second part of the Congress, which makes up the southern portion, is a fourteen-story tower located behind the four-story edifice, housing offices for the congresspeople as well as the library and spaces designated for supporting equipment and technical facilities. The tower is a large monumental cuboid with a square-shaped opening in its lower middle part, resembling a simplified and magnified Arc de Triomphe, thoroughly dominating the surrounding landscape. The postmodern edifice juxtaposing various historical references and freely mixing different colors and materials (dark-red stone, charcoal tiles, and ochre concrete) pleased not only the jury, but according to architect Pablo Allard, also Pinochet himself, who said, "when I saw the models, I knew this was the winner."[38]

Some of the architects who decided not to take part in the competition (as Díaz points out, if we include interns working on the entries, the number comes to approximately 2,000 participants, which adds up to half of the architectural companies registered in Chile) openly criticized those who decided to get involved. Among them was Victor Gubbins, who interpreted the high interest in the competition as a sign of ethical crisis within the profession: "Are we the architects called to fulfill a political and public role in our country?" Gubbins asked. "What is the perception that people and authorities have about our profession? What is the perception we have of ourselves?"[39] Fernando Pérez Oyarzún, another prominent Chilean architect, asked similar questions regarding the competition:

> What is the reason behind the success in participation in a competition on a topic like moving the Congress to Valparaíso that boosted so much criticism from public opinion as well as from the architects themselves? The first, and certainly the less comfortable [answer], might be that as architects we abandoned any conviction, or at least we put them in doubt, in front of the chance of a commission as significant and interesting as this competition....[40]

Díaz describes the propagandistic function of the new building of the Chilean Congress as an effort to signal "a new beginning for Chilean political history" and an attempt to "clean up the past by merging it with the future."[41] In this way, the Congress building is analogous to the Plaza de la Constitución in its effort to "clean up the past" through its classicizing design. As with Undurraga's and Devés's design, the Congreso Nacional de Chile utilizes historical forms that are distant, abstract, and idealized and refers to architectural tradition not to create a sense of continuity between the past and present or to anchor the building in the community which it is supposed to serve, but to craft a desired image of dictatorship. Like the Plaza de la Constitución, the Congreso Nacional de Chile postmodern design evokes the grandiosity of classicism and thus responds to the commission's request for a project that is "austere, dignified and transcendent," in this way departing in intent from the ironic playfulness of Western European or North American postmodern projects. However, the Congreso's evident referentiality plays a significant role in projecting a crafted image of Pinochet's regime as well. With its obvious throwbacks and recuperations of various styles, in line with current architectural trends, the building signals an aesthetic dynamism and an innovative and revived spirit to the Pinochet government. This self-consciously crafted perception inherent to Cárdenas's, Covacevic's, and Farrú's designs undoubtedly appealed to Pinochet's commission, as projecting a more democratic and rejuvenated character was an essential goal of the government which hoped to remain in power after the plebiscite.

How then should a building like the Congreso Nacional de Chile be interpreted? Given the time period and formal qualities of this building, postmodernism seems to be a fitting label to categorize this design. At the same time, the Congreso cannot be described as "playful" in the same sense often ascribed to most postmodern works. With its scale and oversized architectural elements, the Congreso appears serious and solemn, following the aims behind its realization of evoking grandiosity and monumentality. On the other hand, it is not a stretch to call an ancient Egyptian temple planted in a small South American port city an absurdist surreal joke. Moreover, given that just fifteen years prior to entering the competition, Covacevic completed the UNCTAD building – one of the masterpieces of Chilean brutalism and a symbol of Allende's era – the Congreso seems to give an ironic wink (perhaps inappropriate and certainly opportunistic) to an audience versed in architecture and familiar with Chilean architectural discourse. The sense of critical self-reflexivity and the belief in the autonomy of architecture understood as art, distanced from external considerations, are among the fundamental tropes of postmodernism classically understood, which raises the question: can a building like the Congreso, designed not as an autonomous artwork but commissioned to foster a clear political goal and with a clear agenda behind it, still be considered postmodern?

In *Irony; or, The Self-Critical Opacity of Postmodern Architecture*, Emmanuel Petit describes postmodernism as built upon "the attitude of overintellectualization and mental distancing":

> the mindset of postmodernism strove above all for the suspension of intellectual closure. … It appears that the modern period of history in the early to mid-twentieth century, which heralded "clarity," "transparency," and "synthesis" as the utmost virtues for architecture … was followed by a time, when a (willed) intellectual opacity is put forwards in architecture as a way to express the complexities of a self-critical outlook on the worlds of things and ideas. Instead of establishing an unequivocal and direct relationship between sign (form) and signified (message), the opacity of the signifier makes the sign explicit *as* sign or representation.[42]

At first glance, the "opacity" of the signifier would not seem to be a desired quality of a propagandistic building, to say nothing of "self-criticality." However, by uniting contradictory elements – the political motivations that insist viewers treat the building in all seriousness and an ironic play with architectural conventions and expectations – the Congreso certainly operates on various semantic levels. Jencks's notion of "double-coding" (or multiple-coding

46 Postmodernism and the State in Pinochet's Chile

as he clarified this term further[43]) then seems relevant here: for in the Congreso we find a hybrid pluralistic language capable of reaching various audiences and simultaneously convey multiple meanings. Like we will see in some of the other designs in this book, the Congreso provides a peculiar variation of Venturi's "difficult whole" – one in which "complexity and contradiction" are not reduced to formal effects or mere stylistic techniques but are the results of dynamic and often conflicting relations between postmodern notions, social and political agendas behind these designs, and – as Polish examples analyzed in Chapters 3 and 4 show – the disparate goals of architects and commissioners.

Pinochet's efforts to improve his image with a spectacular architectural symbol of his new pro-democratic orientation proved to be unsuccessful. In June of 1989, when it was already known that Pinochet would be stepping down, the dictator traveled to Valparaíso to visit the construction site of the new Congress building. He was welcomed by a crowd of workers chanting "que se vaya!" (leave/get out of here). As recorded in the footage documenting the visit, Pinochet asked the team assisting him to take close-up photographs protesting workers to identify them later.[44] These commands were in fact nothing but empty threats, echoes of Pinochet's former power, as it was clear that Chile had entered a post-dictatorial era.

The examples of the Plaza de la Constitución and the Congreso Nacional de Chile show how postmodernism can retain its core qualities while also working in the service of State power – in this case, in the service of an authoritarian government in a neoliberal age, marshaling the playfulness of Las Vegas to a sincere projection of authority and grandiosity. As we will see in the following chapter, in the very same years, postmodern forms and ideology were also used by architects who opposed the dictatorship and its politics. Such examples demonstrate how postmodernism was a productive platform for multiple ideological stances and political orientations.

Notes

1 For example, see the opinions voiced by architects Smiljan Radic and Alejandro Aravena in Miranda, "Rough, yet poetic."
2 See Talesnik, "Fue el posmodernismo la arquitectura del pinochetismo?," 106.
3 De Simone, "*Caracoles* comerciales."
4 Pérez De Arce, 58.
5 Pérez De Arce, 60.
6 Pérez De Arce, 57.
7 See Reyes, *Diseño urbano inclusivo*, 132–140.
8 See de Castro, *El Ladrillo.*
9 The boom was interrupted by two crises – the first lasting from 1975 to 1977 (with a 20% unemployment rate) and the second from 1982 to 1985, during which unemployment reached 30%.
10 For more on the worker's situation under Pinochet see Winn (ed.), *Victims of the Chilean Miracle.*
11 Klein, "How Power Profits from Disaster."
12 Pertinent legal decree: Decreto Ley No. 1305.
13 Ministerio de Vivienda y Urbanismo, "Política Nacional." In 1985, the document was replaced with a new National Urban Development Policy, in which the State took more responsibility for urban planning. The change was almost entirely symbolic as it wasn't followed by concrete actions or tools allowing the State to take actual active role. For more, see Shapira, "Renovación Urbana," 17.
14 Ministerio de Vivienda y Urbanismo, "Política Nacional," 11. Translation mine.
15 Ministerio de Vivienda y Urbanismo, 11.
16 See *Constitución de Chile de 1980*, Article 24.

17 See Dattwyler, *La vivienda social en Chile.*
18 Preston, *Latin American Development*, 268. See also Weisman, "La Pintana."
19 Rebolledo, "Las olvidadas erradicaciones."
20 For more information on architectural organizations in Chile see Jara Jara, *Ciudad, sociedad y accion Gremial.*
21 More in Jara Jara, 61–63. When discussing the condition of the Colegio under the regime, one cannot forget the kidnappings and murders of its members accused by the regime of leftist affiliations, which occurred with Pinochet's intensified efforts between 1973 and 1976 to rid the country of the opposition.
22 Stern, *Battling for Hearts and Minds*, 62.
23 Stern, *Battling for Hearts and Minds*, 62.
24 Christian, "Chile's Handcuffed Press Can Still Jab at Pinochet."
25 For more on *AUCA*, see Hernández, "La revista AUCA, 1965–1986."
26 Eliash, interview by Lidia Klein (August 23).
27 Rabascall, "Chile's presidential palace basement."
28 Díaz et al., "Docoposmo."
29 The official presentation of the project in *CA* magazine characterized Plaza de la Constitución in a completely different way – as an effort to "respect history, the city, and, above all, its inhabitants" (Undurraga, and Devés, "Remodelación Plaza de la Constitución," 8).
30 Stern, *Reckoning with Pinochet*, 266.
31 Stepan, "The Last Days of Pinochet?"
32 Portoghesi, *Postmodern*, 8.
33 As a result of Law N°18.678 signed in December 24th of 1987. See https://www.leychile.cl/Navegar?idNorma=30064&idParte=.
34 Díaz, "Los arquitectos y la falta de memoria" (English version).
35 Díaz, "Los arquitectos y la falta de memoria" (English version).
36 José Covacevic was one of the designers of the UNCTAD building (the headquarters for the third United Nations Conference on Trade and Development conference), erected in 1972. UNCTAD is one of the most important examples of Chilean modernism and perhaps the most significant building realized under Allende.
37 "Bases y Fallo," 29. Quoted in Díaz, "Los arquitectos y la falta de memoria," 11. Translation by Díaz.
38 Allard, "Traslademos el Congreso," 38. Translation mine.
39 Victor Gubbins, "Mesa Redonda: Descentralización, Edificio y Entorno," *CA* 60 (1990), 68. Quoted in Díaz, "Los arquitectos y la falta de memoria," 10. Translation by Díaz.
40 Fernando Pérez Oyarzún, "Notas críticas sobre el concurso del Edificio del Congreso," *CA* 60 (1990), 41. Quoted in Díaz, "Los arquitectos y la falta de memoria," 10. Translation by Díaz.
41 Díaz, "Los arquitectos y la falta de memoria," 6–7 (English version).
42 Petit, 17.
43 See, for example, Jencks, "What Then Is Post-Modernism?," 21–22.
44 Video available online: https://www.youtube.com/watch?v=i9MagkfOYPg.

2

POSTMODERNISM AGAINST THE STATE UNDER PINOCHET'S DICTATORSHIP

The two architectural realizations commissioned during Pinochet's reign, one which marked the 1980 constitution and the other which marked the plebiscite, both employed postmodern forms in explicitly propagandistic ways. By conveying gravitas and authority through its classical designs and by utilizing a fashionable aesthetic to signal a spirit of innovation, the Pinochet government made postmodernism compatible to its aims. In the very same years, postmodern forms and ideology were also used by Chilean architects who opposed Pinochet's policies. The most significant attempts to use architecture to foster social and political change against Pinochet's regime can be found in the independent collective known as CEDLA (Centro de Estudios de la Arquitectura, Center for Architectural Studies), established in 1977 in Santiago. The group was formed as an effort to reflect on architecture and urban planning in Chile under the military government. After the coup, Pinochet's government replaced the authorities and some of the faculty of major Chilean universities, which, beginning in October 1973, began to be governed by military officers appointed by Pinochet.[1] Additionally, professional associations (including Colegio de Arquitectos) were infiltrated by governmental nominations. Therefore, as the institutions that had previously provided space for architectural discourse were restricted, CEDLA emerged out of a need to create an alternative platform for architectural thought, one less inhibited by political operatives.

In an important sense, the group was formed as a critical response to the neoliberal vision of urban space and architecture promoted by Pinochet. However, at the same time, CEDLA also rejected the orthodox modernist approach to city planning that had been favored by the previous governments of Frei and Allende, even though it also embraced the pro-social postulates of those governments such as the idea that architecture is a social service rather than a commodity driven by profit. For CEDLA, postmodern forms and theories in architecture and city planning provided one way of exploring the possibility of formulating an alternative socially conscious architecture that embraced neither the anonymity of modern design nor the neoliberalism of Pinochet. Postmodernism was thus a way of resisting the laissez-faire norms of the new regime without falling back into the past and repeating the mistakes of modernist urban planning under Frei and Allende.

DOI: 10.4324/9781003179467-3

In the context of Pinochet's Chile, CEDLA's goals of community building and fostering a more egalitarian society were not only social but also political, pushing back against governmental policies that straightforwardly produced atomization and alienation. CEDLA underlined the political character of its proposals by denouncing Pinochet's policies regarding urban space and the architectural formats produced under these policies and by proposing design ideas that would act as a potential remedy to this situation. Since the newly adapted philosophy of neoliberalism was the foundation for the new regime, it should also be emphasized that in Pinochet's Chile "economic" was "political." CEDLA's criticisms of neoliberal urban space dictated by profit were effectively criticisms of the government, so in this sense the CEDLA architects can be understood as oppositional.

At the same time, terms such as "dissent" and "opposition" should be used carefully in the context of CEDLA. The members of CEDLA were not forced into exile – quite the contrary, most of its members were successfully practicing in Chile and not always following the principles declared by the group as we will see with the example of Cristián Boza. In times of heavily controlled public discourse, limits on gatherings, and official bans on oppositional organizing, CEDLA was able to maintain its existence as an independent organization. This was possible not only because the government did not consider architecture as a dangerous field – and hence never put much effort into monitoring architectural discourse – but also because the professional and personal connections of some of the CEDLA members were helpful in supporting the activities of the group. While CEDLA was an independent platform fostering architectural discourse outside of politically controlled academia, its members did not exist in isolation from the academic and professional worlds. They were not directly persecuted by the military dictatorship or faced consequences like torture or imprisonment as was common for many considered to be enemies by Pinochet's dictatorship. Despite these complexities, CEDLA developed a consistent critique of the government's approach to urban space and hoped to counter Pinochet's agenda through their design work and publishing initiatives.

2.1 The Origins of CEDLA and Its Emergence in Santiago

CEDLA was founded in Santiago de Chile in 1977 by Humberto Eliash, Cristián Boza, and Pedro Murtinho.[2] The history of the group dates back to 1975 when Eliash and Boza met at the Architectural Association in London. Eliash was a fresh graduate from Universidad de Chile and Boza held an adjunct teaching position at the Architectural Association. In England, Eliash and Boza established contact with Fernando Castillo Velazco, one of the most prominent proponents of modernist architecture in Chile and the former president of Pontificia Universidad Católica de Chile (1967–1973), but who had been removed from office in 1973 by Pinochet's government and forced to leave the country because of his socialist beliefs. The idea of CEDLA evolved during frequent meetings and discussions between the three architects, but the group was only materialized when Eliash and Boza decided to return to Santiago in 1977 to establish their professional practices.[3]

In London, Boza and Eliash had discussed the paradigms for architecture and urbanism that departed from the modernist approach that had shaped their education as architects and their early careers in Chile. For these architects, that approach was represented by CORMU's flagship designs – namely, Remodelación San Borja, and the winning proposal for the Santiago Poniente competition. Boza, who had briefly worked at CORMU after graduation, describes the time working there as one of the experiences that caused him to reconsider his approach to architecture as well as his future interest in postmodernism:

> One day in 1972, my director at CORMU asked me and my friend to go and buy wooden blocks. We had no idea why we were doing this, but we got the blocks and returned to the office. When we came back, we finally learned what they were needed for – they were used as models for buildings, he just took these blocks and arranged them evenly on the ground. I thought he must be joking! How can you build the city from wooden blocks like that? That moment made me start thinking about what "the city" is and what "city planning" is.[4]

Boza's experience at CORMU, in his telling, prompted a desire to think about architecture and urbanism differently. Although the CEDLA members criticized CORMU's modernist paradigms and reductive approach to the city, at the same time they shared one view fundamental for the organization – namely, that architecture is a social service. Pedro Murtinho, another founding member of CEDLA, sums up the group's attitude toward CORMU:

> San Borja and Santiago Poniente were symbols of CORMU's approach to the city based on the worst paradigms of modernism and Le Corbusier's urbanism of the isolated tower as a solution to urban problems. There was no reflection behind it and we were against it. ... We stood with CORMU's message of building for the people, working for the people, instead of subjecting architecture to market rules. But their approach to planning wasn't well thought through.[5]

Similarly, Eliash states that

> CORMU promoted something we wanted as well – urban renewal – but they realized it in a fundamentally different, modernist, way. But we were supportive of the idea that the State takes responsibility for planning, and doesn't give the city entirely to private hands as we saw under Pinochet.[6]

CEDLA's criticisms of CORMU's realizations were not based on disagreements with the view of urban planning as a social mission with a long-term goal of creating just and egalitarian urban environments, since, in Boza's words, "CEDLA shared with CORMU a pro-social idea of the city."[7] The disagreement was based on the design philosophy applied to achieve these goals. For CEDLA, modernist solutions such as high rises and the elimination of the street were alienating, antisocial, and incapable of building community through architecture. Postmodern forms and theories, by contrast, would offer a vision of an inclusive city, avoiding the failed promises of modernism.

While founded on the criticism of modern paradigms embodied by the design methods promoted within CORMU, the crucial impulse for the emergence of CEDLA arose in response to the neoliberal policies of Pinochet. As the free market philosophy was applied to urban space, Santiago and other Chilean cities became populated with architectural formats harmful to the social fabric. A characteristic example of this are *caracoles* (literally, "snails"): commercial centers adapting the form of Frank Lloyd Wright's Guggenheim Museum in

New York for retail purposes, and which were built abundantly in the 1970s and 1980s in Chilean regional capitals, especially Santiago. With small stores owned or rented by separate individuals and arranged around a spiral pedestrian ramp unfolding around a central void, caracoles created isolated spaces separated from the city while appropriating the traditional functions of the street.[8] In order to attract customers, the architecture of caracoles was spectacular and clearly distinguished from its surroundings – examples vary from two massive, connected cylinders of Dos Caracoles (Sergio Larraín García-Moreno, Ignacio Covarrubias and Jorge Swinburn, 1978) to a bizarre form resembling an Aztec pyramid in La Pirámide del Sol (1976, Octavio Soto de Angelis, both in Santiago).

These constructions might be called postmodern in their own right with their historical references and playful design. Although they cannot be described as explicitly political propaganda like the Plaza de la Constitución and the Congreso Nacional de Chile discussed in Chapter 1, they were nonetheless profoundly associated with Pinochet's Chile. The interiors of these caracoles, with gaudy sculptural chandeliers, colorful neon lights, and an abundance of gold and colorful tiles, were designed to evoke luxury and the image of a "Western" commercial center.

Caracoles were a social phenomenon and not just an architectural type. As a result of the rapid rise of unemployment caused by the market opening to imported goods and broader financial crises sweeping the country, many Chileans opened their own small businesses (stores and services) as a way to survive under this new economic reality. Caracoles arose as an architectural response to this need. At the same time, as architectural historian Liliana de Simone noted, caracoles were "symbolic constructions" and symbols of the "awaited and

Figure 2.1 La Pirámide Del Sol In Santiago De Chile (1976, Octavio Soto De Angelis) (Diego Antonio Vilches).

Figure 2.2 Interior of Dos Caracoles building in Santiago de Chile (1977, Sergio Larraín García-Moreno, Ignacio Covarrubias, and Jorge Swinburn) (author).

expected progress, imbued with the discourses of modernization advocated by the military regime."[9] While they performed pragmatic architectural functions as retail spaces, they were also monuments of the new neoliberal society with individual entrepreneurship as its foundation. As Germán del Sol noted in *ARS*, an architecture magazine run by the CEDLA group,

> A walk through Santiago and other [Chilean] cities is enough to notice the appearance of new architecture … Mayan and Aztec pyramids covered with stainless steel, [with] clean facades of crystal and bright mirrors which … hide the building and defy gravity giving it an ethereal appearance. This architecture, which is being realized with many, often excessive, means … seems to have borrowed the principles which govern them from the laws of the market, transforming it into a merchandise ready to be consumed.[10]

Del Sol's statements are concluded with Eliash's cartoon showing *La Pirámide del Sol* building and two people standing in front of it. "Maya?" – asks the first figure. "No! Friedman" – answers the second.[11]

For CEDLA, caracoles were symptomatic of the destruction of public space and the elimination of its social and community-oriented potential under Pinochet's rule. As caracoles gradually took over urban space and replaced typologies like streets or city squares that had traditionally fostered egalitarian social interactions between people of different incomes and social statuses, they became symbols of new Chilean urban space ruled by profit. By contrast, CEDLA's interest in the postmodern revival of traditional typologies

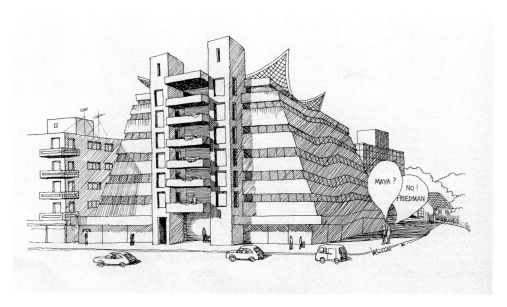

FIGURE 2.3 Cartoon by Humberto Eliash, published in "Vanguardia y Post Modernismo en Chile," *ARS* 4 (1981), 28.

was a statement against the commodification of urban space – urban space turned into "a merchandise ready to be consumed"[12] – as embodied by new commercial spatial formats.

Before the coup, Boza and Eliash's intention was to connect their career work as practicing architects in Santiago with pedagogy and conceptual work, and they planned to pursue these goals within university structures. However, upon returning to Chile, they found that the politicized character of post-1973 educational institutions made that goal impossible. In Chile, they were joined by Pedro Murtinho, who shared their interest in architectural theory and who already had an established position in Santiago as a co-owner of Larraín Murtinho y Asociados studio (founded in 1963). As a group of three they established the scope, goals, and structure of CEDLA. The group disseminated its ideas through publications, exhibitions, conferences, and meetings held at a townhouse located on Pedro de Valdivia 872, the main seat of the group. Between 1977 and 1990, CEDLA managed to invite major South American and international architects (Justo Solsona, Juvenal Baracco, Michael Graves, Aldo Rossi, Peter Eisenman, and Sue Rogers, among others) for discussions and lectures, with the intention to undo the isolation of Chilean architectural discourse during the dictatorship.

Reflecting on the main goals of CEDLA and its emergence in Santiago, Boza, Eliash, and Murtinho emphasize its political character and its strong anti-government position. Murtinho describes CEDLA's goals in the following way:

> CEDLA was a critical movement concerned with architecture, but also with the state of the country. It brought strength and energy to criticize the current situation – the situation reduced to consumerism, mercantilism and capitalism. I am not a communist. But the Chicago school that took over the country together with the start of the

dictatorship was terrible. We weren't political in the sense that we weren't linked to any political party, but CEDLA was a social project. It was a statement against the neoliberal treatment of the city as commodity, and in this sense it was oppositional.[13]

Eliash describes the political nature of the group similarly:

CEDLA was a political project. We treated architecture as a social agent. Chilean society at that time was very divided and the neoliberal politics produced two things that we were strongly opposing. The first was segregation, which pushed low-income people outside the city limits and welcomed only the middle and upper middle class in the city center. The second was that Pinochet's neoliberalism produced isolation, the society was becoming increasingly disintegrated and people were losing a sense of community. In this sense, CEDLA and Santiago Poniente were social and political statements, statements against that.[14]

The major platform that expressed the importance of postmodern theories for CEDLA – and more generally the major platform for communicating all ideas and projects developed by members of the group – was a magazine released approximately once a year. Its first issue appeared under the name of *CEDLA* in 1977, and the following were published as *ARS: Revista del Centro de Estudios de la Arquitectura*. *ARS* had eleven issues, which were published between 1978 and 1990.

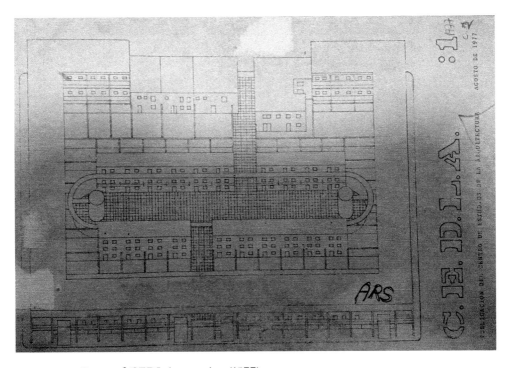

FIGURE 2.4 Cover of *CEDLA* magazine (1977).

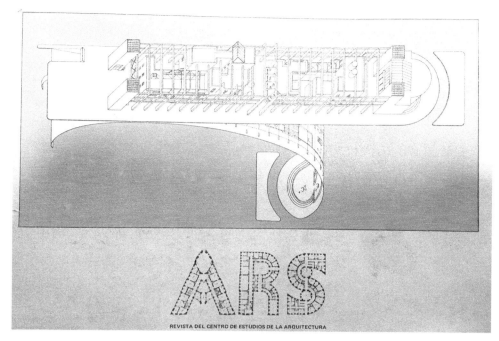

FIGURE 2.5 Cover of *ARS* 1 (1978).

The magazine was distributed among architectural circles in Chile and other South American countries and was financed from the resources of CEDLA members as well as from advertisements of companies operating in the Chilean architecture industry.[15] *ARS* published articles written by CEDLA members as well as invited contributors. The scope of texts included general reflections on theory of architecture and urban planning but held an especially strong focus on postmodern theories, discussions of recent realizations and projects in Chile, as well as analyses and critiques of the government's approach to urban space. In the final two issues (in 1989 and 1990), *ARS* began to expand its scope to look at Latin America more broadly, but primarily the magazine focused on Chile, analyzing the possible architectural solutions that could counter the neoliberal ideology gradually destroying Chilean cities and society. As one essay authored by CEDLA from a 1984 issue reads,

> In a few years we have experienced the boom and decay of a neoliberal economic system, based on the apparatus created by the military regime. ... For architectural culture, this period ... may have been more damaging than the inexorable scarcity of resources (economic and architectural) that we always struggled with.[16]

In the same issue, Cristián Fernandez Cox diagnosed this situation as the time of "populist ethics and aesthetics ..., the aesthetics of the market."[17]

The postmodern theories promoted by the CEDLA members were presented as possible tools for countering architecture shaped by the neoliberal ideology of the military government. As its members emphasize, CEDLA's interest in postmodernism was not primarily

56 Postmodernism against the State under Pinochet's Dictatorship

formalist or commercial in orientation, as was common among Western architects of the 1970s and 1980s. Postmodernism for CEDLA signified not the repetition of historical forms, but an exploration "of our roots, and of how the city functions."[18] In Boza's words, for CEDLA, "postmodernism was not only about columns and friezes. It was about regaining our identity. ... We did not agree with the military government. We were talking about liberation, about bringing our country and its particular architecture back."[19] This manner of embracing postmodernism as a way of "regaining identity," "liberation," and "bringing our country back" can be contrasted with the signaling of classical grandiosity and of dynamic referentiality in the cases of Plaza de la Constitución and the Congreso Nacional de Chile. While in those cases, postmodernism's aesthetics of the surface functions as a means of propaganda, for Boza and CEDLA, postmodernism would be envisioned as a means of reviving the sense of community and character of Chile through typologies that encouraged social interactions across class and income lines.

This approach to postmodernism can be seen in CEDLA's flagship project, an alternative design for the Santiago Poniente area. According to Eliash, Santiago Poniente represented CEDLA's goals to avoid the "segregation, which pushed low-income people outside the city limits," and "Pinochet's neoliberalism [which] produced isolation" and a disintegrated sense of community:

> In our projects, like in Santiago Poniente, everything happens on the street, activities are mixed, society mixes, the architectural heritage is protected and intermingles with new buildings. We simply saw the city as integrated on many levels, both in a formal and social sense.[20]

The revitalization of Santiago Poniente, which drew upon postmodern design principles, was the first project developed by the group. It was presented in the first issue of *ARS,* and became widely known as a manifesto of the group's principles and design philosophy.

2.2 CEDLA's Project for Santiago Poniente

In 1972, Allende's administration announced a competition, organized by CORMU, for the Western area of central Santiago (Santiago Poniente). The winning proposal, a rational modernist plan designed by a group of Argentinean architects associated with la Universidad Nacional de La Plata (Emilio Sessa, Enrique Bares, Santiago F. Bó, Tomas García, and Roberto Germani), was abandoned with the coup in 1973 (see discussion of this design in Chapter 1). Several years later, in 1976, Patricio Mekis, the mayor of Santiago, announced plans for the revitalization of Santiago Poniente. Mekis, who was appointed as mayor of Santiago by the military dictatorship and held this position from 1976 and 1979, was devoted to the ideas of protection and restoration of historical buildings in the city center. CEDLA saw this as an opportunity to introduce their vision for the revitalization of this neighborhood in which the idea of preserving the historic tissue was crucial. Using the occasion of the first edition of La Bienal Nacional de Arquitectura exhibition, organized in 1977 by the Colegio de Arquitectos in Santiago, the members of CEDLA presented their project for Santiago Poniente. While they were still in London in 1975, Boza and Eliash had prepared a critical response to the results of CORMU's competition – the modernist design of Sessa et al. – and sketched an alternative proposal for the revitalization of this area. That initial design served as the basis for the project that CEDLA developed two years later in 1977 and introduced to the broader public at the Bienal Nacional.

CEDLA's project for Santiago Poniente embodied its philosophy and was treated as a manifesto of sorts for the group both by its members and by the broader public. The proposal represents an approach familiar from critical texts of postmodernism, such as Venturi's, Scott Brown's, and Izenour's *Learning from Las Vegas* and Rossi's *The Architecture of the City*, deploying the postmodern revival of traditional typologies and spatial solutions. The revitalization plan included housing for 38,000 people, 300 offices, 400 commercial enterprises (such as stores and services), five daycares, two schools, and two community centers, all distributed in the surface of 69 hectares and with density between 550 and 600 inhabitants per hectare. On a formal level, the main idea behind the project was to create continuity with the existing architecture of the site by relying on traditional spatial typologies and using historical architectural forms and materials. At the same time, CEDLA emphasized the social potential of these postmodern techniques, and saw the role of historical forms not only as respecting the context and history of the neighborhood but above all as enabling community building and the identification of inhabitants with the space they lived in. For CEDLA, historical models provided more familiar and relatable environments than abstract, modernist forms, and thus responded better to the social challenges of post-coup Chile – namely, to the increasing social segregation based on economic differences exacerbated by Pinochet's policies. In CEDLA's interpretation, traditional typologies known from historical cities, revived by the postmodern movement, were the means of fostering a more egalitarian society. In Boza's words,

> Our position was: no to segregation, yes to the interchange of people. We tried to achieve this by creating public spaces based on traditional typologies, like street or square, and ensuring mixed-use spaces that encouraged people to interact. The design of Santiago Poniente was based on three typologies: the street, the square, and the boulevard as places where people can meet, discuss, integrate and mingle. ... Our goal was to defend the old tissue and to foster the integration of the people in the city. We were against segregation and against the fact that low-income inhabitants were pushed to the peripheries of Santiago. We wanted to mix people with different incomes.[21]

The first step was a careful study of the site (presented both in *ARS* and exhibited at the Bienal) in the form of drawings, photographs, and descriptions. The architects began by documenting the architecture of twenty-seven blocks constituting Santiago Poniente in drawings and photos and creating an isometric representation of the site. Subsequently, CEDLA discerned typologies basic for Santiago Poniente: manzana (block); plaza (square); cité (housing unit with continuous façade); plazuela (little piazza); edificio patio (courtyard building); rambla (boulevard); and pasaje (passage).

Each of the types were documented and described in terms of its history, its place in the development of Santiago and other Latin American cities, and the role it played for the community on different scales – for example, plazas and plazuelas as spaces of meeting and exchange between inhabitants from different parts of the city, or courtyards of edificios patios as spaces guarding the privacy of families dwelling in them. The characterizations of spatial types essential to Santiago Poniente were supplemented with detailed studies of their elements, such as crossings of the passages or connectors between buildings and streets. This

58 Postmodernism against the State under Pinochet's Dictatorship

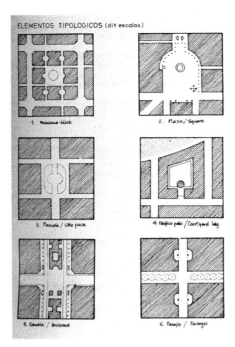

FIGURE 2.6 Typological study of Santiago Poniente (CEDLA, 1977), published in Boza, et al., "Tema II La ciudad de Santiago proposición para Santiago Metropolitano," *AUCA* 34 (1978), 74.

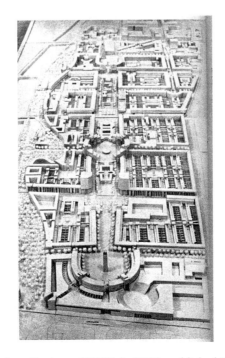

FIGURE 2.7 Model of Santiago Poniente (CEDLA, 1977), published in Boza, et al., "Tema II La ciudad de Santiago proposición para Santiago Metropolitano," *AUCA* 34 (1978), 75.

detailed study of Santiago Poniente was an essential part of CEDLA's proposal, as the leading principle of the design was to "achieve typological continuity with existing site"[22] and consequently to preserve and create spaces focused on building community and fostering social bonds in a city with increasing separation between inhabitants of different economic classes.

The spine of CEDLA's plan for Santiago Poniente is la Rambla, a commercial boulevard of approximately 50 m width, stretched between Plaza del Mercado from the North side and

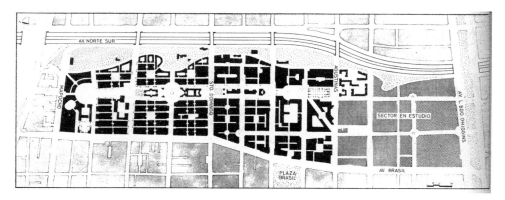

FIGURE 2.8 Plan for Santiago Poniente (CEDLA, 1977), published in Boza, et al, "Tema II La ciudad de Santiago proposición para Santiago Metropolitano," *AUCA* 34 (1978), 74.

FIGURE 2.9 Cristián Boza's sketches for Santiago Poniente (1978) published in Boza, Arquitectura, los dibujos previos, 34–35.

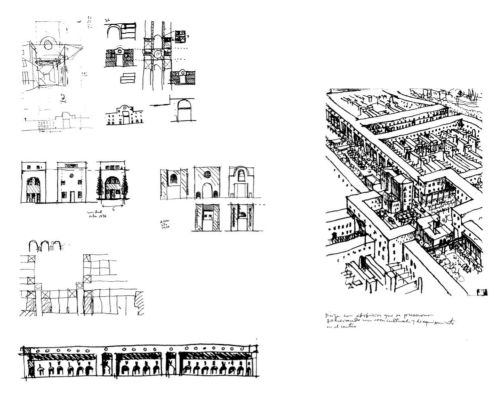

FIGURE 2.10 Cristián Boza's sketches for Santiago Poniente (1978) published in Boza, Arquitectura, los dibujos previos, 36–37.

Basilica del Salvador from the South, and interrupted by piazzas and squares. In the plan, La Rambla consists of existing buildings, renovated and adapted to commercial purposes, and newly constructed five-story buildings, the lowest level of which houses stores, offices, and services. The streets parallel to la Rambla lead to manzanas (blocks) of Santiago Poniente, occupied by existing and new buildings of edificio patio (courtyard building) type, as well as small urban parks, piazzas, and interior passages connecting housing and services with squares and piazzas. CEDLA's aim was to achieve high urban density without the use of high-rise architecture while preserving existing architecture. In order to blend with the historical tissue in scale and proportions, the proposed buildings were between two and six stories high. In their project description, CEDLA emphasized the role of traditional typologies in community building and creating platforms of interactions for inhabitants. "Small and big squares," reads the project description, "generated from existing typologies are forms of organization and identification on the scale of the neighborhood or block. They are sites of encounters par excellence."[23]

A crucial element in the typology used by CEDLA was the street, which the architects regarded as an essential urban element that constitutes the city understood not only as architectural but also as social form. One of the major goals of Santiago Poniente was thus to "recuperate the concept of the street as a channel ... of activity more than just a simple connector"[24] and as such encourage community building and oppose "Pinochet's neoliberalism [which] produced isolation."[25] CEDLA's treatment of the street as a site of encounter capable of strengthening the social fabric by promoting diversity and encouraging encounters between strangers coming from different social, cultural, and economic backgrounds recalls Jane Jacobs' theories outlined in *The Death and Life of the Great American Cities*. According to Jacobs, a well-functioning city offers a "most intricate and close-grained diversity of uses that give each other constant mutual support, both economically and socially."[26] Diversity can be achieved through four generators: mixed uses, permeability, variety in the built environment, and high density. Even though the description of Santiago Poniente doesn't mention Jacobs specifically, these four rules, in addition to the emphasis on the importance of street in community building, are essential for CEDLA's project.[27]

The integration of people of different social and economic statuses, declared by the CEDLA members as one of the main goals of Santiago Poniente, was, to a large degree, aspirational, as it could not be realized without the support of state-level urban development strategies. In its intention, public spaces and traditional urban forms such as piazzas and streets were supposed to stimulate social interactions between usually separated groups of people, but under the reality of Pinochet's policies that displaced the urban poor out of prominent urban locations, these goals were unattainable. As Eliash comments,

> in our vision of the city, we wanted to mix uses, functions, and, most importantly, different economic strata of society. But we didn't have the actual tools to make it happen. It was mostly wishful thinking, given the market-driven reality of that time and the reality in which the military government was cutting the limbs of the state and giving more power to the private sector. Only some years after the fall of the dictatorship did I manage to put these ambitions of social integration into practice.[28]

Even though Santiago Poniente could be materialized only in models and visualizations, it was nonetheless a strong statement against the dominant ideologies of city planning in Chile of that time and a critique of the urban injustice caused by the commercialization of city space.

CEDLA's projects, especially Santiago Poniente, generated heated debates and animated Chilean architectural circles in times that were unfavorable to questioning the status quo regarding both the organization of urban space and society more generally. The presentation of Santiago Poniente, both in *ARS* and the Bienal, provoked contrasting reactions. As Boza recalls, while the students were mostly very enthusiastic, "older architects couldn't understand this, and they were throwing shoes at us [during the Bienal]."[29] The Chilean architectural establishment, predominantly represented by architects sharing the modernist approach to urban space, reacted to the emergence of CEDLA and Santiago Poniente as the group's project-manifesto mostly with hostility, or at least skepticism. In 1978, the twenty-second issue of *CA* (Revista del Colegio de Arquitectos Chile) – one of the two major architectural magazines during this period (see Chapter 1) – began with a welcome note to CEDLA. The editors of *CA* made clear that although they wished CEDLA luck, they "don't share [the group's] proposals." "Together with these sincere wishes of success and following postulates of plurality which inspire *CA*," the editors decided to "give space to the opinions of Monserrat Palmer, which are radically different than those of CEDLA."[30] Palmer, a consistent proponent of modernism in architecture, did not mention CEDLA specifically in her

62 Postmodernism against the State under Pinochet's Dictatorship

contribution, but criticized recent interest in reviving older historical architectural forms as articulated in the theories of Aldo Rossi or Leon Krier. Palmer diagnosed the appearance of these forms in Chile as misguided and not suited for the specificity of local context: "These are their problems. Not ours," stated Palmer as a conclusion for her article.[31] The addressee of these criticisms was clearly CEDLA, as CEDLA was the only group in Chile advocating an urban philosophy openly based on postmodern paradigms and theories.

Despite the skepticism expressed by the Colegio de Arquitectos in their official magazine, both the presentation of Santiago Poniente during the Bienal and events (such as meetings and discussions) organized by CEDLA in their headquarters attracted large numbers of followers. CEDLA was supported mainly by students, but appealed also to a few established architects previously associated with the institutions of Allende's era. Apart from Fernando Castillo Velazco, who, according to Boza and Eliash took a critical part in the foundation of the group, one of the most prominent architects sympathizing with CEDLA was Nicolas Garcia, the former director of CORMU during Allende's presidency. According to Eliash, the involvement of architects like Castillo Velazco and Garcia was not surprising, and confirmed that, despite their differences in formal approach, "there was an affinity in spirit between CEDLA and CORMU."[32] As mentioned before, for Eliash, Boza, and Murtinho, CEDLA was guided by the same pro-social agenda CORMU once had. This "affinity of spirit," however, should not be overstated, because of the fundamental difference in scope and nature of these two organizations – an independent research institute on the one hand, and a state-funded organization responsible for urban development on the other – as well as in their different attitudes to rationalistic modern designs.

2.3 Social Housing

One of the fields severely impacted by the neoliberal policies of the military government was social housing.[33] The state agencies developed under Frei and Allende with the goal of implementing long-term strategies of providing affordable housing solutions were dissolved by the Pinochet administration. Typically, social housing projects commissioned by the newly established state organization (SERVIU) were make-shift solutions in remote locations lacking proper infrastructure and characterized by low-quality architecture. Built by private construction companies, these projects were designed to maximize profit rather than to promote the social good. Between 1985 and 1986, CEDLA formulated its response to the critical situation of social housing in urban peripheries and published it in the sixth and seventh issues of *ARS*.

As a point of departure, the architects provided an analysis of social housing complexes commissioned by SERVIU in peripheral regions of Santiago, such as la Granja and San Joaquin. They highlighted its main problems from poor infrastructure and lack of access to education and the low quality of architecture. SERVIU did not favor any particular typology or design solution and their housing commissions were to a large degree dictated by cost optimization rather than any preexistent design philosophy. In CEDLA's words, the housing realized by SERVIU was focused on the "mere production of built square meters [in order] to feed the statistics."[34] Mass housing complexes were typically laid out on a uniform grid with identical, barrack-like single family housing units devoid of any public space. Another typical example of SERVIU housing realized in Santiago's urban peripheries was made up of monotonous multi-family housing units formed by identical cuboid blocks. An example

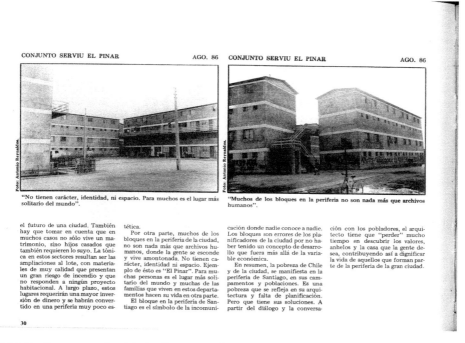

FIGURE 2.11   Fragment of article by Derry Hearly, "Los arquitectos deben perder el tiempo," on the condition of social housing in Chile, published in *ARS* 7 (1986), 30.

of the latter type was the El Pinar housing complex located in the San Joaquin neighborhood of Santiago, which was analyzed by CEDLA in one of their case studies.

In the seventh issue of *ARS*, El Pinar was described as

> nothing more than a human repository, where people are stored. [Such housing] has no character, identity or space, … it is the loneliest place in the world. … A [housing] block on the outskirts of Santiago symbolizes lack of connection, in which nobody knows anybody. These blocks are errors of the city planners who did not have any idea for development that went beyond the economic variable.…[35]

CEDLA described the poor conditions of social housing realized by SERVIU as a consequence of

> real estate speculation, of the venality of some professionals, of the economic voracity and of social insensitivity which are … the result of the mechanistic application of a policy that does not care about the number of victims sacrificed on the altar of the Market.[36]

CEDLA stated clearly that the root of the problem lies in the political situation in Chile, which "allows for the domination of a very small elite and marginalization of the majority."[37] At the same time, the group criticized not only the authorities for implementing the politics of social and urban segregation but also the architects who, instead of creating decent living spaces, took advantage of the flawed social housing system under Pinochet. "Architects," reads *ARS*, "need some ethical reflection on our actions in the urban periphery":

> It is a fallacy to declare that our discipline has little capacity to [act in that matter]. … New constructions are signed by professionals, and a large majority of them are, regretfully, the result of the absence of thought and dedication to this kind of work. … It is our responsibility to acknowledge the difference between what is legal and what is just. Many of the disturbances permitted by building norms could be eliminated with an internal sense of decency.[38]

CEDLA's efforts were focused on what could be done within the existing models of the housing market, as a necessary change of direction in state policies was unachievable in the near future.[39]

The next step of addressing the problem of social housing was to provide tools for its improvement. For CEDLA, postmodern theories and design tools were helpful in tackling the problem of low-quality housing within the existing framework. In the seventh issue of *ARS*, CEDLA emphasized the need for a better understanding of Chilean urban peripheries as a first step toward better designs respecting the specificities of local contexts. CEDLA intended to challenge the common notion that "the characteristic qualities of the urban periphery are its amorphous nature and lack of defined structural elements" and encouraged approaching the "disorder of the periphery" as "the order which we don't understand" and as an "internally organized cosmos."[40] While the authors do not mention specific texts that guide their approach, their characterization of the urban periphery is framed in a way that is very similar to that of the Strip in *Learning from Las Vegas*. For the authors of *Learning from Las Vegas*, the Strip should not be dismissed as a chaotic kitschy environment that needs to be fixed; instead, it deserves the attention of architects and urban planners as a complex system with its own internal logic. Quoting Henri Bergson who described disorder as "all order we cannot see," Venturi et al. argue that the Strip presents a "complex order," which is not "easy" or "rigid" but instead based on inclusion and the juxtaposition of "seemingly incongruous" elements in constant flux. As a result, "it is not an order dominated by the expert and made easy for the eye" but nevertheless a logical system that can be understood if we learn to read its codes.[41] While the nature of order in Las Vegas, based on visual communication subjected to the rules of a car-centered Strip, is radically different than the one studied by CEDLA in urban peripheries, the principle remains the same: architects should learn from the seemingly chaotic vernacular environments instead of replacing them with their own limited idea of order.

In a series of drawings following these statements, CEDLA analyzed the urban peripheries of Chilean cities by distinguishing their basic typologies – from different forms of organization of streets to the nodes of social importance for the community (such as soccer fields).

While CEDLA does not mention any particular methodology or theory that informs these analyses, the attention to commonplace spatial patterns clearly recalls Alexander's studies from *Pattern Language*. Like with *Learning from Las Vegas* and *Pattern Language*, the studies of urban peripheries published in the seventh issue of *ARS* are to a large extent

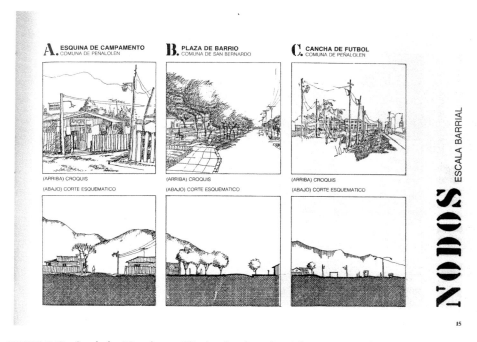

FIGURE 2.12 Study by Humberto Eliash of nodes of social importance from Eliash, "La periferia dibujada," published in *ARS* 7 (1986), 15. Drawings by David Neri and Dante Novoa.

conducted through images, and further, drawings play important roles as tools for spatial analysis.

Not only were CEDLA's proposed solutions to housing problems drawn from postmodern ideas, but also was CEDLA's diagnosis of the problem itself, as it was posed as a communication issue. "No doubt there is a crisis of communication between the codes used by the inhabitants of the peripheries and those of the architects trained academically with different aesthetic and cultural values," reads the seventh issue of *ARS*.[42] The recognition of the lack of understanding between educated, refined experts and the "common people" with different cultural backgrounds and expectations – bridging the gap between "low" and "high" culture – was one of the founding diagnoses at the basis of the postmodern turn, particularly as described by Jencks.[43] For CEDLA, successful housing solutions would need to operate within the codes of both design professionals and users, as in Jencks's "double-coding," and postmodernism offered a way to achieve that. To a large degree, double-coding functioned as a marketing strategy in North America and Western Europe. The over-sized swan on top of Michael Graves's hotel for Disney or the playful Italian Renaissance and Baroque references in Charles Moore's Piazza d'Italia were relatable and understandable both for architectural connoisseurs and for the "common people." Since the designers were able to communicate with very different audiences, they also maximized their chances for commercial success. CEDLA likewise emphasized the need to operate within the codes of experts and users, but did so in a completely different noncommercial context, deploying the postmodern concept of double-coding in order to solve a particular social problem.

In the seventh issue of *ARS*, CEDLA presented a few specific built examples of low-cost housing which realized the group's postulates of providing better quality living space rooted in postmodern ideas. One of them, the Parque Santa Elvira housing complex for 3,200 people, was located in the La Florida neighborhood on the southeastern outskirts of Santiago and was realized in 1985 by a team of architects led by Pedro Murtinho (Ricardo Contreras, Luis González, Humberto Eliash, and Santiago Raby).

The neighborhood was dominated by old country estates and farm houses and the architects wanted to create a housing complex, which, unlike the homogeneous units built by SERVIU, would respect and revive the rural character of the site. The site was divided into ten blocks. Each of the blocks consisted of two-story single-family housing units grouped around a central square with leisure and recreational functions (such as playgrounds). Additional housing units were distributed in five blocks separated from the ten main blocks by a narrow passage (Pasaje Los Sauces) with greenery. The architectural design was based on the postmodern principle of using local materials (clay bricks and wood) and spatial forms traditional for the site (low rural houses with enclosed courtyards). Therefore, by using local materials and familiar formal language, Santa Elvira was designed as a relatable environment capable of communicating with nonprofessional users (inhabitants) by speaking with their code. As in other projects designed by CEDLA, a crucial part of Parque Santa Elvira was the existence of common public spaces, which were lacking in the vast majority of low-cost housing built during Pinochet's times.

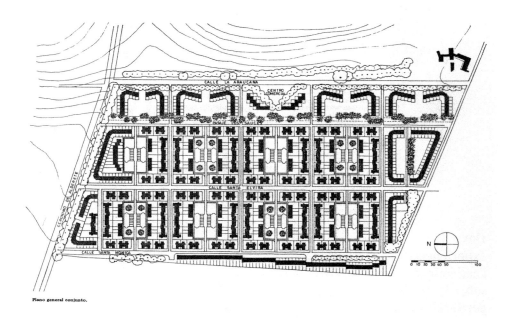

FIGURE 2.13 Site plan for Parque Santa Elvira housing complex in Santiago de Chile (Pedro Murtinho, Ricardo Contreras, Luis González, Humberto Eliash, and Santiago Raby, 1984), reprinted in Murtinho, et al., "Parque Santa Elvira," 57.

FIGURE 2.14 Corner of a building in Parque Santa Elvira housing complex in Santiago de Chile (Pedro Murtinho et al., 1984–1985) (archive of Pedro Murtinho).

FIGURE 2.15 Buildings in Parque Santa Elvira housing complex in Santiago de Chile (Pedro Murtinho et al., Ricardo Contreras, Luis González, Humberto Eliash, and Santiago Raby, 1984–1985) (archive of Pedro Murtinho).

FIGURE 2.16 Street view of Parque Santa Elvira housing complex in Santiago de Chile (Pedro Murtinho et al., 1984–1985) (archive of Pedro Murtinho).

Due to financial issues, in the final realization these public spaces were drastically reduced: "In this project," says Murtinho,

> we really fought hard with the investor. We fought because he didn't understand our principles of urbanism and social dwelling, and he was interested only in the commercial aspect. When we said that we wanted 30% of the project to be taken up by public space he simply said no way and insisted that it needed to be reduced to 5%.[44]

Even though the original program was drastically curtailed, the architectural quality of Santa Elvira housing stands out among low-cost housing realizations in Chile under Pinochet.

CEDLA's approach to low-cost housing is marked by respect for local tradition (in form and material), an emphasis on the importance of images as means of spatial analysis, and double-coding as broadening access to architectural understanding. These practices were drawn explicitly from postmodern principles in order to design higher quality living spaces that countered the monotonous and utilitarian designs of SERVIU. Similarly, its use of traditional typologies (piazzas, squares, the street) in its design for Santiago Poniente exemplifies a form of postmodernism dedicated to the social good, opposing the forms of city planning that arose out of the neoliberal logic of the free market new to Chile. In this way, for CEDLA, throughout the twelve years of its existence, the postmodern turn in architecture brought the promise of a socially engaged architecture aimed at opposing the destructive policies of Pinochet's regime.

2.4 Dissent and Compliance

In projects like Santiago Poniente, CEDLA used postmodern ideas as tools to pursue social and political agendas in ways intended to challenge the status quo. At the same time, it is important to remember that the division between architectures endorsed by the State and architectures against the State during Pinochet's dictatorship is bound to be nuanced and that unambiguously characterizing CEDLA as "oppositional architecture" risks oversimplifying matters. While its program was pursued mostly through unrealized projects and theoretical debates published in *ARS*, most members of the group ran successful architectural practices outside of the group. Some of their work in the 1970s and 1980s directly corresponds to debates conducted within CEDLA – for example, the Parque Santa Elvira discussed above. However, in other instances, these architects realized a number of private and commercial buildings that do not exhibit the same social and political engagement as was fundamental for CEDLA.

Cristián Boza, for instance, was one of the main organizers within the group, but he was also an owner of one of the most successful architectural studios during Pinochet's regime. Boza's studio designed many of the buildings that shaped the new corporate and neoliberal image of Santiago. With formal allusions to neighboring architecture, simplified classicized elements in designs like Las Americas office building (completed in 1987) and CODELCO (Corporación Nacional del Cobre de Chile, National Copper Corporation of Chile) headquarters (1982–1983), and the use of local artisanal materials like red terracotta cladding in Eve commercial center (1981), in his numerous corporate realizations Boza used postmodern aesthetics very differently than he did as a member of CEDLA. In these buildings, postmodernism was employed not as a tool for "liberation" or "bringing our country back" (contrary to Boza's declaration quoted above) but as a formal language of architectural complacency with the neoliberal agenda of the regime. Moreover, in 1987, Boza took part in the competition for the Chilean Congress organized by Pinochet's administration.[45] This discrepancy between theory and practice of some of the group's members (Boza's case is the most controversial but not the only example) is one reason why some Chilean architects remain skeptical of CEDLA's agenda.[46]

Despite these complexities, CEDLA as an organization exhibited a commitment to pushing for social and political change through spatial and architectural designs. Through their projects, publications, organized conferences, and symposia, CEDLA interpreted postmodernism in a subversive way and used postmodern concepts – such as the revival of traditional urban forms – as tools to foster community and social bonds that they hoped would eventually contribute to overturning the regime and the return of democracy.

2.5 Chile's Distinctive Postmodernism

Chilean architecture allows us to emphasize some ways in which postmodernism can be used politically, due to the country's particular political-economic context. First, the case of Chile between 1973 and 1990 presents how an economic (*laissez-faire*) context is not politically neutral but needs to be actively defended and propagandized; as a result, postmodernism becomes both a passive byproduct and an active contribution of the government simultaneously. Chile thus helps us see how the capitalist context means that postmodernism *is* political, for in this case, the neoliberal ideology needs to be defended (and is indeed contested). At the same time, in designs that work against the government, we see the pro-social potential in postmodernism at work, particularly in the uses of traditional typologies.

In some ways, Chilean postmodern realizations uphold the familiar diagnosis of postmodernism formulated by Habermas, McLeod, and Jameson: indeed, many exemplify what McLeod has referred to as "pseudohistorical nostalgia, the fabricated traditions [and] the pandering to a nouveau-riche clientele" and a general complacency with neoliberal market forces.[47] However, they are also coupled with political aims we do not usually find in the canonical Western European or North American examples. As the economic system is here a site of political contestation, postmodern designs either legitimize that economic system as a part of a political structure or oppose it by leaning into postmodernism's pro-social potential. If the propagandistic efforts of the Plaza de la Constitución and the Congreso Nacional de Chile come closer to the "pseudohistorical nostalgia" and "fabricated traditions" described by McLeod, they also do so in order to emphatically generate support for a particular regime.

Chilean architecture in the decades of the 1970s and 1980s simultaneously went with the logic of the market and against it, both realizing the government agenda and challenging it. The convoluted and contradictory paths of architectures analyzed in this chapter prove how flexible and susceptible to differing ideological uses postmodernism was. Indeed, this feature is itself quintessentially postmodern. Chilean postmodernism recalls Robert Venturi's description of postmodernism as "hybrid rather than pure," and "compromised" and "distorted" instead of "obvious."[48] The resulting irony is not merely playful, but rather a necessary consequence of the differing social and political motivations, messages, and connotations implicated in the design. In these ways, Chilean postmodernism insists upon a broader narrative for the history and theory of postmodernism, one that is more attuned to the complex relationships between architecture, capitalism, and the neoliberal state in a location that has witnessed economic and political developments quite different than familiarly traced in Western Europe and North America.

Notes

1 Legal decree: Decreto Ley 50, October 1, 1973. Full text: https://www.leychile.cl/Navegar/index_html?idNorma=5702.
2 Other members include José Gabril Alemparte, Pablo Astaburuaga, Fernando Boza, Miguel Catillo, Ricardo Contreras, Hernán Duval, Luis González, Eugenio Guzmán, Guillermo Hevia, José Larraín, Teresa Lima-Campos, Carlos López, Roberto López, Jorge Luhrs, Ignacio Martínez, José F. Muzard, Rodolfo Opazo, Andrés Pinto, Santiago Raby, Eduardo Walker, and Diana Wilson (as listed in the editorial page of the 1977 issue of CEDLA).
3 Castillo Velazco could not join them, as he remained in political exile. Eliash and Boza underline the importance of Castillo Velazco's support for the emergence of CEDLA (see interviews with Humberto Eliash and Cristián Boza published in Appendix). Another crucial figure who influenced CEDLA's emergence and program was Fernando Montes, a Chilean architect working in France, who in 1977 established contact with Boza and proposed to give a series of presentations on postmodern architecture and theory to the CEDLA circle.
4 Boza, interview by Lidia Klein.
5 Murtinho, interview by Lidia Klein (September 1).
6 Eliash, interview by Lidia Klein (September 7).
7 Boza, interview by Lidia Klein.
8 The buildings were owned and administered by individuals or companies who were responsible for their maintenance. Individual retail units within caracoles were either rented or owned. In the latter case, owners paid monthly maintenance fees to the building's administration.

9 De Simone, "Caracoles comerciales." Translation mine.
10 "Vanguardia y Post Modernismo en Chile," 28. Translation mine.
11 "Vanguardia y Post Modernismo en Chile," 28.
12 "Vanguardia y Post Modernismo en Chile," 28.
13 Murtinho, interview by Lidia Klein (August 30).
14 Eliash, interview by Lidia Klein (August 23).
15 In 1979, CEDLA tried to implement a different way of financing the magazine. With the distribution of third issue, CEDLA attached a letter asking the recipients to pay for the magazine, but as it proved unsuccessful, the architects continued to finance it through advertisement and their own money.
16 "Editorial," 7. Translation mine.
17 Cox, "Universalidad y peculiaridad en la dimension simbólica," 15. Translation mine.
18 Murtinho, interview by Lidia Klein (August 30).
19 Boza, interview by Joaquín Serrano, 165. Translation mine.
20 Eliash, interview by Lidia Klein (September 7).
21 Boza, interview by Lidia Klein.
22 "Remodelación Santiago Poniente," 15. Translation mine.
23 Boza et al., "Tema II La ciudad de Santiago proposición para Santiago Metropolitano," 74. Translation mine.
24 Boza et al., 74.
25 Eliash, interview by Lidia Klein (August 23).
26 Jacobs, *The Death and Life of Great American Cities*, 14.
27 It should be noted that Jacobs's emphasis of diversity is often reduced to a purely aesthetic, superficial dimension and its economic dimension is often overlooked. Examples of such misinterpretations of Jacobs are present in the theories of Richard Florida and Joel Garreau. Indeed, Jacobs is often blamed for promoting conservative urban philosophy leading to gentrification. However, as Robert Fitch argues in *The Assassination of New York*, economic diversity is central to Jacobs's argument and in this sense, her fight was not only about modernism, but capitalism as the real destructor of the cities. See Fitch, *The Assassination of New York* (London: Verso Books), 1993, 27–29.
28 Eliash, interview by Lidia Klein (September 7).
29 Boza, interview by Lidia Klein.
30 "Saludamos a *ARS*" (pages not numbered). Translation mine.
31 Palmer, "Urbanismo, ideologias y dependencia" (pages not numbered). Translation mine.
32 Eliash, interview by Lidia Klein (September 7).
33 By social housing (*vivienda social*), I mean affordable housing solutions provided by the State with the goal of remedying inequalities. The term overlaps with and is often considered to be synonymous with public housing.
34 Arriola, "Editorial," 7. Translation mine.
35 Healy, "Los arquitectos deben perder el tiempo," 30. Translation mine.
36 Arriola, "Editorial," 7.
37 Arriola, "Editorial," 8.
38 Arriola, "Editorial," 8.
39 As Hernán Duval writes, "Every proposal to overcome the current urban crisis needs to be supported by systemic solutions based on participation and cooperation, to which appropriate architectural typologies and urban solutions can be applied." Duval, "Periferia metropolitana," 10. Translation mine.
40 Eliash, "La periferia dibujada," 11. Translation mine.
41 Jacobs, *Learning from Las Vegas*, 52–53.
42 Eliash, "La periferia dibujada," 11.
43 Jencks, *What Is Post-Modernism?*, 14.
44 Murtinho, interview by Lidia Klein (August 30).
45 It should be noted that the ambiguity of Boza's position is true also for other architects. For example, other CEDLA members (including Pedro Murtinho and Humberto Eliash) also submitted their proposals for the Chilean Congress. Moreover, Cristián Undurraga and Ana Luisa Devés, the architects of Plaza de la Constitución, were very closely connected to CEDLA's circle.
46 See, for instance, interviews with Fernando Pérez Oyarzún, published in the Appendix.
47 McLeod, "Architecture and Politics in the Reagan Era," 23.
48 Venturi, *Complexity and Contradiction in Architecture*, 16.

3

SOCIALIST POSTMODERNISM IN THE POLISH PEOPLE'S REPUBLIC

The phrase "state-supported socialist postmodernism" may sound oxymoronic. In cultural and architectural theory, postmodernism is framed as following the "cultural logic of late-capitalism" (Jameson) or "the architecture of post-industrial society" (Portoghesi). Following these widespread assumptions, it would be logical to conclude that in Poland, postmodern architecture could appear only in the 1990s after the transition to a free market economy. If postmodern architecture is inseparably connected to capitalism, the political and economic context of Poland – which between 1947 and 1989 was a socialist country functioning under the name of Polish People's Republic (Polska Republika Ludowa, PRL) – could not provide appropriate conditions for postmodernism to develop.

Moreover, the ruling Polish Socialist Party had a clear vision for official architecture supported by the State. In its first years, the official style of the PRL was described as "socialist realism," which in the late 1950s was replaced by industrialized late modernism. Therefore, in the late 1960s, Poland was not only a country with an industrial socialist economy but also a country where the official vision for architecture was based on technocratic late modernist ideals opposed by Western postmodernism. Despite these conditions, however, postmodern currents were not only present in Polish architectural discourse and practice since the 1970s but also were embraced by the Party and used for propagandistic purposes. This official acceptance of Western architectural trends allowed their circulation and eventually (as we will see in Chapter 4), contrary to the government's intentions, made possible their use against the State.

3.1 Postmodern Architecture and Propaganda in the Polish People's Republic

As postmodern forms were very different from the industrialized building styles promoted as the appropriate architectural expression of the socialist republic, the State authorities needed to provide a rationale for their use. In order to better understand the conditions under which postmodern notions were introduced on Polish ground, it is crucial to outline the basic mechanisms of State propaganda in socialist Poland. The intensity of State

DOI: 10.4324/9781003179467-4

propaganda efforts in the PRL has varied throughout its history. Especially powerful in the first years after the end of World War II, the machine of cultural propaganda noticeably slowed down after Joseph Stalin's death in 1953. In the late 1940s and early 1950s, during the early years of the Polish People's Republic, the Polish Socialist Party expressed a strong interest in culture as a tool capable of shaping the minds and attitudes of citizens. For every field of cultural production, from architecture to painting, literature, film, and graphic design, the Party issued manifestos with guidelines providing clear rules to be followed in order to create artworks compatible with the official ideology of socialism. Each work of art was supposed to carry socialist content and use realist forms comprehensible to the working masses, thereby representing the goals of the new style of "socialist realism" (socrealizm).[1] Architecture and urbanism were seen as especially important pieces of this project because of their scale and public character. In the decades following 1953, cultural propaganda was less forceful, its power gradually waning.

In March 1956, during a meeting of the Association of Polish Architects (Stowarzyszenie Architektow Polskich; SARP), socialist realism was declared to be no longer the official style of the PRL. From then on, state-commissioned buildings needed to be erected using industrialized construction methods based on prefabricated concrete elements and a quick assembly schedule. The primary goal of Polish architecture was defined as providing mass housing to the working class, and modern industrialized building was seen as a mean to realizing this postulate in the most efficient way.[2]

The late socialist State did not produce declarations as strong and straightforwardly written as the early manifestos. This does not mean, however, that culture – and especially architecture – ceased to be of interest for the Party. Throughout the entire period of the existence of Polish People's Republic, all cultural production was controlled for ideological suitability by the Main Office for the Control of Press, Presentations, and Public Performances, referred to hereafter as the GUKPPiW (Główny Urząd Kontroli Prasy, Publikacji i Widowisk), an institution existing between 1949 and 1989. Documents regarding architecture and urban planning were screened by GUKPPiW and required the censors' approval before publication. Even though the majority of architects were not Party members, the official statements of SARP were always carefully worded to affirm architecture's role in building socialism. For example, in the resolution accompanying SARP's centenary in 1977, the Association declares,

> we are aware of the weight of our responsibilities. … [Our] activity in the People's Republic of Poland started with the realization of all the postulates of architectural circles, which could not be fulfilled in capitalism. Thus we advanced the development of architecture as an art serving the whole society. Urban planning has been advanced, housing has become common for everyone. The State patronage of architecture opened possibilities for realizing programs of scale and content unimaginable before. Moreover, architects and the SARP contributed to, first, a rebuilding of the country [after the war], and then to the process of building a country already chasing the top ten industrialized countries in the world. … The bond present in SARP solidifies this awareness of the social responsibility of the profession of architecture, as well as the sense of our responsibility for the realization of social commissions for architecture that serve the needs of the people and the socialist development of Poland. … We will continue to improve the art of architecture for the good of our socialist homeland.[3]

74 Socialist Postmodernism in the Polish People's Republic

Two years later, on the occasion of the 35th Anniversary of the People's Republic of Poland, similarly flattering words came out from Polish architectural circles:

> In this year we are celebrating the 35th anniversary of the People's Republic of Poland. During these years our architecture has attained the status of a social service ... The change in political system has freed us from the nightmare of building speculation, while at the same time has created the conditions for controlling spatial development. The material base was provided for by economic growth. The State organizations for designing – design offices – were called into being, thus putting an end to the prospect of unemployment, once very drastic in the architectural milieu. Never before in Polish history had we built so much, and never has the outlook for the future been so propitious.[4]

Open declarations like these, which affirmed close ties between the government and architects, were not as frequent in late socialist Poland as they were during the early years of PRL, but their presence attests to the close connections between politics and architecture even in the 1970s and 1980s. Architecture was a powerful tool for the Party throughout the entire history of the Polish People's Republic. Due to its connection to economy and industry, it was seen as an important element in forming the image of the State, as it demonstrated progress and advancements of the living conditions of the PRL's citizens. New architectural realizations, such as housing estates, factories, or public-use buildings provided tangible proof for how the country flourishes under socialism. New projects were eagerly presented by state-controlled media and outlets such as the Polish Film Chronicle (Polska Kronika Filmowa) – a short propagandistic newsreel obligatorily shown in cinemas before each film screening. These resources leave no doubt as to the Party's interest in architecture as a tool for propaganda, even in the absence of manifestos or directives outlining its socialist goals. The most valuable and revealing accounts of continued state pressure are interviews with architects active in that period and the architectural publications in late socialist Poland. These latter sources provide evidence that the government was not indifferent toward new architectural tendencies and that it appropriated them for its own ideological goals.

3.2 *Architektura*

A document crucial for understanding the architectural discourse of the period is the journal *Architektura*. *Architektura* was published by the SARP on a monthly basis between 1947 and 1980, and bimonthly from 1980 through 1989. *Architektura* was the most important and widely read architectural magazine in socialist Poland and functioned as the country's major platform for architectural discourse. As with every book and magazine published legally in socialist Poland, each issue needed to be checked for the appropriateness of its content and authorized. Each issue was sent to the GUKPPiW and waited upon approval by the censors. After positive review, the magazine was sent back with a censors' stamp of approval authorizing its publication. If the content was not approved, depending on the gravity of the problem, the consequences varied from resubmitting the issue to more serious actions, including the possibly of a publishing ban, possibly of several years, for the author of the material. Although it was more common in the early years of the PRL, having a publication banned remained a real possibility as late as the 1980s.[5] As a result, even though most of the editors and contributors were not members or even supporters of the Party (and some of them, like Czesław Bielecki, were active in the underground opposition), the content of the magazine had to recognize the ideological line of the government.

In the Polish architectural press, the term "postmodernism" was first used in 1979 in the May/June issue of *Architektura*.

The cover featured a large photograph of Charles Moore's *Piazza d'Italia* in New Orleans – the first time that a contemporary building appeared on typically abstract covers of this magazine. Below the photo, contrasting sharply with its white background, was a caption in black reading, "what next?" The cover announced the main goal of the publication: to diagnose the situation of contemporary architecture and reflect on its future. As the editor's opening note reads:

> When we observe the development of contemporary architecture, we ask the above question [what next?] more and more frequently. Although a whole new language was created to define the phenomena occurring in architecture, a radical solution does not seem to be at hand. As a continuation of the same subject, *Architektura* wishes to present the achievements of a group of architects who are said by critics to have surpassed the threshold of Modernism. … Some misgivings about solutions introduced into world architecture by Post-modernism may arise when we go back to the beginnings

FIGURE 3.1 Cover of *Architektura* 379–380 (1979) with Charles Moore's Piazza d'Italia in New Orleans.

of Modernism. ... Therefore ... we are publishing a picture of the creative path of several classics of Soviet architecture – the Romantic Modernists.[6]

Although works by postmodern architects had been presented occasionally in *Architektura* before, the May/June 1979 issue not only mentions for the first time the term "postmodernism" but also provides a characterization of the movement, mainly through reprints of two articles on contemporary architecture published in magazines *Baumeister* and *Time*. However, the editors of *Architektura* complemented these Western accounts on postmodernism with the audacious suggestion that postmodernism had Soviet origins. An article on the Soviet "Romantic Modernists" by Yevgeny Myelnikov in this issue presented the major works of the Vesnin brothers – Aleksey Shchusev, Konstantin Melnikov, and Boris Iofan. Myelnikov praised their "colorful individuality," "influence of national traditions," "creative individuality," and a search for "new artistic forms in architecture" – elements that would fit very well into most descriptions of postmodern architecture.[7]

Buildings like Konstantin Melnikov's Rusakov *Workers' Club in Moscow* (1928) indeed show some similarities with the later formal experiments of postmodern architects. While an analogical argument could be made using Le Corbusier's chapel of *Notre Dame du Haut* in Ronchamp (1954) or the works of German expressionists such as Erich Mendelsohn or Hans Poelzig, the journal does not mention any of those Western examples, rather choosing to focus on Soviet architecture exclusively, in effect sending a message that postmodernism originated in the USSR. As this issue of *Architektura* was planned as an introduction

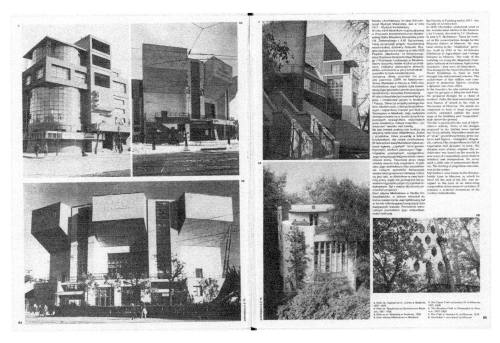

FIGURE 3.2 Fragment of Yevgeny Myelnikov's article "Romantic Modernists" published in *Architektura* 379–380 (1979), 84–85.

of postmodernism to Polish architects, the decision to suggest its Soviet genealogy is a meaningful gesture. By demonstrating that postmodernism was invented in Soviet Moscow rather than "learned from Las Vegas," the editors made it possible to view postmodern architecture not as a potentially dangerous Western, imperialist, and capitalist imposition, but as a phenomenon of close, familiar, and ideologically suitable roots.[8]

A similar effort was undertaken by *Architektura* a year prior. Although it did not mention the term "postmodernism" explicitly, issue 3–4 of 1978 was devoted to the discussion of the crisis of modern architecture. Half of the issue is comprised of a fifty-page essay, "Continuity in Architecture" by Czesław Bielecki, which praised cities of the past and criticized twentieth-century cities for the destruction of the urban tissue.

Bielecki's argument is developed both by the text (with numerous references to authors with important connections to theories of postmodernism, such as Christopher Alexander, Jane Jacobs, Kevin Lynch, Robert Venturi, and Umberto Eco) and by dense visual material – schemes, drawings, and illustrations of architecture from the past. In a Venturi-esque style, the images flow in a continuous stream usurping page space and dominating the text. Both the message and the form of a visual/textual collage earned the essay's reputation as the "Polish manifesto of postmodernism."[9] In the "Afterword" to the issue, the editor Jerzy Bruszewski made sure that the potentially dangerous content of Bielecki's essay would not be interpreted as a statement against the socialist State. As the continuity in architecture praised by Bielecki was broken by the industrialized late modern architecture chosen by the socialist State as its architectural expression, the essay could have been easily taken as openly oppositional, but in his afterword, Bruszewski stresses the merits of modern architecture in

FIGURE 3.3 Fragment of article by Czesław Bielecki, "Continuity in Architecture," published in *Architektura* 3–4 (1978), 28–29.

78 Socialist Postmodernism in the Polish People's Republic

providing housing for the masses while also acknowledging its flaws – "uniformity, clichés, shoddiness, low standards."[10] Further, the editor remarks that although Bielecki's theses might seem controversial, his "main claims are true" and that they are a remedy for the technocratic and demiurgic ambitions of contemporary architects.[11] Bruszewski concludes his afterword by reassuring readers that Bielecki's postmodern postulates fulfill the intentions of the Party:

> The return to the game rules in architecture suggested by Bielecki instead of the technocratic "fixing" of our neighbors is also characteristic of our times. In Polish conditions, this means a consistent trend resulting from permanent improvement in the functioning of socialist democracy in all domains of the country's life, evidently including also the sphere of architectural creation.[12]

Bielecki's architectural practice cannot be separated from his underground oppositional activity in the 1970s and 1980s. His architectural criticism of centralized, industrialized architecture was a direct statement against the political system that had implemented this (in his view) oppressive mode of architectural expression. As he stated in 1991, "standardization and prefabrication were methods of communization."[13] Architectural efforts against those forms represented oppositional activity against the regime. Architectural circles were well aware of Bielecki's engagement in the opposition and his unequivocal criticisms of socialism; likewise, Bruszewski's remarks in the "Afterword" did not have any real persuasive power to convince the magazine's readers that Bielecki's statements corresponded with the efforts of the Party. Those empty and purely rhetorical remarks were, nevertheless, enough to obtain the censorship's seal of approval and maintain the safe status of *Architektura* as a magazine expressing ideologically correct values. This is a perfect example of what Alexei Yurchak, theorist of culture in Soviet and post-Soviet Russia, described as a "performative shift," which he considers as characteristic of late socialism – a condition in which "the performative dimension of ritualized and speech acts rises in importance (it is important to participate in the reproduction of these acts at the level of form), while the constative dimension of these acts become open-ended, indeterminate, or simply irrelevant."[14] Both Bruszewski and the readers of *Architektura* took part in a performative ritual of State observance while being perfectly aware of Bielecki's real intentions.

The two issues of *Architektura* discussed here provide valuable leads for the reconstruction of the Polish socialist state's approach to postmodern architecture. We can find further evidence of the relation between the State and these new architectural currents by attending to the words of architects who worked in late socialist Poland. One of the most active architects in that time was Romuald Loegler. He describes these relations in the following way:

> After 1981 … one could observe social and political changes aiming to "humanize" the present system. The government … started to articulate the need to humanize architecture. It was associated with the critique of mass housing units … in order to show that the Party cares about the people. That was the first moment when I noticed the government starting to declare the need to move away from concrete slab housing. There were opinions that one way to achieve that is to return to the city, to the philosophy of architecture returning to historical forms, in other words the notions used by postmodernism. … With these declarations of the Party, one could immediately

notice an increased interest in notions such as the street or the piazza in the city within architectural circles.[15]

Loegler emphasizes that for the socialist Party the stated interest in the citizens' well-being was strictly instrumental. He believes that while the architects were interested in new postmodern currents for various reasons, this interest was eagerly appropriated by the Party's propaganda:

> From one side, architects were looking for new paths, but from another, the Party was eagerly using this as an occasion to create its image as caring and citizen-friendly. ... Those efforts were a part of the general directive which the Party realized in every voivodeship [collection of counties] in order to strengthen the bond between the nation and the Party. The real threat for the government was not the attitude of ten architects, but thousands of angry people.[16]

The last line from Loegler's statement reflects an essential element of the role of postmodern architecture in late socialist Poland: postmodern architecture – which introduced a human scale, focused on spaces fostering social interaction, and created more visually exciting architectural environments – was a perfect tool in the Party's effort of appeasing "thousands of angry people." Although in the 1970s and 1980s architecture was rarely a tool for direct propaganda as it had been during the Stalinist times, it was still important for the government as a "relief valve," helping to ameliorate growing social tensions.

3.3 Na Skarpie Estate (Centrum E)

The appropriation of postmodern architecture by the late socialist State can also be seen in architecture competitions. One example of this can be seen in an invitation-only competition for a housing estate "Na Skarpie" (Centrum E) in Kraków's eastern-most neighborhood, Nowa Huta. The competition was organized in 1985 by Kraków's SARP and commissioned by the Cooperative Housing Association DZB Budostal. The winning proposal was submitted by a team lead by Loegler (with Wojciech Dobrzański and Michał Szymanowski), at that time an acclaimed architect known for prominent church realizations (St. Jadwiga Church in Kraków, with Jacek Czekaj, 1983–1989) and residential buildings (several townhouses in Kraków). At that time, Loegler was an exceptional figure in the Polish architectural scene. Not only did he run one of the first private architectural offices in Poland, but he also was an active organizer and animator of architectural discourse and in 1985 initiated the first Biennale of Architecture in Kraków, which provided one of the very few platforms for international architectural exchange in late socialist Poland. Loegler's career is also unique because of his extensive international experience, starting during his studies at the Kraków University of Technology (Politechnika Krakowska) from which he graduated in 1964. As a student, he received scholarships in Finland and France and between 1973 and 1974 he was an intern at Karl Schwanzer's architectural studio in Vienna. In the 1970s and 1980s, Loegler worked in Syria as a member of state design agency Miastoprojekt Kraków, where he experimented with postmodern ideas and forms that later influenced his projects in Poland, such as Na Skarpie Estate.[17] Commenting on the political uses of postmodern architecture by the Party, Loegler states, "thanks to the postmodern design philosophy, which permeated not only Polish architectural circles, but as I mentioned also the Party, projects such as the competition for Nowa Huta could emerge."[18] He notes that

> the rules [of the competition] were defined by the Main Architect, [Zbigniew] Zuziak, a man who, simply by virtue of his position, was associated with the Party, and they were defined in a way that fit into the propaganda of humanizing architecture, about which I spoke before. For example, there was a recommendation to include pitched roofs, or that the buildings should have some architectural detail, like a 'historicizing' railing in the balconies.[19]

The goal of the competition was to design a housing estate providing necessary services (grocery stores, daycare center) and recreational spaces (buildings for culture and leisure). Additionally, because the city planned for the creation of a lagoon connecting Na Skarpie and the Vistula river (less than a mile away), the organizers requested a proposal for an architectural program of the hypothetical future riverfront.

Nowa Huta was a site of particular interest and significance for the Party. It was originally designed in 1949 by a team of architects and urbanists led by Tadeusz Ptaszycki for the workers of the Lenin Steelworks steel plant.

Nowa Huta was built as a socialist ideal city and was erected by the working class for the working class. It occupied a prominent role in political propaganda, described as "the pride of the nation," "the forge of our prosperity," and "a work of Polish-Soviet friendship."[20] As it was designed according to the principles of socialist realist urban design, Nowa Huta's plan and architecture were based on traditional forms. Its fan-shaped layout with hierarchical

FIGURE 3.4 Plac Centralny in Nowa Huta housing estate in Kraków (1952–1956, Tadeusz Ptaszycki and team) (TomRollauer, 2016 CC BY-SA 4.0 license).

streets leading to the main square, Plac Centralny, and buildings with abundant references to renaissance and classical architecture makes Nowa Huta one of the most complete examples of socialist realist urbanism. Three decades after its design, Nowa Huta was transformed from the icon of socialist planning and social engineering to a symbol of social unrest and became a hub for the rising opposition: in the 1980s, Nowa Huta was one of the crucial strongholds of the Solidarność (Solidarity) movement and a site of massive protests and demonstrations of the workers and students, especially intense between 1981 and 1983.[21] The competition for Na Skarpie in 1985 was then used by the Party to show its concern with the well-being of Nowa Huta citizens and to tame popular discontent through attractive design that would contrast with the monotonous landscape of late socialist Polish housing architecture. As Loegler recalls, the competition's role was "to appease dangerous social unrest among the workers and the Party wanted to show that they care about Nowa Huta."[22]

Notably, in contrast to other architectural competitions in late socialist Poland, the rules for Na Skarpie did not mention the use of prefabricated systems as an obligatory condition. As for the construction method, it specifies only that "all building materials and the construction technology need to be generally available for realization in Kraków."[23] Loegler explains that the organizers did not mention the prefabricated building technology explicitly, because

> it had really bad press, it was an epitome of everything bad and evil in Polish architecture at that time. They obviously avoided mentioning 'prefabricated technology' deliberately, as the goal was to create an impression of breaking up with the inhumane architecture, not continuing it.[24]

Although the competition in its written official form does not mention any particular design philosophy or "style" as preferable for the future realization, the invited architects received clear guidelines directly from the organizers. Loegler states that

> the competition was organized in a moment when the people knew that the system was fragile. The Party tried to resolve social tensions by showing its caring side and declared its attention to the people by the attempt to "humanize" architecture. They wanted architecture that would become a landmark in Poland. Zbigniew Zuziak [Main Architect of Kraków, 1984–91] informed the organizer, the Cooperative Housing Association, that the entries should be postmodern proposals. But it wasn't official. It was stated unofficially and was not a part of official guidelines because everybody knew that postmodern architecture is expensive, for example due to its attention to detail and building materials.[25]

Postmodern architecture was the preferred style of the organizers and this wish was satisfied with the winning entry, prepared by Loegler and his team.

The plan for Na Skarpie shows the housing complex organized in a comb-shaped layout. The shaft of the comb is formed by seven-story housing blocks adjacent to the busy Jana Pawła avenue and Nowa Huta's main square, Plac Centralny (to the northwest). The teeth, made up of five-story blocks, open to extensive areas of wild greenery and, beyond that, the river. Four-story housing buildings are also situated between the main blocks of this part, forming a curved line along the South, parallel to the planned river bank. On the Northern

82 Socialist Postmodernism in the Polish People's Republic

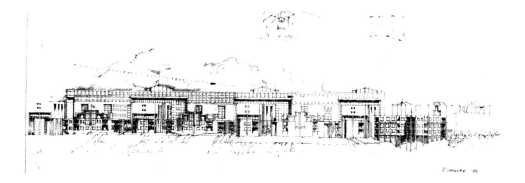

FIGURE 3.5 First-prize-winning proposal for Na Skarpie Estate in Kraków-Nowa Huta (1985, Romuald Loegler, Wojciech Dobrzański, and Michał Szymanowski) (archive of Romuald Loegler).

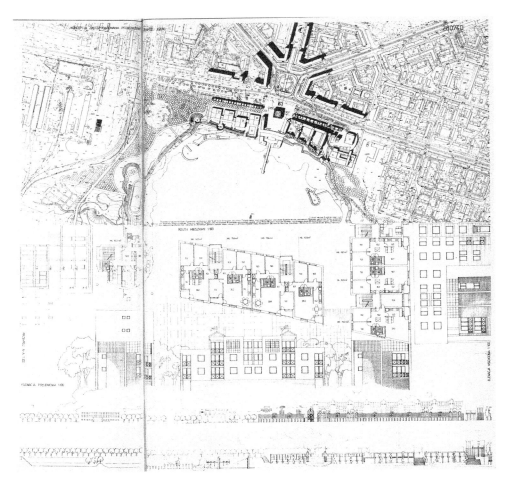

FIGURE 3.6 Na Skarpie Estate in Kraków-Nowa Huta, site plan, c. 1986 (Romuald Loegler et al.), reprinted in Loegler, "Konkurs SARP na rozwiązanie zespołu mieszkalnego," 54–55.

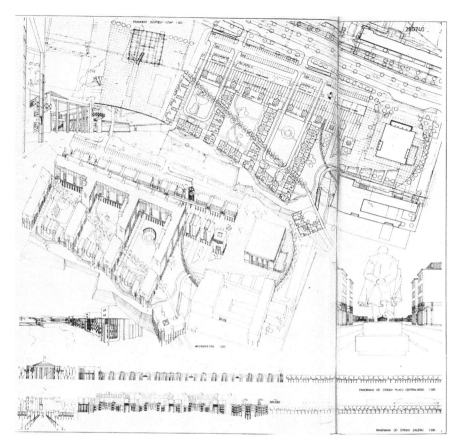

FIGURE 3.7   Na Skarpie Estate in Kraków–Nowa Huta, site plan, c. 1986 (Romuald Loegler et al.), reprinted in Loegler, "Konkurs SARP na rozwiązanie zespołu mieszkalnego," 56–57.

side, along the avenue and in front of the housing blocks, Loegler's team placed a lower passage of retail buildings providing necessary services, such as schools, which supplement the extant infrastructure of Nowa Huta. This also served as an acoustic barrier for the housing complex. Additional services like stores, cafes, restaurants, and daycare facilities are placed in the tall first floors of housing buildings.

Usually, the rules for competitions for new mass housing complexes in late socialist Poland limited the building method to "wielka płyta" ("large slab"). Wielka płyta provided economic efficiency and short construction times due to its high level of standardization as the basic modules were large concrete panels with precut elements such as windows. Loegler's team decided to use "wielki blok" ("large block") – a more open system in which basic modules are smaller and more diverse, allowing for more flexibility. With the use of this relatively flexible system of prefabricates, the architectural forms used in Na Skarpie could be diversified. Buildings on the South end, facing the river, are supported on thin round pillars and have slightly curved avant-corps. The façades of the buildings facing the city on the North end have lower parts cut with simple rectangular arcades, housing stores, and services. In most of the buildings, staircases are accentuated by avant-corps, glass bricks,

FIGURE 3.8 Na Skarpie housing estate in Kraków-Nowa Huta, aerial view from the South (1987–1995, Romuald Loegler et al.) (archive of Romuald Loegler).

FIGURE 3.9 Na Skarpie housing estate in Kraków-Nowa Huta, South end (1987–1995, Romuald Loegler et al.) (archive of Romuald Loegler).

FIGURE 3.10 Balconies at Na Skarpie housing estate in Kraków-Nowa Huta, (1987–1995, Romuald Loegler et al.) (author).

or panel windows. Details, such as precast balconies with geometrical cuts or gable roofs supported by asymmetrical diagonal beams, add to the formal complexity to the space of Na Skarpie.

The monotony of grey concrete slabs is broken by the use of color (pink and blue). While colorful façades are abundant in Western postmodern architecture of the 1970s and 1980s, in the Polish building industry, color was seen a luxury, which increased costs without improving function, and were thus superfluous. Because of the unavailability of outdoor façade paints on the Polish market, Loegler's team used poster colors as pigments added to regular white paint. As Loegler recalls,

> [expectations were] confronted with the scarcity of available materials. … In that time … the external walls needed to be painted using one (the only available) white paint which then was pigmented with poster paint in the chosen color. After one big rain, everything was washed away. I recently told this story at a conference in Berlin and the audience simply did not want to believe it possible, they thought I was joking. Well I wasn't joking, it was definitely possible in socialist Poland.[26]

Though this may be quite unthinkable to architects unfamiliar with the market reality of Eastern Europe under late socialism, it is a telling example not only of the "shortage economy" but also of the do-it-yourself approach common for Polish architects in late socialism.[27]

The simplified, geometrical shapes and classicizing design solutions of Nowa Huta recall the realizations of Aldo Rossi, Mario Botta, or the Krier brothers. The complex borrows from baroque urban plans by creating theatrical scenographic effects. The diverse planes of façades and their sculptural details unfold slowly while walking from the North to the East end. Since the hierarchical, axial composition of baroque cities was one of the most common references for planners of socialist realist cities, including Nowa Huta, this way of composing Na Skarpie was another method of linking the new development with existing architecture forms in a playful, postmodern way.

The design for Na Skarpie is also rooted in ideas promoted by the IBA (International Building Exposition) organized in West Berlin between 1979 and 1987. In 1986, Loegler took part in one of IBA's design seminars in Berlin-Kreuzberg, which resulted in the realization of a multifamily building completed in 1993.[28] In that simple four-story building with a façade cladded with red brick grid laid over a white plastered wall Loegler experimented with basic urban typologies (street, courtyard) and subtle historical references (window openings, use of brick) in an attempt to acknowledge both the history of the site (partly destroyed during the World War II) and contemporary architectural language. This emphasis on continuity between past and present achieved thanks to the use of traditional typologies, as well as the exploration of basic geometric figures (square and rectangular shapes organizing the façade), can also be found in Na Skarpie. Resonances of the IBA can be traced, for example, in a four-story L-shaped building with bay windows and balconies flanking central glazed staircase. Loegler called this building "Urban Villa" (Willa Miejska), using terminology broadly circulating within IBA.

Loegler's original (unrealized) plan of Na Skarpie included an "urban loggia" – a square, roofed area defined by simple classicizing arcades.

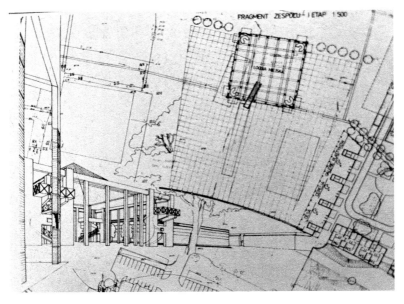

FIGURE 3.11 Unrealized design for "Urban Loggia" from Na Skarpie Estate in Kraków-Nowa Huta, c. 1986 (Romuald Loegler et al.), reprinted in Loegler, "Konkurs SARP na rozwiązanie zespołu mieszkalnego," 56.

The loggia was intended as a space for spontaneous social activities and interactions integrating the local community. As Loegler describes it,

> the intention was to create a new version of public spaces for interactions and gatherings known from historical cities – a nucleus of the urban. In our project, it was designed as an urban theatre, a free and open platform for spontaneous activities, mainly for the local community, as well as a space for pre-planned shows or concerts. But the main point was to create a place where people could meet and talk without forcing them and without imposing anything, a place that simply invites everyone to be there. … It was a symbolic way to give this space to the people and to encourage them to interact and cooperate without imposed regulations or rules, to free them from how people were taught to act in socialism, always on command, in a pre-programmed way.[29]

The loggia was linked with Nowa Huta's Plac Centralny, the district's monumental, representative square, designed as a site for parades and carefully choreographed marches praising the communist state. The concept of the representative square was one of the dominant examples of how socialist realist urbanism became subordinated to propagandistic aims. Loegler's loggia enters into a dialogue with Plac Centralny by its use of simplified classical forms, although in a notably critical way. Its modest, approachable scale is starkly antithetical to the pompous monumentality of socialist realist representative city squares. Its politics is also very different in its emphasis on spontaneity and in its bottom-up initiative. As Loegler says,

> Plac Centralny was formed according to the ideology of its period. … It was planned as a social space, a site for mass demonstrations showing the power of the working class people. … This was our point of departure, as we decided to reinterpret its programmed content and refer it to a different scale. [We wanted to] give this space a different meaning: to reject banners, mass marches, and replace them with the ordinary person, in his natural scale, cleaned from all this pompousness.[30]

In one of the first plans for Nowa Huta in the late 1940s, its designers had planned to situate a theatre building on Plac Centralny. "We replaced it with an unprofessional theatre initiated by the people themselves," recalls Loegler.[31] The "urban theatre" was not restricted to high-brow cultural events, but included

> actions of various types, actions which would help to bring back natural, urban tendencies. All that is needed is the right scale to attract vendors, buyers, or even casual drunks – all this is normal, human, it happens in cities and should be happening in Nowa Huta too.[32]

The urban loggia was never realized, as "nobody wanted to invest in an empty space without a clear function assigned to it."[33]

Na Skarpie was therefore seen as an agent of change in different ways by the government and by the architects themselves. Nowa Huta was intended to demonstrate the Party's openness and its willingness to improve the living conditions of the working class in times of increasing social unrest, threatening the existence of socialist state. The new housing development in Nowa Huta was a chance to show the Party's caring face and to appease the inhabitants of the neighborhood, which was a site of major worker's strikes between 1981 and 1983. At the same time, Loegler's team took advantage of the relatively flexible competition rules as an occasion to create a more democratic design:

> We tried to create spatial remedies for social atomization and the anonymity of living in a mass-produced, homogeneous housing estate by focusing on common spaces. Our goal was to create a bond between the people, and also identification of the inhabitants with the place they live in.[34]

Na Skarpie's postmodern features certainly recall those theorized by Rossi, Jencks, and Portoghesi in their common emphasis on historical referentiality and traditional typologies. But also, as we saw with the Congreso Nacional de Chile (though in quite a different way), the design takes advantage of postmodernism's capacity for double-coding. In one sense, it seeks to revert to traditional typologies in building public spaces that would assist community building and in another sense in its playful referentiality and inviting presentation it served to communicate the amiable intentions of an unpopular government. These are codependent: the architects depended upon the government for the approval of the building's design and the success of the design for the people directly benefited the government. This leaves the complex with intrinsically ironic qualities, but the irony here is not simply playful; rather, it is a necessary and natural byproduct of the different motivations of the architect and the State.

The construction of Na Skarpie started in 1987, two years after the competition, when the downfall of the old system was already imminent, and it was completed in 1995. The persuasive power of bold postmodern forms proved to be weaker than the rising social dissent in Nowa Huta and the rest of the country. The sculptural and bright façades painted with poster colors failed to convince the people of the Party's concern for the citizens' well-being and failed to restore their faith in socialism. A year later, in May 1988, Nowa Huta was the site of a much more immediate form of persuasion than architecture – the government's brutal suppression of the Lenin Steelworks' workers' strike.

With the changes caused by the crisis of Modernism and by the rise of postmodernism in architecture and urban planning permeating Polish architectural circles, the Party reacted strategically by reframing postmodernism as rooted in Soviet origins and reflecting "a consistent trend resulting from permanent improvement in functioning of the socialist democracy."[35] Rather than a capitalist, potentially reactionary, import, it was represented as homegrown and compatible with socialist ideals. Postmodernism helped the government formulate a necessary response to the growing criticism of mass-produced housing and to renew the Party's image as caring for its citizens. These efforts to "humanize" architecture (as Loegler characterized it) with the use of postmodern principles appeared in a precarious political moment of social unrest. Acceptance or – as the competition for Na Skarpie shows – even the promotion of postmodern architecture offered the Party a chance to salvage its image.

Ultimately, postmodern architecture proved incapable of appeasing "thousands of angry people," but the government's positive attitude toward postmodern currents made postmodernism in Polish architecture possible. The official acceptance of postmodern notions, in turn, allowed their use by architects in anti-communist statements, as will be discussed in Chapter 4.

Notes

1 The manifesto of the architecture of socialist realism was issued in 1949 as "Rezolucja Krajowej Partyjnej Narady Architektow w dniu 20–21 czerwca 1949 r. w Warszawie" in Architektura 6–8 (1949): 162.
2 Ogólnopolska Narada architektów, xviii. See also materials from IX Plenum PZPR in 1954, where the issue of the industrialization of building was raised.
3 "Nadzwyczajny Walny Zjazd SARP," 8. Translation mine.
4 Zwoliński, "Biuro Projektów Budownictwa Ogólnego 'Budopol,'" 4. Translation mine.
5 For example, architectural historian Marta Leśniakowska was given a five-year ban in 1981. See Leśniakowska, interview by Lidia Klein.
6 Bruszewski, "Od redaktora: Co dalej?," 23. Translation mine.
7 Myelnikov, "Romantic Modernists," 77, 82, 85, and 86, respectively.
8 A similar suggestion appeared two issues before; the works of soviet architect Ivan W. Zholtovski were juxtaposed with those of Philip Johnson. See Zholtovski and Myelnikov, "The Classics of the Soviet Architecture."
9 Leśniakowska, interview by Lidia Klein.
10 Bruszewski, "Posłowie od redaktora," 76. Translation mine.
11 Bruszewski, "Posłowie od redaktora," 77.
12 Bruszewski, "Posłowie od redaktora," 77.
13 "Architektów kłopoty z wolnością," 28. Translation mine.
14 Yurchak, Everything Was Forever, Until It Was No More, 26.
15 Loegler, "Rozmowa z Romualdem Loeglerem," 154. Translation mine.
16 Loegler, "Rozmowa z Romualdem Loeglerem," 155.
17 See Stanek, Postmodernizm jest prawie w porządku [Postmodernism Is Almost Alright].
18 Loegler, "Rozmowa z Romualdem Loeglerem," 173.
19 Loegler, "Rozmowa z Romualdem Loeglerem," 157.
20 Aman, Architecture and Ideology in Eastern Europe During the Stalin Era, 151.
21 See Lasota et al., "Małopolska i Świętokrzyskie."
22 Loegler, "Rozmowa z Romualdem Loeglerem," 154.
23 Loegler, "Konkurs SARP na rozwiazanie zespolu mieszkalnego," 53. Translation mine.
24 Loegler, "Rozmowa z Romualdem Loeglerem," 154.
25 Loegler, "Rozmowa z Romualdem Loeglerem," 154.
26 Loegler, "Rozmowa z Romualdem Loeglerem," 160.
27 Hungarian economist Janos Kornai coined this term to characterize socialist centrally planned economies of the eastern block. For Kornai, chronic shortages typical for late socialist states in the 1970s and 1980s were flaws embedded in the system itself rather than results of singular planning mistakes. See Kornai, Economics of Shortage.
28 Block 2 (plot between Dessauer Straße, Stresemannstraße, and Bernburger Straße). The seminar was invite-only and included members of the Association of Polish Architects (Wojciech Dobrzański, Wojciech Kosiński, Andrzej Wyrzykowski, Stanisław Denko, Robert Kuzianik, Krzysztof Lenartowicz, Jacek Czekaj, Daniel Karpiński, Wojciech Obtułowicz).
29 Loegler, interview by Lidia Klein.
30 Loegler, "Konkurs SARP na rozwiazanie zespolu mieszkalnego," 61.
31 Loegler, "Konkurs SARP na rozwiązanie zespołu mieszkalnego," 61.
32 Loegler, "Konkurs SARP na rozwiązanie zespołu mieszkalnego," 61.
33 Loegler, "Rozmowa z Romualdem Loeglerem," 160.
34 Loegler, "Rozmowa z Romualdem Loeglerem," 160.
35 Bruszewski, "Posłowie od redaktora," 77.

4

POSTMODERNISM AND DISSENT IN SOCIALIST POLAND

As we have seen in the previous chapter, because the Party embraced postmodernism as "a consistent trend resulting from permanent improvement in the functioning of socialist democracy," postmodern ideas could circulate freely in architectural discourse as ideologically safe.[1] This meant that, paradoxically, postmodern architecture in late socialist Poland could present anti-government statements not despite but because of its acceptance by the government. Indeed, the embrace of postmodernism by the Party also allowed their use by architects with anti-communist sentiments and, as the example of Romuald Loegler's Na Skarpie Estate shows, this coexistence of opposing ideological interpretations and contrasting uses of postmodern architecture was possible even within a single realization.

The architects using postmodern forms and ideas as tools to oppose the vision of society and urban space imposed by the politics of the Polish People's Republic cannot be described as a homogeneous group. Some of them, like Czesław Bielecki, translated postmodernism into a strong oppositional message against communist and socialist values. Others, like Loegler or Marek Budzyński, opposed the Polish socialist government, but not socialist principles. For them, postmodernism was a tool to achieve social change by slowly transforming the oppressive system from within. This chapter explores these diverse practices and shows how postmodern architecture was used as a political platform by architects who believed in the possibility of social and political change through architecture.

4.1 Oppositional Postmodernism: Czesław Bielecki and the DiM Group

In late socialist Poland, it would have been hard to find a more politically engaged architect than Czesław Bielecki. In addition to his architectural practice, Bielecki had (and still has) a parallel career in politics, beginning as an oppositional activist in socialist Poland and, after the political transformation of 1989, becoming a conservative right-wing politician. Bielecki strongly opposed not only the Polish socialist government but also the industrialized architecture of late modernism, which he saw as "a method of communization."[2] With articles such as "Ciągłość w architekturze" ["Continuity in Architecture"], which introduced Polish readers to key postmodern concepts, Bielecki became one of the

DOI: 10.4324/9781003179467-5

first proponents of postmodern ideas in Polish architecture.[3] As Loegler states, "Czesław Bielecki used postmodernism as an anti-systemic statement against the government. He was able to translate it [postmodernism] in a political way and create a manifesto that fit right into those times of tremendous change."[4]

From the 1970s up to the fall of communism, Bielecki was an active member of the anti-government opposition. Starting in 1979, he was a collaborator of *Kultura Paryska* (Paris Culture), a leading Polish-émigré cultural magazine published in Rome and then Paris, and which was an important platform for the anti-communist opposition.[5] He was also active in various anti-government underground movements and organizations in the country, including Polska Walcząca (Fighting Poland) between 1970 and 1979 and Polskie Porozumienie Niepodległościowe PPN (Polish Accord for Independence) from 1979 to 1980. In 1980, Bielecki became a member of the Solidarność movement. Arrested in 1968, 1983, and 1985 (with one of the charges being an attempt to overturn the political system), Bielecki became the most vocal opponent of the regime in Polish architectural circles. In 1980, Bielecki was the main initiator of the DiM ("Dom i Miasto" [House and City]) group, which emerged after discussions held during one of the SARP's meetings in Gdańsk, and existed for roughly four years, comprising over twenty members. The group's name was intended to signal a postulated shift in design priorities from concrete panel housing units and large-scale housing estates to architecture and urbanism rooted in traditional forms such as the "house" and the "city." DiM did not produce any actual urban or architectural designs and their theories were presented only in documents.

FIGURE 4.1 DiM Charter (1981, DiM group) (archive of Czesław Bielecki).

During the International Congress of Architecture, which was hosted by SARP in Warsaw in 1981, the DiM group curated an exhibition on the reconstruction of Warsaw after WWII and distributed their manifesto – a single-page document entitled *Karta DiM (DiM Charter)*.

DiM's participation in the Congress was officially supported by Solidarność, and the Charter was printed by the organization with its stamped logo.[6] The document was distributed to visitors of the Congress as a large-format leaflet, available in English, Polish, German, and French. The *DiM Charter* does not mention postmodernism explicitly, but its critique of modernist architecture and urban planning is saturated with ideas fundamental for the postmodern turn in architecture. The title is a polemical reference to *The Athens Charter*, which the authors blame for "breaking the continuity of culture" and "the destruction of traditional city."[7] Through ten sections of the document (Architecture and Politics; Between Collectivism and Individualism; The Responsibility for the Crisis in Architecture; Continuity in Architecture; Urban Planning, Monumental Architecture and City Fabric; Architecture is Art; The Language of Architecture; Social Role of the Architect; Memento), the authors reveal their vision for architecture and the city as standing in "fundamental opposition to the documents issued by the Association of Polish Architects, SARP."[8]

The *Charter* begins by characterizing architecture as a socio-political problem and describes contemporary architecture as dominated by "totalism" (an obsolete expression for totalitarianism) due to its reliance on standardization and prefabrication. As a remedy, the *Charter* states that "it is necessary to bring back continuity in architecture, finding the meaning of [forgotten] words from the architect's toolkit, such as style, modus, and canon," for "the goal of practicing architecture is not the creation of new terms, but the reinterpretation of the eternal phenomena of house and city."[9] Besides this return to history and traditional values in architecture, the *DiM Charter* draws on an array of postmodern theories although without referring to specific authors or books. Echoing works such as Rowe and Koetter's *Collage City* or Venturi's *Complexity and Contradiction in Architecture*, DiM claims that "the city is simultaneously a composition and a collage. The ideas of monumentality and urban fabric exist as a contrast." In the passages that follow, the authors state that the modernist "concept of architecture as science of technology deprives it from its role as culture generator and myth creator" and that "aesthetic functions are architecture's raison d'être." Further, indirectly referring to Alexander's *Pattern Language*, the authors state that

> reducing architecture to function deprives it of its role as a medium in social communication. In the moment when the pattern language was substituted with newspeak of precast concrete houses, settlements and pavilions, the city started to be illegible, monotonous, and death for its inhabitants. It is possible to build a city only using the elementary patterns of interiors, houses, streets, and piazzas as a basis.[10]

In the *DiM Charter*, architecture is framed as an artistic (rather than purely technical) discipline and a communication act that plays an important cultural and social role due to its myth-making potential.

These postmodernist values presented in the document were for the DiM group inseparable from its anti-socialist message. The authors argue against "nationalization in the name of fighting chaos" and call for the respect for private property, stating that "urban planning is auspicious for social life only when it is paired with the ownership of one's territory" and that "in the name of aesthetic coherence the architect cannot deprive individuals the right to express their personality, to spontaneous actions, to choice." In DiM's manifesto, the right for aesthetic choice, limited or non-existent in the reality of the uniform state-funded architecture of late socialist Poland, is inseparably connected with politics and economics. The optimal conditions for architecture are guaranteed by the free market economy, as artistic freedom can be achieved only by "the limitation of the state monopoly in building, [fostering] healthy competition among professionals, [having] the possibility to choose the client and the architect." Architectural freedom is a social and political postulate as "in a democratic society there cannot be art without competing artistic agendas." This message is amplified by the concluding paragraph of the *DiM Charter* ("Memento") stating that "the solidarity against the totalitarian threat of the individual and nation reminds us today that architecture can be humane and beautiful only when it is created by free citizens serving a free society."[11]

The openly political, anti-government, and pro-capitalist character of the *Charter* makes it a unique document in late socialist Polish architecture. DiM's anti-communist message, which "fit right into those times of tremendous change," combined with the attractive ideas of postmodernism, resonated among Polish architects and contributed to Bielecki's reputation as actively engaged in both pro-capitalist political activity and the dissemination of postmodern theories.[12] DiM's postulates were noticed and interpreted as political statements both by Polish architectural circles and international observers. The *Charter* was recognized by Paolo Portoghesi who had a chance to read the translated version of the document during the International Congress of Architecture in 1981. In the introduction to *Postmodern*, Portoghesi argues that "postmodern theses have deep roots in the present human conditions," which "is confirmed today in the document on architecture issued by the Polish union Solidarity":

> This text accuses the modern city of being the product of an alliance between bureaucracy and totalitarianism, and singles out the great error of modern architecture in the break of historical continuity. Solidarity's words should be meditated upon, especially by those who have confused a great movement of collective consciousness [postmodernism] with a passing fashion.[13]

Similarly, in *The Story of Post-Modernism*, Charles Jencks mentions that members of the Solidarność (Solidarity) movement were in touch with him in 1981 when he visited Warsaw. Jencks mentions Poland as one of the countries "behind the Iron Curtain where Modernism was at its most virulent and mandated as a total approach to the environment."[14] He recalls that Polish, Hungarian, and Czech architects became especially interested in postmodernism and that soon after, "by the mid-1980s just about every country with a totalitarian apparatus, and underground, joined the movement."[15] Jencks does not specify who exactly was in touch with him during his visit in 1981, but Bielecki confirms that he and other members of the DiM group met with Jencks during the International Congress and discussed the group's manifesto.[16]

During the four years of its existence, the DiM group issued a few more documents on architecture and urban planning. Apart from the *DiM Charter*, the crucial one was *Ways to Solve the Housing Problem* (*Drogi Rozwiązywania Kwestii Mieszkaniowej*), published sometime between 1981 and 1984 (exact date unknown), and, like the *DiM Charter*, was distributed as a leaflet with the Solidarność logo. As in the *DiM Charter*, the document considers "the city as a result of socio-economic processes" and links modernism (which denied the "traditional city with houses built along streets and squares") with "totalitarian systems."[17] According to this document, the disastrous condition of architecture in late socialist Poland can be repaired only by a radical shift toward capitalism: "the introduction of free market mechanisms" will allow "all social and economic subjects to take part in the free market game" and make space for "social and economic initiatives, which are now paralyzed by the existing state monopoly. ... It is time to stop supporting unprofitable behemoths and accept the existence of small private initiatives and cooperatives." This postulated change from the socialist economy to the free market model is again tied to the shift from the modernist paradigms of design to the traditional urban forms promoted by postmodernism. More so than in the *DiM Charter, Ways to Solve the Housing Problem* stresses that urban design should be focused on the question of the street as

> the street unites the vital functions of living, trade, services and communication in the most economical way. Meanwhile, the most oppressive quality of [late modernist] housing estates is the separation of functions contrary to our tradition and psychological expectations; real streets cannot be materialized in them as they lead "from nowhere to nowhere."

In contrast to the politics of the late socialist Polish housing models focused on collectivity (multi-family housing units), the document prioritizes individuals, their families, and their need for personal space. Instead of anonymous mass housing estates, the politics of housing should be based on

> houses for many generations, [which] reduce the need of social housing in the future. [The owner] is responsible for the maintenance of building and surrounding greenery .... Therefore, with the aid of an appropriate strategy of mortgages, we should create conditions optimal for the development of individual houses.

This model is possible only "under the condition of decentralization, when freedom of choice will be possible." DiM univocally rejects the Party's efforts toward the "humanization" of architecture, which, as Loegler's example of Na Skarpie shows, were used by the architects as occasions to pursue their own progressive design ideas within state-funded investments. For DiM, late socialist architecture and its politics could not be simply changed or improved but should be rejected altogether:

> as long as the pluralism of social and economic life doesn't develop freely, architecture is doomed to monotony. Sculptural forms of buildings or murals and other efforts to 'humanize' architecture are, in the centralized economy, only treatments of symptoms without curing the real disease.[18]

DiM's reflections on architecture and urban space were continued by an informal seminar group organized by Bielecki after his release from prison in 1986. Its participants, meeting once every few months in Bielecki's workshop in Warsaw, were mainly practicing architects, architecture critics, and intellectuals invested in urban space. The group did not have any formalized structure or program, but the discussions were focused on postmodern architectural theories read and interpreted in political contexts. The political agenda of the meetings was clear. As Marta Leśniakowska (architecture critic and one of the participants) put it, the meetings were "pleasant seminars during which we were saving the world, architecture, and the homeland from the commies."[19] As Leśniakowska says, the seminars "had a strong political dimension. The closer it was to the downfall of communism, the more chances we saw in creating new social forms with architecture and urbanism. It was strongly political."[20] The participants discussed readings by Christopher Alexander (one of the members, Jacek Zielonka, was in the process of translating *Pattern Language*), as well as canonical postmodern texts by authors like Venturi and Jencks. Leśniakowska stresses that the members of the group were not interested in postmodernism as a new style, based on superficial and formalist references to history. Instead, postmodernism was a way to think about the city in a radically different way than it was promoted by the Polish socialist state. As she describes,

> for us, in Poland, the interest in postmodernism was different than in the West. It was a chance to revive the traditions of Polish architecture instead of the universalist international language of modernism. Postmodernism wasn't for us a matter of form, a matter of façade. We were interested in how the city works, we wanted to return to traditional urban forms such as streets, quarters or squares. For us, the form was an expression of ideological and political attitudes. We understood postmodernism as a chance for the renewal of architectural vocabulary. We believed that the return to detail, to human and urban scales …, to traditional thinking about the urban fabric – very different from the oppressive character of late socialist architecture – would shape new kinds of social relations.[21]

As Leśniakowska stresses, this postmodernism needs to be interpreted differently than in the most common Western understanding – as "an expression of ideological and political attitudes." As we saw with Chile, the economic order is not politically neutral but needs to be defended or contested. If with Pinochet's regime, the neoliberal ideology needed to be defended by the State through propagandistic postmodernism, then with DiM in Poland, the anti-socialist (for Bielecki, explicitly pro-capitalist) message needed to be pushed by the dissenting coalition of architects who saw postmodernism as paving the way to "shap[ing] new kinds of social relations" and eventually changing the political system.

After the transition of 1989, as the political context changed radically, the seminars were no longer organized. The discussions held during the seminars were not transcribed and there are no sources documenting the meetings. Nevertheless, Bielecki's most well-known book, *The City Game* (published in 1996), which its author characterizes as "written in the shadow of post-totalitarianism and postmodernism," is based on key ideas developed during these meetings.[22] *The City Game*, described by a critic as "an optimistic manifesto of liberal politics, in which the authorities, architects and investors build a consensus and create a new, better, marketized living space,"[23] provides an accurate summary of the anti-socialist and free market oriented ideology of both DiM and the seminars led by Bielecki. For Bielecki, postmodernism provided a chance to materialize these ideas in urban space and to create architecture that would eventually generate new anti-communist forms of social life.

96 Postmodernism and Dissent in Socialist Poland

4.2 Reforming the System from within: Marek Budzyński and the Legacy of Socialist Realism

No other figure or group used postmodern currents as part of an oppositional strategy in so strong or evident a fashion as Bielecki and DiM. Meanwhile, even though the majority of architects and urbanists, as well as artists, academics, and intellectuals, were supportive of the anti-government opposition and the Solidarność movement, the State remained their major employer. This meant that the centralized state-controlled nature of the profession of architecture in socialist Poland limited the possibilities of real oppositional engagement to strictly underground activity if one wished to remain a practicing architect. Moreover, not everyone wanted a radical overturn of the system or believed that socialism should be rejected all together. It was common to believe that the desired and long-awaited social and political change did not necessarily mean the rejection of socialist values and the unequivocal acceptance of the ideology of Western capitalism. Such opinions were expressed widely, also within the Solidarność movement.[24] It was also not uncommon among the intelligentsia, including architects, to look for possible changes in the political and economic system that would have an evolutionary rather than revolutionary character and would incorporate, instead of unequivocally reject, socialist ideas.

In Chapter 3, we saw how Romuald Loegler's designs sought to counteract the "social atomization and the anonymity of living in a mass-produced, homogeneous housing estate" that had been the consequence of governmental policies, but was only able to do so because of the government's eagerness to project a pleasing image of itself. We can find a similar case in Marek Budzyński, an architect who believed in the possibility to reform the system from within by making use of the approval of the State. Although the first case was framed in the context of pro-state postmodernism and the case of Budzyński is framed in the context of dissenting postmodernism, both can be understood from the opposite perspective as well: these are cases in which postmodernism allows both functions to work simultaneously. They are simultaneously cases of attempting to reform the system from within, as well as cases of the government pushing postmodernism to superficially present a positive image of itself.

Indeed, in keeping with the desire to push evolutionary rather than revolutionary change, Budzyński placed his hopes in the formulation of a "third way" between socialism and capitalism. As he stated when describing his activity in the 1970s and 1980s,

> I was very socially engaged, I was organizing workshops on local democracy and this has always been my passion. I believed that we [Poland] could be a real model of connecting socialism and capitalism. Despite the opinions that they are completely contradictory, I think that they can be united in a creative way, just as I believe in the union of contradictions in general. At that time, I believed it would work out, but the problem was, I think, the fact that we – both the elites and society – weren't prepared to formulate a socio-liberal system. Making use of democracy, we gave ourselves over to neoliberalism, which destroys democracy.[25]

Reflecting on his architectural practice in late socialist times, Budzyński expressed his belief in the political dimension of design and placed his efforts within a broader attempt to fix the imperfections of socialism:

> Designing, both then and now, has a political or even macroeconomic character. We were living in the times of real socialism, which didn't have much in common with

the ideas of true socialism. But in the 1970s, there was a strong will to modify the system.[26]

For Budzyński, postmodern concepts were useful tools to create a bridge reconciling contradicting systems of communism and capitalism. The city served as a possible platform for such union.

One way to achieve this reconciliation was by emphasizing some aspects of postmodern architecture that could be found in Poland's architectural past. Specifically, for Budzyński and others, the ideas and forms observed in Western postmodernism thorough the 1970s and 1980s could be identified in the doctrine of socialist realism present before the advent of industrialized late modernism in the late 1950s.[27] Returning to socialist realism offered a way to resist the industrialized late modernism that was not dependent solely on the discourse of postmodernism discussed by Western architects but that was anchored in familiar and local trends. Socialist realism was proclaimed in 1934 in the Soviet Union during the First Congress of Soviet Writers as the official style of Soviet culture. The goal of art was defined as depicting "reality in its revolutionary development" and artists were to become "engineers of human souls."[28] In Poland, socialist realism was presented as the official artistic doctrine in 1949 during IV National Meeting of the Delegates of Polish Association of Artists (ZPAP) in Katowice and as the official architectural style during the Meeting of Union of Polish Architects (SARP) in the same year.[29] Architecture was considered as holding a privileged position among other arts. As we can read in a manifesto authored by Edmund Goldzamt, a leading ideologue of socialist realism in Polish architecture,

> The architect of socialism is not only an engineer of edifices and streets, but also an engineer of human soul. It has the possibility to impact human masses everywhere and always – his duties are therefore broader than those of writer or musician. He needs to express in his creations, in shapes, openings, divisions, dynamic of forms and surfaces, ideas of contemporaneity – not "ideas" of beauty or construction or sophisticated formal elegance, but social ideas for which human masses work and live.[30]

Continuing the tradition of Gesamtkunstwerk, and opposing the modernist ideas of medium specificity, architecture was also seen as enabling the synthesis of visual arts – as both sculpture and painting, integrated in the form of a building.[31] Architecture's primal function was defined as reflecting the ideology of socialism. It was expected to be "realist," the "faithful reflection of social reality" and founded on a belief in the "social foundations of architecture, which does not – as idealists claim – organize the space, but provides a spatial framework for social processes."[32] In order to

> express social and material content and perform its pedagogical and ideological role, architecture needs to use forms which are simple and accessible for the masses. Art belongs to the people! It is deeply rooted in the masses, and thus it should be comprehensible for them, loved by them![33]

To achieve such an understanding, architects should use familiar forms from the historical repertoire, rejecting the abstract paradigm of avant-garde.[34] Thus, based on Lenin's claim that "there is no need for inventing a new, proletariat culture. We should develop good patterns basing on existing cultural heritage considering the standpoint of Marxism and the conditions of the proletariat's work and struggle,"[35] Goldzamt defined the desired architect's attitude toward the past as to "creatively refer to the best patterns from the history of Polish and world architecture."[36] According to the theoreticians of socialist realism, "socialist content cannot be expressed in any way other than by using national forms, and without those national forms socialist content is impossible to express."[37] Therefore, the definition of socialist realist architecture was encapsulated in the short constantly repeated slogan, "socialist in content, national in form."[38] The architecture of socialist realism was considered as a firm opposition against functionalism[39] (a building should express ideology, not function), constructivism (as being "empty" and "degenerated"[40]) and eclecticism.[41] The new style was presented as "not imitation and stylization, not eclectic mélanges of styles, but deep assimilation of means and compositional rules achieved by old architecture with the purpose of expressing completely new social content."[42] Through its motivation to draw from the historical repertoire and oppose rigid functionalism, we can see how an architect like Budzyński might see socialist realism as containing some of core qualities of postmodernism.

One of the flagship projects of socialist realist city planning, in which, according to Budzyński, we can discern some quasi-postmodern features, was Muranów, a neighborhood in Warsaw built on the rubble of a Jewish ghetto (razed to the ground at the end of World War II) between 1948 and 1956.

Designed by Bohdan Lachert, Muranów represents an intimate urban form with numerous references to historical styles, mainly classicism and renaissance. Muranów is situated

FIGURE 4.2 View of Muranów neighborhood in Warsaw (1948–1956, Bohdan Lachert) (Szczebrzeszynski, public domain).

along the broad John Paul II Avenue (Aleja Jana Pawła II), which divides the neighborhood into East and West parts. Despite its busy location in the city center, Muranów offers calm inviting spaces thanks to small-scale residential buildings with historicizing detail, narrow walking paths, picturesque courtyards, and an abundance of greenery. In Budzyński's words, "Muranów is an excellent urban project, a perfect ... integration of housing complex with the city. The west came up with such solutions only thirty years after, with postmodernism."[43] Budzyński extrapolates the example of Muranów by formulating a more general claim on the connection between socialist realism and postmodernism:

> Isn't it true that, to some extent, a great part of socialist realist legacy is actually postmodern? We have a lot of both bad and good examples of socialist realist architecture, and when it is well-made it could be taken as postmodern, without reservations! And, why couldn't we take this entire socialist realism just as a forerunner of postmodernism? Why do we judge socialist realism as being so bad if the intentions of postmodernism and socialist realism were so similar?[44]

While on a formal level, Polish postmodern realizations do not seem to resemble works of socialist realism, the emphasis on creating relatable and familiar urban environments based on solutions known from historical cities and the belief in the social and political importance of design carries important similarities to the "assimilation of means and compositional rules achieved by old architecture with the purpose of expressing completely new social content" declared by Goldzamt over twenty years earlier.

Budzyński is not alone in analogizing socialist realism and postmodernism. In his essay "Postmodernism or Socialist Realism? The Architecture of Housing Estates in Late Socialist Czechoslovakia," Maroš Krivý argues that "the historico-phenomenological turn in late socialist architecture drew on two intellectual sources: contemporaneous Western postmodernism and postwar domestic socialist realism."[45] He focuses on late socialist housing estates in former Czechoslovakia, which, as we will also see with the case of Budzyński's North Ursynów, were attempts to "humanize" residential architecture with the use of historic typologies and renewed interest in meaning, communication, and phenomenology in architecture. Krivý shows that architects of housing estates in Czechoslovakia realized during the 1970s and 1980s sourced these notions not only from postmodern theories and projects but also from the architectural tradition of socialist realism.

It would be a stretch to interpret Soviet Bloc postmodernism as a part of the longue durée of socialist realist architecture or as a straightforward continuation of traditions of socialist realism. However, the legacy of socialist realism was influential, and not just for Budzyński, but also for many other architects experimenting with postmodernism in the 1970s and 1980s, even those who may not have shared Budzyński's appreciation for this style.[46] Crediting its legacy also helps us recognize how features of postmodernism were, if partly imported from Western sources, not entirely unfamiliar to architects. Moreover, Budzyński's praise of socialist realism is consistent with his hopes to reconcile communism and capitalism; the architect rejects the modernist dogmas of the late socialist Polish People's Republic not directly through postmodernism – a new architectural current that emerged within a very different economic and social reality – but through a quintessentially socialist style that happens to share qualities with the Western postmodernism that appeared after socialist realism was introduced.

4.3 North Ursynów: City, Church, and Continuity

The most important example realizing Budzyński's theories and his desire to find a "third way" is the North Ursynów housing estate in Warsaw, planned for 40,000 inhabitants, and designed in collaboration with Jerzy Szczepanik-Dzikowski and Andrzej Szkop as well as a vast team of assistant architects and sociologists. Budzyński started working on North Ursynów when he was just 33 years old. By that time he was already a recognized architect and had won major national and international competitions (the railway station in Tychy in 1960, Victory Monument in Playa Girón, Cuba in 1963). In 1970, he received a month-long stipend in Denmark and, after completing it, worked in an architectural studio led by Sven Högsbro. In Denmark, he gained experience designing housing complexes (for example in Nivröd, 1970). At the end of 1971, Budzyński was contacted by Szczepanik-Dzikowski and Szkop who, as part of a design team led by Ludwik Borawski, in 1970 won the competition for North Ursynów organized by SARP. After Borawski's death in November 1971, the team was looking for a new lead architect and offered Budzyński to take up this role. Budzyński agreed to accept the offer and move back to Poland under the condition that the design would be conceived from scratch, undoing the earlier plans made under the guidance of Borawski.

The construction began in 1975 and the first residents arrived in 1977. Ursynów was planned as a "city within/in the city" – an urban unit independent from Warsaw, but connected to it by the subway. The self-sufficient character of Ursynów was achieved by providing all infrastructure and functions necessary for its inhabitants, such as schools, daycares, a post office, numerous stores, street markets, and other services. It was also planned to provide a sizable number of workplaces for its residents. One of Budzyński's core goals was to design a residential estate that counteracted the negative social results of prefabricated mass housing. This dissatisfaction with late modernist housing estates is visible in the first major presentation of the design for North Ursynów in *Architektura* in 1975, which begins with an introduction summing up opinions on mass housing expressed by architectural circles and the general public from the early 1970s.[47] The introduction starts with the assertion that using industrial building methods is the only feasible solution for the housing problems and that "the understanding of this truth is at the basis of housing policy in Poland, because we have to construct 7.3 million new dwellings by 1990."[48] Although late-modern mass housing estates

> transformed the spatial environment of man, giving him sun and air … the results were often not equal to the intentions. … Uniform houses, arranged in a uniform pattern, produced a depressing monotony. The results of losing the correct scale were becoming increasingly noticeable. … The uniformity and monotony of housing areas is becoming intensely felt. The identical lay-outs, consisting of identical houses with identical detail, are becoming increasingly anonymous, lacking individual identity …. The need for a different approach to the design of house areas is becoming more and more evident. … The housing areas have become dormitories …. There is a growing need to create an integrated spatial environment of intermixed residential, shopping, cultural, educational, and other social functions. To develop urban areas, which … would represent fragments of the town as a whole. The notion of "a street" is being again recognized, a street … full of life, facilitating social contacts with an attractive

Postmodernism and Dissent in Socialist Poland **101**

programme of differentiated functions. There are various attempts to create new residential areas adequately meeting the present-day demands. One of them is the project for North Ursynów, a Warsaw district, presented on the following pages.[49]

While his design sought to counteract the effects of the government's housing policies, at the same time, Budzyński was only able to realize these goals through the approval of Edward Gierek's government. Gierek, who replaced Władysław Gomułka as the First Secretary of the Polish Worker's Party in 1970 and held this position until 1980, eagerly used infrastructural and architectural realizations like North Ursynów as evidence of successful governance and the overall progress and advancement of the country. Presenting North Ursynów in this way was crucial in times of rising social tensions and dissatisfaction with the deteriorating economy. North Ursynów was indeed one of the flagship projects realized in late socialist Poland under Edward Gierek's leadership.

The construction of North Ursynów was covered in numerous articles in magazines and daily newspapers, as well as by the Polska Kronika Filmowa (Polish Film Chronicle).[50] In one of the materials produced by the TVP (Telewizja Polska, the only TV station in socialist Poland), North Ursynów is visited by Edward Gierek and the delegation of Party representatives. Walking through the construction site, Gierek says,

> I am observing the construction of this estate from the very beginning. We don't know how [the buildings] will look on the inside, but if it will be as pretty as it is on the outside, I think that the people will be happy.

"Comrade secretary, it is likely that the interiors are even prettier!" one of the construction supervisors quickly adds.[51] The Ursynów estate received special attention from the government and itself functioned as a tool for Party propaganda just as much as the Polska Kronika Filmowa and TVP newsreels did themselves. Gierek, by overseeing the construction site himself, showed his personal involvement in the living conditions of the inhabitants of North Ursynów and, by extension, Polish citizens in general. Through the design of a new citizen-friendly housing estate with experimental urban solutions, the Party had a chance to improve its image.

Gierek liked to emphasize the importance of architecture for the Party and praised Ursynów as an example of architecture focused on social needs. On June 1, 1977, the SARP delegation was received by Gierek for a consultative meeting before the VII Plenary Session of the Party organized under the slogan, "For a Better Quality of Work and the Life of the Nation." The introduction to *Architektura* 5–6 (1977), written by SARP's president, Jerzy Buszkiewicz, was devoted entirely to discussing the meeting. Architects presented their "views on the problems of new housing" and, as Buszkiewicz stressed, Gierek "listened to them with understanding." In his presentation, Gierek emphasized the need to

> preserve the beauty and functionality of historical cities, and the continuation of this historical tradition in new urban forms. ... Comrade Gierek spoke approvingly about the results of some of the last housing realizations, for example housing estates in Wrocław or Warsaw, such as Ursynów. This approval pertained to [the architects'] endeavor to create housing estates of distinct character and achieving a diversified and [more] intimate dimension of prefabricated building technologies. Comrade Gierek

102 Postmodernism and Dissent in Socialist Poland

> emphasized that housing architecture is a national problem. … On behalf of SARP, I reassured the First Secretary of KCPZPR, comrade Edward Gierek … that Polish architects are consistently engaged [in this mission].[52]

The plan for the North Ursynów estate emerges therefore in the context of the Party looking for ways to improve its perception by the people, but also within a specific milieu in Polish architecture, marked by a growing dissatisfaction with prefabricated mass housing. In the project statement, Budzyński outlined the major goals of Ursynów and presented them as part of wider political goals and promises declared by the Party under Edward Gierek's leadership:

> The design of North Ursynów was and is synchronized with the decisions for accelerated socio-economic development of the country [as well as the declaration of] opening ways for initiatives [and] the general devaluation of the old standards, norms, requirements, and bureaucratized institutional actions. [It is tied to] the moment of searching for new forms of action, defining goals and ways of achieving them, awakening inspirations and setting ambitious challenges. This moment of struggle, high hopes, and will, [this moment of] meaningful, not just formal, undertakings.[53]

For Budzyński, the general idea behind Ursynów was "continuation," which is to say continuity between past and present, as "the design for Ursynów is not an attempt to find something 'new.' It is an attempt to materialize and realize well known 'truths.'"[54] The progressive ideas underlying Ursynów were thus undertaken with a respect for the past and under the sanction of the government. In this way, for both the architects and the government, the goal of Ursynów was to influence social reality with the use of architecture, although both parties understood this differently.

Although Ursynów was realized in the obligatory prefabricated concrete panel system, it was planned as a social and urban experiment breaking with the model of loosely distributed, disconnected housing units arranged according to a clear, geometricized plan. Instead of a rigid outline based on straight lines, which would have been typical for late socialist modernist housing estates, the plan of North Ursynów by Budzyński's team is based on organic, irregular lines of housing units of different heights and lengths. The ground level is diversified by artificial hills, slopes, and elevations created with the soil removed during the construction process. The units are placed along both sides of Komisja Edukacji Narodowej – the main communication artery connecting Ursynów with the rest of Warsaw. The curves and bends created by the units allow for interior urban spaces that are much more cozy and intimate than the vast open spaces known from late modern housing estates. The lines of housing units are interrupted by narrow openings for small pedestrian streets and alleys connecting the units with the rest of the complex.

North Ursynów was built using two systems of prefabricates: Szczecin, based on a 4.8 m/2/4 m concrete slab, and WK-70, offering slabs in a range of sides between 2.4 m and 6 m. The first – the Szczecin system – allowed for slight diversification of the slabs' texture by adding surface elements such as white granite chips, which were used in some Ursynów's buildings. With the use of a more flexible systems of prefabricates, which allowed at least some formal diversity, the designers hoped to achieve a housing complex significantly different from most of architecture in late socialist Poland.

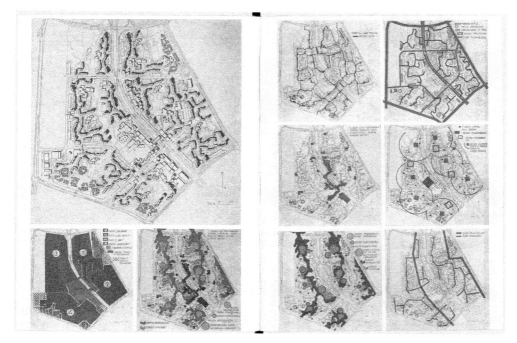

FIGURE 4.3 Plan for North Ursynów housing estate with functional schemes analyzing placement of zones for pedestrians, public transit, and services such as schools, daycares, stores, and community centers (Marek Budzyński, Jerzy Szczepanik-Dzikowski, and Andrzej Szkop, 1971–1975), reprinted in *Architektura* 326–327 (1975), 38–39.

The main intention of the designer's team was to return to the ideals of traditional urban space, especially the street, and recreate them within a socialist city. In this way, although the design is quite different from Muranów or other examples of socialist realism, we can see a similar intention in drawing from the repertoire of historical urban forms in order to achieve socially progressive goals. As we can read in "Rehabilitacja Ulicy" ["The Rehabilitation of the Street"], an article describing the objectives behind Ursynów's design, "the leading principle for us was to achieve functional and spatial continuity …, we tried to create a new urban tissue for Warsaw. It is realized, inter alia, in our attempt to restore the concept of 'the street,'" as a result of which "the buildings are not dominating over the space, but are integral parts of it."[55] Reflecting these priorities, the apartment blocks of various heights and lengths are situated along narrow streets. The ground level was planned for stores, restaurants, and services ensuring functional diversity and "intricate minglings of different uses," in this sense following Jane Jacobs's guidelines on the components of well-planned, living cities. The pedestrian traffic is privileged within the entire complex:

> The speed of a walking pedestrian is a natural speed for registering [urban] phenomena and sensing the space. … The pedestrians' attention is concentrated above all in the spaces for stores and services. Therefore, when designing the façades, we are thinking not in terms of singular buildings but of street frontages, especially their ground floors. The variability of the space and its individual character play the most important

role in the identification of residents with "spatial spheres," such as neighborhood, block, street, courtyard, house …. Such identification is crucial for the residents' well-being. … The ground floor decides the character of the street. … The most important elements are on the level of the pedestrians' sight. … The ground floor is the closest to the human scale … it provides a natural terrain for human interactions.[56]

The project descriptions for North Ursynów are saturated with the rhetoric known from works of such thinkers as Jacobs and Alexander, even though its planners did not refer to their theories explicitly. However, Budzyński admitted in an interview thirty years after designing Ursynów that Jacobs was an especially vital point of reference: "When I was thirty years old," he says,

> Jane Jacobs was a crucial figure. Everyone involved in Ursynów knew who she was, we were reading and using her theories. … She had a strong influence [on Polish architects in the 1970s]. Christopher Alexander as well …. His attempt was to create the city from patterns meaningful for groups and individual users of space. He noticed them, named them and showed that this is how you design the city. … I need to admit that he had a strong influence on me.[57]

One of the ways Ursynów's postmodern design stands out in relation to other Polish mass housing designs is through its ability "to allow the inhabitants to take part in the shape, form, and use of their spatial environment [as well as to] give them a bigger spectrum of

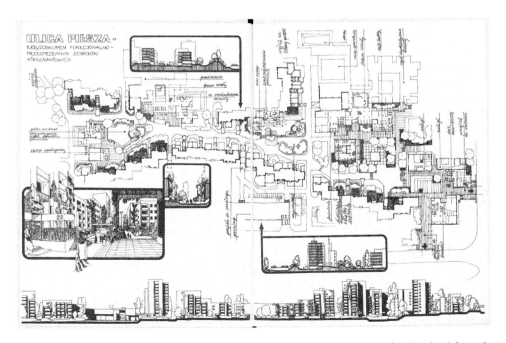

FIGURE 4.4 Study of North Ursynów pedestrian street (Marek Budzyński, Jerzy Szczepanik-Dzikowski, and Andrzej Szkop, 1971–1975), reprinted in *Architektura* 326–327 (1975), 44–45.

choice" and to "adjust the initial spatial organization to its unpredicted, organic transformations."[58] It is thus distinguished by its focus on the role of individual users, flexibility, and the return to traditional urban patterns. Indeed, one of the crucial components of Ursynów was the idea of the participation of the inhabitants in the process of design. User participation – promoted by Western postmodernists as a part of the broader move toward a more egalitarian, democratic architecture – was a controversial idea in the reality of late socialist Poland. The centrally managed process of design and production of architecture as well as the rather rigid prefabricate system did not present auspicious conditions for user participation. It is notable then that the Ursynów designers insisted on inviting future users to the process of design. As the team wrote in 1971,

> The architect's role is to serve the society. The architect's work is a stimulator of desires, needs and possibilities. Today's social consciousness … allows the architect to create in collaboration with the users. We want the future inhabitants of Ursynów to take part in the creation of the city from the very beginning. There should be a bond between designers and inhabitants. … We think that it is necessary for the well-being of the people who will live there. They need to know that everything was done there for them.[59]

After the first residents moved in to Ursynów, they were encouraged to participate in the life of the neighborhood by organizing events in community centers or taking care of shared gardens. These activities were animated by a team of sociologists led by two urban sociologists, Krzysztof Herbst and Waldemar Siemiński, helping the first tenants to meet each other and to make use of spaces designed for their interaction. The ideas of local engagement and the encouragement of social life were therefore integral parts of Ursynów's plan. Initially, Herbst postulated the creation of an Office for Apartment Selection (Biuro Wyboru Mieszkań), an intermediary institution working for the improvement of communication between designers and inhabitants. The users would communicate their particular needs to the officers, who would gather and organize them into a formalized proposal.[60] As Herbst says,

> We needed to reconstruct the space of the community. Communist concepts of housing were targeted to destroy the community as settlement and settlement as community. Our designing was essentially conspiring. For me [the Ursynów planners' work] was like a revelation. And I was contributing sociological thinking to it: ways to prevent crises and conflicts. For example, common laundry rooms. I knew from Sweden that those kinds of spaces greatly enable human interactions, they make people meet with each other.[61]

Although the Office for Apartment Selection never existed as a formalized entity, the team managed to consult minor elements of the design directly with the users. As Herbst recalls,

> Budzyński accepted practically every idea, including the wildest ones. … Fence the lawn with car tires cut in half – sure, go ahead, insert glass panels on your balcony – yes. As long as there is life, as long as the inhabitants arrange this space for themselves and for their likeness.[62]

106 Postmodernism and Dissent in Socialist Poland

The progressive plan aimed to stimulate the urban character of Ursynów. As Szkop recalls,

> we assumed that it [Ursynów] should be a city, not a huge housing complex. This is the difference. We used references to historical projects we knew from the lectures on history of architecture. … We solved many problems thanks to the solutions from the past. And you can see traces [of this thinking] in Ursynów: urban patterns, streets, the ways we developed the area.[63]

The team's design narrows the streets and diversifies the monotonous, concrete housing units with elements such as roofing, arcades, or stairs with railings. One of the traditional, pre-modern urban patterns key for Ursynów's design team was the model of a housing unit with services and stores located in the first floor and thus accesible from the street. This idea was heavily limited not only by the reality of the post-socialist economy in which, as Szkop commented ironically forty years after Ursynów's design, "there was nothing to trade,"[64] but also by the necessity of the use of prefabricated concrete modules. Concrete slabs not only made traditional retail solutions such as storefronts impossible but also limited the possible surface of stores and services. The designers struggled to overcome these limitations by erecting rows of retail pavilions attached to housing buildings.

Another important element diversifying North Ursynów was the greenery, developed with landscape architect Irena Bajerska. The ground of North Ursynów was initially flat, and the designers decided to diversify its surface by raising selected areas and create hills of different dimensions. The main goal in the landscaping of Ursynów was to preserve existing trees as well as to plant new ones to create spaces with wild-looking greenery rather than neatly organized modernist parks. In Ursynów, trees and plants were not reduced to "the lungs of the city," or a merely functional element serving the hygienistic purpose of providing oxygen and supporting healthy living functions, as they had been presented in modernist documents such as *The Athens Charter*; rather, trees and plants were treated as sculptural elements shaping the architecture of the complex. Creepers like ivy and grapevine, for which the coarse structure of the concrete slabs was a perfect ground, allowed the external walls to function as vertical gardens.

One of the settlement's most prominent spaces is a large city square with a sculptural church (Church of the Ascension of Christ), both of which were designed in 1980 by Budzyński, Zbigniew Badowski and Piotr Wicha.

The church was intended to bring a sense of historical continuity into an estate erected from scratch, and the square was planned to recreate the role traditionally played by local town markets and to become "the most prominent town square, which will concentrate the life of the entire population of Ursynów."[65] As Budzyński says,

> We decided that the church in Ursynów should be a symbol of the continuity of culture, Polish identity, that it should at the same time be a symbol of the connection between the past and a progressive social ideology. We found it important … especially in Ursynów, within a newly emerged city fabric. … [Ursynów] was made from abstract forms produced in the factories of houses. In Ursynów there was no time for coming of age and "accretion," for changes and growth. … Additional problems arose with the simplifications made during the construction process and with the adjustments required by the primitive methods available for construction.[66]

FIGURE 4.5 Ascension Church in Warsaw-Ursynów, (1980–1985, Marek Budzyński, Zbigniew Badowski, and Piotr Wicha) (Adrian Grycuk, distributed under CC BY-SA 3.0 pl license).

Ursynów's church and square were therefore attempts to save some of the leading design principles of Budzyński's team, which were lost in the realization process. Squat proportions, foundations made of stone, and low simple portal columns recall examples of Romanesque architecture, while flowing curves of buttresses and the façade recall both provincial baroque and gothic forms. Architects juxtaposed historical motifs with modern architectural language – the plain surface of the façade combined with an entrance shaped in the form of cross, and the roof and exterior walls of the aisles covered with copper sheet or bijou precast concrete detail of the portal.

The architects put special emphasis on building materials and saw the realization of the church as an opportunity for the revival of traditional craftsmanship. Their intention was to work with natural materials such as brick, stone, or wood rarely used in the industrialized reality of Polish late socialist architecture:

> We wanted to return these to society with the church. Both the materials and the craftsmen who still know how to use them. Carpenters, masons, stonemasons and their apprentices. These professions are basically destroyed and it would be wonderful if here they could find employment as well as some sort of protection from Ursynów's inhabitants.[67]

The postmodern tactics utilized in the Ascension Church, from its sculptural artistic form to the eclectic mélange of architectural styles and the return to craftsmanship and artisanal building materials and techniques, were intended to help create a continuity with tradition and to establish a stronger bond between North Ursynów's space and its users.

FIGURE 4.6 Concrete details of Ascension Church in Warsaw–Ursynów, (1980–1985, Marek Budzyński, Zbigniew Badowski, and Piotr Wicha) (author).

The fact that the most eye-catching sculptural and artistic form within a rather monotonous (despite the designers' efforts) landscape of Ursynów is a church building is itself meaningful. Despite its declared secularity, the late socialist Polish state reluctantly tolerated new church constructions, partly because most of the Party members were still personally tied to religious traditions and partly because prohibiting church realizations could easily trigger further protests. Facing the rise of the opposition led by the Solidarność movement especially during the 1980s, the Party could not risk instigating more dissent. Another factor that influenced the Party's attitude toward new church buildings was the liberalization of the regime under Gierek's leadership. As a result, the state was willing to provide plots of land for the purpose of new church construction, provided that the community would be responsible for the design, materials, and building. Church realizations in late socialist Poland were therefore mostly bottom-up initiatives. They were executed thanks to the initiative and participation of church community members, usually outside the system governed by the Main Office of Urban Planning, but with the approval of the State. As a consequence, not only were new church realizations allowed, but the number of churches erected in Poland between 1979 and 1989 significantly exceeds church realizations in any European country during those years.[68]

Despite the silent approval of new church realizations granted by the State, it is crucial to note that at the same time, the Catholic Church in Poland was a strong center for the anti-communist opposition. New churches were resonating symbols of the spirit of Polish religiosity despite the proclaimed secularity of the socialist state, and thus an important tool of resistance against the communist system. This anti-systemic message was further strengthened by the emergence of the Solidarność movement and the election of the anti-communist Polish cardinal Karol Wojtyła as Pope in 1978. Postmodern forms of churches constructed in the 1970s and 1980s – often historicizing and boldly sculptural – thus posed a strong contrast to the rigidity of late socialist housing estates and served as perfect vessels for oppositional messages. Both members of the Catholic community and the clergy were skeptical toward unfamiliar late-modern architectural forms too closely associated with omnipresent mass-produced housing, an expression of the socialist utopia of modernization. Instead, they preferred buildings resembling historical, traditional, and regional architecture, embodying the continuity of the Christian spirit in place of late-modern architecture, which recalled socialist attempts of secularization.

Additionally, church buildings served not only religious purposes. Usually constructed with the active participation of local parishioners, they served as community cultural centers, vital places for discussions, meetings, film screenings, and exhibitions. The Ascension Church was no exception. Avoiding both literal architectural quotations and pastiche, the architects designed a massive temple in which numerous historical references and allusions served as showcases for the solid tradition of Catholicism in Poland, attempting to portray its endurance even in the declaratively secular times of socialism. In this sense, the presence (and prominence) of a historicizing church building in Ursynów's landscape sent a strong dissenting message. At the same time, when Budzyński described the church in an interview in *Architektura*, conducted when the building was under construction (quoted above), he suggested that it is not opposed to, but rather harmoniously connected with the socialist reality. Therefore, even though in socialist Poland church buildings were seen as anti-government statements, Budzyński emphasized its function as a symbol of "continuity" and "connection between the past and a progressive social ideology." This move is understandable both for practical reasons (even during the loosening of the regime Budzyński could not declare open dissent against the state in his architecture) and given Budzyński's philosophy of political architecture based on the ideas of reconciliation, continuity, and the organic integration of opposite values.

The North Ursynów housing estate can be clearly distinguished from other mass housing projects of the time also through its presentation in the distinctively attractive visual material used. Instead of the usual way in which projects were presented in *Architektura* – with cold technical drawings, plans and axonometric drawings, sometimes accompanied by a rather formal photo of the authors – North Ursynów's presentation made a powerful visual statement. The visualizations of the project, drawn by Budzyński, Szczepanik-Dzikowski, and Szkop in black, blue, and bright pink, show Ursynów's spaces as lively, dense places with housing of different heights covered with wild-looking creepers, common spaces such as playgrounds or neighborhood clubs, as well as services like shops, restaurants, bars, and cafes with neon signs of major Polish brands of that time such as "Hortex" or "Pollena" and even "Coca-Cola."

The presence of the Coca-Cola slogan in particular is a meaningful detail, given the brand's role in Gierek's plan of opening the country to the West. In the 1950s and 1960s, Coca-Cola, an obvious symbol of Western capitalism, had been described by propaganda

110 Postmodernism and Dissent in Socialist Poland

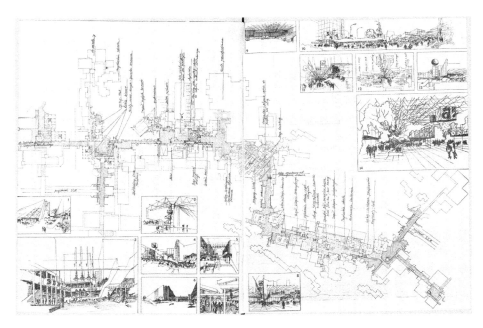

FIGURE 4.7 Spatial and functional analysis of North Ursynów, showing placement of stores, schools, services, and cultural and recreational spaces, reprinted in *Architektura* 326–327 (1975), 62–63.

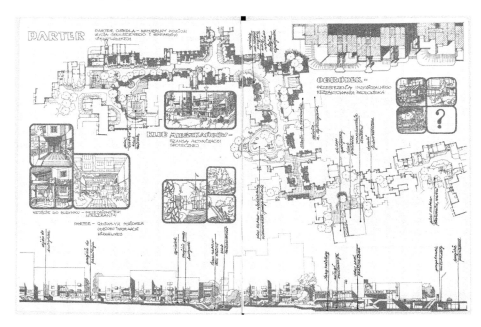

FIGURE 4.8 Study of North Ursynów's pedestrian level, including private spaces (gardens) and public spaces (community club, playgrounds) (Marek Budzyński, Jerzy Szczepanik-Dzikowski, and Andrzej Szkop, 1971–1975), published in *Architektura* 326–327 (1975), 42–43.

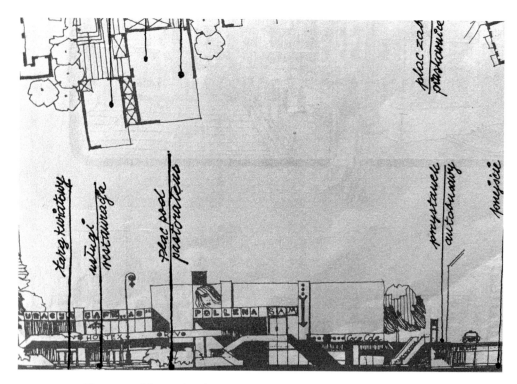

FIGURE 4.9   Close-up of the study of North Ursynów's pedestrian level, including a Coca-Cola sign on a storefront (Marek Budzyński, Jerzy Szczepanik-Dzikowski, and Andrzej Szkop, 1971–1975), published in *Architektura* 326–327 (1975), 43.

press as "liquid pest."[69] The Party had warned Polish citizens of the dangers of the imperialist way of life with the popular slogan, "the enemy lures you with Coca-Cola," and the beverage was absent from Polish stores.[70] In December 1971, very soon after Gierek's team took over, the government bought a license to produce Coca-Cola locally. Instead of overwhelming monotonous concrete wilderness, which dominated the landscape of late socialist Poland, Ursynów's visualizations promised a vibrant city with an integrated local community of inhabitants surrounded by greenery and spending free time in neighborhood clubs and even enjoying the once-forbidden imperialist soda.

The texts of Budzyński and the other designers of Ursynów are illustrated not only with drawings, maps, plans, and models but also with numerous pictures showing young architects at work at the design studio, sketching studiously and explaining ideas to others, walking through Ursynów's muddy ground, laughing while carrying a toddler-size bathtub filled with picnic food, or barbecuing sausages and drinking beer on the site of Gierek's flagship mass housing undertaking.

All of this sent a clear message: Ursynów is an unprecedented project and a break from the inhumane and intimidating late socialist housing estates. The pictures of joyous and enthusiastic young architects suggested a real change in approach to architecture.

112 Postmodernism and Dissent in Socialist Poland

FIGURE 4.10 Architects of North Ursynów housing estate on a site visit, c. 1972 (Nina Smolarz), reprinted in *Architektura* 326–327 (1975), 59.

FIGURE 4.11 Architects of North Ursynów at work, c. 1972–1975 (Nina Smolarz), reprinted in *Architektura* 326–327 (1975), 26.

When completed, Ursynów was considered only a partial success. The reality of late socialism was fundamentally different than in socialist Denmark where Budzyński's design philosophy had been shaped:

> In Denmark, I had a chance to carefully observe how a truly open society works, a society, which is based upon the ideas of social democracy. There, the housing defined streets and piazzas, together with the network of services fulfiling inhabitants' needs – laundries, neighborhood clubs, cafes, small daycares. … It was really hard to realize this concept given the primitive prefabricated system, which didn't allow us to design along the functional and emotional needs of the future users.[71]

As Piotr Wicha recalls, "there is not a single place in Ursynów completed in accordance with the original project."[72] Less than twenty percent of the services planned in the initial design were realized. Out of the twelve planned piazzas, only one was fully realized. As Budzyński said in an interview held in 1984,

> Ursynów was designed with an assumption that there is a centralized, grand, supple and well-functioning institution, which builds the city fabric. … As it turned out,

real investment possibilities of the State are close to zero when it comes to services for the people.[73]

Economic constraints were paired with the limitations posed by prefabricated technology and despite designers' efforts to diversify the façades, spatial complexity was rather impossible to achieve. Moreover, the failures of North Ursynów's realization are further accentuated by the contrast between the monotony of prefabricated housing units and the Ascension Church with its organic historicizing forms, red brick, and the attention to architectural detail.

Despite the intentions of its designers, the crude precast concrete dominates the landscape of Ursynów to such a degree that references to traditional and historical urban forms are not easy or obvious to identify.

The designers' efforts to diversify the complex by, for example, choosing curves and bends rather than straight lines to organize its plan, introducing different heights of the housing units or using various textures of concrete slabs, did result in a living environment of significantly higher quality than the vast majority of housing estates in late socialist Poland. Nevertheless, because of the material and building technology used, Ursynów still overwhelms with the monotonous grayness of precast concrete and repetitiveness of boxy forms of housing units. Despite the designers' intentions, Ursynów resembles a set of building blocks, much like many late modernist mass housing estates. Additionally, the ideal of a

FIGURE 4.12 North Ursynów housing estate in Warsaw, (1972–1977, Marek Budzyński, Jerzy Szczepanik-Dzikowski, and Andrzej Szkop) (Gophi, distributed under CC BY-SA 3.0 license).

114 Postmodernism and Dissent in Socialist Poland

walkable street needed to accommodate to reality, as the planned two-floor parking spaces were never built and Ursynów's streets were soon taken over by parked cars. Not all spaces designed for social interaction worked out either. Budzyński recalls that when the people realized that one of the construction sites in their vicinity prepared the ground for a street market, they strongly protested against it.[74] Also the collective laundry buildings never truly operated, since it turned out that, as Herbst put it, "Poles hate to show up with their dirty laundry in public spaces."[75]

The practice of Budzyński shows that the use of postmodern notions such as the return of the street and pre-modern urban forms in late socialist Poland did not necessarily mean a revolutionary gesture against the system (as in the case of the DiM group), but could also function as an attempt to reform it from within. North Ursynów also demonstrates how, for Budzyński, just as communism and capitalism were not irreconcilable but instead could be "united in a creative way," architectural postmodernism does not necessarily need to be considered as standing in a sharp contrast with socialist architecture. In this way, North Ursynów offers another example of how postmodernism can be a convenient vehicle for offering different meanings to different parties: on the one hand, evidence of socialist future-oriented prosperity and the progress occurring under Gierek, and on the other hand, the possibility of fixing the imperfections of socialism through solutions rooted in an architectural past and breaking with industrial modernism. Gierek could benefit from endorsing a state-of-the-art housing estate that evoked the openness and prosperity of his government. Meanwhile, for Budzyński and his circle, it functioned as a response to the failures of socialist government and to the shortcomings of the model of prefabricated housing.

4.4 Poland's Distinctive Postmodernism

Na Skarpie Estate (Centrum E) and North Ursynów are both parts of a broader attempt to introduce postmodern thought and forms into housing estates made using rigid prefabricated systems. Such design experiments merging the idea of a city of a small human scale with the model of large-scale central planning and a homogenizing building method are characteristic of many projects realized in the 1970s and 1980s in Poland. Another such design is the Zielone Wzgórza (Green Hills) housing complex near Poznań, designed in 1982 by a team lead by Jerzy Buszkiewicz. Instead of the late modern global ideal of an objective, impersonal "machine for living," the designers proposed an intimate picturesque estate with narrow streets and piazzas encouraging social life beyond the "minimum existence." Diverse houses of different scales, often covered with mansard roofs successfully created an impression of a small-scale pre-modern town – a feeling almost convincing, but only for an inattentive visitor overseeing uncanny details, such as façades made from prefabricated slabs and concrete dormers. Another notable example of a design that merges late-modern industrialized technology of concrete panel housing systems and uniformity with postmodern inclinations toward local historical allusions and diversity is the Radogoszcz-East housing estate in Łódź, designed by Jakub Wujek and Zdzisław Lipski in 1979–1985. Both Wujek and Lipski were known for their interests in postmodernism evidenced both by their design practice and publications such as their analysis of fundamental architectural vocabulary (corners, roofs, gates, etc.) based on typology observed in premodern architectural forms published in *Architektura*.[76] This return to the traditional language of architecture is fundamental for Radogoszcz-East. Instead of designing blocks of flats in arrangements subordinated to the rules of the *Athens Charter*, architects decided to create several small quarters-colonies organized around internal courtyards-gardens. Each colony was to be developed by a different architect so the buildings and spaces between them would be diversified.[77]

It should be noted that many of the architects introducing postmodern notions to Polish prefabricated housing sympathized with the opposition, and some, like Wujek, suggested that their use of postmodernism was intended as a gesture against the government.[78] Since such statements can rarely be reconstructed entirely from written resources and the main tool to use in these analyses are interviews, the work of deceased architects (Wujek) is difficult to analyze. While in many cases oppositional intentions behind the use of postmodern ideas and forms in prefabricated housing in late socialist Poland cannot be unequivocally confirmed, examples like Na Skarpie and North Ursynów show that it was not uncommon to interpret postmodern notions influencing state-funded mass housing estates as a political statement.

While Budzyński's strong and explicit appreciation for socialist realism is rather unique among Polish architects, his attempt to use postmodern notions as a way to reform the system is echoed in other architects like Loegler. Loegler makes this comparison explicitly:

> the intentions behind my projects, such as Centrum E or Prądnik Czerwony are parallel to Budzyński's intentions in Ursynów. This idea [of architecture as a medium for social change and an attempt to change social relations witin the possibilities of late socialism] is analogical, no doubt. Of course, there are differences – like in Ursynów the greenery was one of the major elements to provoke social interactions. In our projects, we tried to create spatial remedies for social atomization and the anonymity of living in mass-produced, homogeneous housing estates by focusing on common spaces. Our goal was to create a bond between the people, and also identification of the inhabitants with the place they live in.[79]

For both projects, the postmodern revivals of traditional spatial solutions and historical traditional urban forms were means of contributing to social and political change.

Loegler and Budzyński both used the Party's efforts to present itself as more people-oriented through promoting more "humane" housing estates to realize their own agendas. Bielecki and the DiM group, in turn, outright rejected any collaboration with the regime and decided to disseminate their vision for architecture only through the discursive means of manifestos and discussions. Both of these ways of using architecture as a platform for political activism had their limitations. Bielecki's ideas were circulated only within architectural circles and remained purely speculative until the transition to the market economy in 1989. Loegler and Budzyński managed to materialize their ideas, but their realizations diverged significantly from their original plans. Most of the spatial solutions that had socially progressive agendas weren't realized. At the same time, both Na Skarpie and North Ursynów proved to be successful in the goals of community building and identification of the inhabitants with their living space. Na Skarpie remains a sought-after location in Kraków's real estate market. A great number of Ursynów's original tenants still live there, and the neigborhood is one of the most popular in Warsaw. Numerous book publications, blogs, and websites on Ursynów's architectural and social history – mostly created by its inhabitants – are also vital signs of its importance for the community.

116 Postmodernism and Dissent in Socialist Poland

Poland's postmodern buildings and designs from the 1970s and 1980s play complex roles between state approval, architects seeking to rectify the consequences of the State's damaging policies, and the possibility (as we saw with Budzyński) of a "third way" between communism and capitalism. An important reason postmodernism was able to play some of these roles was that it was able to be interpreted as having ideologically safe origins, either in the Soviet "Romantic Modernists" or in the legacy of socialist realism. With respect to the latter, the social function of architecture, as opposed to the functionalist approach of modernism, could unite socialist realism with the ideas of Jacobs, Venturi, and Rossi.[80]

Crucial for the emergence of postmodernism in Polish architecture is that due to the government's decision to embrace this current rather than reject it as a Western capitalistic trend hostile to socialism, the architects were able to use postmodern forms and ideas freely. Often, as demonstrated throughout this chapter, these uses were not ideologically neutral but were aimed to counteract or amend features and implications of the current political system. Like some of the examples in the Chilean context, the susceptibility to "multiple-coding" and the ability to speak to different audiences means that postmodernism could achieve contradicting goals and that these different goals were not met with skepticism or criticism by either party. Postmodernism was embraced by actors with opposing agendas as a current that could help achieve not only their architectural but also their social and political goals.

Notes

1　Bruszewski, "Posłowie od redaktora," 76. Translation mine.
2　"Architektów kłopoty z wolnością," 28. Translation mine. Bielecki himself, despite his reputation as one of the most recognized postmodern architects in Poland, insists on describing his architectural practice as "eclecticism," not "postmodernism."
3　Bielecki, "Ciągłość w architekturze." Translation mine.
4　Loegler, "Rozmowa z Romualdem Loeglerem," 156. Translation mine.
5　Bielecki was publishing his articles under pseudonym (Maciej Polecki) and was never identified as their author by Polish socialist government. In addition to *Kultura Paryska* he collaborated with several underground oppositional magazines in Poland (*Maly Konspirator* and *Tygodnik KOS*, among others).
6　Solidarność did not have any specified beliefs regarding architecture or urban space. Nevertheless, Bielecki mentions that many of their core members – such as Zbigniew Bujak, Wojciech Kulewski or Krystyna Zachwatowicz – recognized the importance of architecture and its connection to politics. See Bielecki, interview by Lidia Klein.
7　Dom i Miasto, *Karta DiM*. Translation mine.
8　Czesław Bielecki, email message to Lidia Klein, July 9, 2016.
9　Dom i Miasto, *DiM Charter*.
10　Dom i Miasto, *DiM Charter*.
11　Dom i Miasto, *DiM Charter*.
12　Loegler, "Rozmowa z Romualdem Loeglerem," 156.
13　Portoghesi, *Postmodern*, 8. Since none of the members of DiM preserved the English version of the "DiM Charter" in their private archives, I use my own English translation of the Polish document.
14　Jencks, *The Story of Post-Modernism*, 250.
15　Jencks, *The Story of Post-Modernism*, 250.
16　Czesław Bielecki, email message to Lidia Klein, July 9, 2016.
17　Dom i Miasto, *Drogi Rozwiazywania Kwestii Mieszkaniowej*. Translation mine.
18　Dom i Miasto, *Drogi Rozwiazywania Kwestii Mieszkaniowej*.
19　Marta Leśniakowska, email message to Lidia Klein, July 8, 2016.
20　Leśniakowska, interview by Lidia Klein.

21 Leśniakowska, interview by Lidia Klein.

22 Bielecki, *Gra w Miasto*, 185. Translation mine.

23 Woś, "Gra w miasto." Translation mine.

24 Karol Modzelewski and Jacek Kuroń, both leading oppositionists in the People's Republic of Poland, are the most prominent examples. For more on the socialist beliefs within members of Solidarność movement see: Jadwiga Staniszkis, *Poland's Self-Limiting Revolution* (Princeton, NJ: Princeton University Press, 1984); Alain Touraine, *Solidarity: The Analysis of a Social Movement: Poland 1980–1981* (Cambridge: Cambridge University Press, 1983); and Jan Sowa, *Inna Rzeczpospolita jest możliwa! Widma przeszłości, wizje przyszłości* (Warszawa: WAB, 2015).

25 See Budzyński, "Rozmowa z Markiem Budzyńskim," 58. Translation mine.

26 Budzyński, "Architekt jako urbanista," 73. Translation mine.

27 Budzyński's suggestion is not isolated and the analogies between postmodernism and socialist realism were drawn by many theoreticians. For example, Boris Groys wrote that "Beginning with the Stalin years ... Soviet culture, Soviet art, and Soviet ideology became eclectic, citational, 'postmodern'" (Groys, *The Total Art of Stalinism*, 108). However, it is unlikely that Budzyński is aware of this body of research.

28 Zdhanov, "Soviet Literature."

29 Its premises and ideological program were defined mainly by Roman Piotrowski and Edmund Goldzamt. See Roman Piotrowski, "Stanowisko architekta" [Architect's Statement] in *Komunikat SARP* [Communications of the Society of Polish Architects], 1947, numbers 10 and 12; and Goldzamt, *O polską architekturę socjalistyczną*.

30 Goldzamt, 26. Translation mine.

31 Goldzamt, 27.

32 Goldzamt, 21.

33 Goldzamt, 28.

34 Goldzamt, 35.

35 Goldzamt, 29.

36 Goldzamt, 29.

37 Goldzamt, 31.

38 The character of "national form" was never unequivocally specified. Instead, it was a rather elusive concept with no clear characteristic provided. As Goldzamt wrote,

> there is no eternal national character, constant for every generation. The national character is a reflection of specific living conditions of the nation in any given moment that is class development specificity, geographical surrounding, and population density. There are no constant, immutable features of national culture and architecture. But in any given moment is architecture a reflection of a contemporary reality of the society. ... By reproducing faithfully how Polish nation expresses our epoch, embodying its progressive ideas – we will create its national architecture.
>
> (Goldzamt, 32)

39 Goldzamt, 21.

40 Goldzamt, 28.

41 Even from such short fragments we can see the general qualities of the rhetoric shaping most of socialist realist manifestos: the lack of specific directions and practical guidelines, the proliferation of platitudes, and the most general possible statements, susceptible to various interpretations. How can architecture "provide a framework for social processes"? What is the difference between the idea of "national" architecture and, for example, high-modernism, much criticized by the same authors, in which architecture was also seen as the epitome of the present, and, moreover, a tool capable of reflecting and instigating social change? It is therefore legitimate to claim that the theory of architecture of socialist realism was largely founded upon negation – declarations of what it "should not be" instead of what it should be. See, for example, Waldemar Baraniewski, "Ideologia w architekturze Warszawy okresu realizmu socjalistycznego," *Rocznik Historii Sztuki* 22 (1996): 231–260, and Wojciech Włodarczyk, *Socrealizm. Sztuka polska w latach 1950–1954* (Paris: Libella, 1986).

42 Goldzamt, 30.

43 Budzyński, "Betonowe Dziedzictwo." Translation mine.

44 Budzyński, "Rozmowa z Markiem Budzyńskim," 24.

45 Krivý, "Postmodernism or Socialist Realism?," 74.
46 Socialist realism impacted not only architectural practice but also architectural education, and in this sense its influence can be seen even after its official rejection in 1956.
47 See Budzyński, "Ursynów Połnócny." In *Architektura*, the first articles expressing dissatisfaction with the condition of industrialized mass housing buildings appeared in 1971.
48 Gliński et al., "Swiatowy Kongres," 10. Translation mine.
49 Gliński et al., 12–20.
50 Two episodes of Polska Kronika Filmowa were devoted to North Ursynów: PKF 27/1979, PKF 3/1988.
51 *Edward Gierek na Ursynowie*. Translation mine.
52 Buszkiewicz, "Spotkanie konsultacyjne," 7. Translation mine.
53 Budzyński, "Ursynów Północny," 25.
54 Budzyński, "Ursynów Północny," 25.
55 Szkop, "Rehabilitacja Ulicy," 41. Translation mine.
56 Szkop, 41.
57 Budzyński, "Rozmowa z Markiem Budzyńskim," 13–14.
58 Budzyński, "Rozmowa z Markiem Budzyńskim," 25–26. The architects sought also other than architectural means to establish symbolic connections between Ursynów and the city. For example, in the early days of Ursynów's design, the architects tried to create a lapidarium of Warsaw's townhouses in Ursynów. See "Kościół na Ursynowie Północnym w Warszawie," 62.
59 Borawski et al., "Dzielnica: młode miasto," 2. Translation mine.
60 Herbst, "Propozycje socjotechniczne," 27.
61 "Najbardziej ludzka sypialnia," 67. Quoted in Pańków, *Bloki w słońcu*, 82. Translation mine.
62 "Najbardziej ludzka sypialnia," 67.
63 Pańków, *Bloki w słońcu*, 82. Translation mine.
64 Pańków, 109.
65 "Kościół na Ursynowie Północnym w Warszawie," 64. Translation mine.
66 "Kościół na Ursynowie Północnym w Warszawie," 66.
67 "Kościół na Ursynowie Północnym w Warszawie," 69.
68 There were approximately 2,500 churches erected in Poland between 1979 and 1989, according to the data provided by Komisja Episkopatu Polski (The Commission of the Polish Episcopate). This number does not include chapels and small branch churches (approximately 5,000). See: *Komunikat nr 35 Komisji Episkopatu Polski ds. Budowy Kościołów*, discussed in Basista, *Betonowe dziedzictwo*, 156. See also: Andrzej Majdowski, "Piśmiennictwo do stanu badań nad architekturą sakralną w Polsce," *Nasza Przeszłość* 106 (2006): 283–293, and Cichońska et al., *Day-VII Architecture*.
69 Literally: "liquid potato beetle." Communist propaganda claimed that the potato beetle had been introduced in Poland, East Germany, and Czechoslovakia to cause famine and economic crisis. During the Cold War, the Warsaw Pact countries launched a common campaign called "The War Against the Potato Beetle."
70 For more, see "Bąbelki i socjalizm z ludzką twarzą."
71 Budzyński, "Architekt jako urbanista," 74. Translation mine. Romuald Loegler speaks similarly about his experience as practicing architect in Finland in multiple interviews.
72 Budzyński et al., "Pasaż Ursynowski – dyskusja," 41. Translation mine.
73 Budzyński et al., "Pasaż Ursynowski – dyskusja," 31.
74 Budzyński et al., "Pasaż Ursynowski – dyskusja," 32.
75 "Najbardziej ludzka sypialnia," quoted in Pańków, 88.
76 Lipski and Wujek, 18–40.
77 Ultimately, due to the limited time and budget as well as the lack of support and understanding for the design principles shown by local authorities, the realization differs greatly from the initial project. The neighborhood in Łódź, finally designed entirely by Wujek and Lipski, is in the end a homogeneous, unified entity of buildings of similar volume constructed from concrete panel systems, slightly diversified by modest architectural detail.
78 Wujek, "Rozmowa z Jakubem Wujkiem," 116–117.
79 Loegler, interview by Lidia Klein.
80 It is also worth mentioning Rossi's own appreciation for socialist realism in architecture, most famously expressed when he called Karl-Marx-Allee (originally Stalinallee) in Berlin "Europe's last great street."

CONCLUSION

Postmodernism as a Political Form

Architectural styles or tendencies can rarely be unequivocally ascribed to a single ideology or political orientation. Postmodern architecture is no exception. Although best known in Western European and North American realizations inseparable from the economic and political conditions of late capitalism, the uses of postmodern forms and theories worldwide have been various. Given that Western Europe and North America still dominate scholarship on architectural history and shape its canon, it is not surprising that postmodernism is seen as politically disengaged and passively confirming the neoliberal status quo. Postmodern architects are understood as preoccupied with form, not ideology, and current incarnations of postmodern revivalism confirm this view. However, in countries such as Chile and Poland, postmodern buildings were consciously ascribed social and political roles. Colorful façades with a wide range of historical references or urban forms based on the revival of traditional typologies were used as tools for either promoting or resisting social and political reality, both by regimes in power and by forces oppositional to them. As we have seen in Chapters 1 and 3, in the 1970s and 1980s, postmodern architecture was used for propagandistic purposes – in the first case by Pinochet's regime in Chile and in the second case by the socialist government of the Polish People's Republic. At the same time, as discussed in Chapters 2 and 4, architects in these two countries practiced versions of politically and socially engaged postmodernism that could counter the agendas of the ruling regimes.

In most of the case studies analyzed in this book, the contrasting agendas of governmental and oppositional forces mingled and overlapped with each other. In many Polish cases, such Marek Budzyński's North Ursynów in Warsaw or Romuald Loegler et al.'s Na Skarpie in Kraków, postmodern forms were used both by the government to build a positive image of the State and by the architects to pursue a counter-government agenda. This complexity is especially stark in Chile with the example of the CEDLA group and some of its members, like Cristián Boza, who was simultaneously one of the most active CEDLA members and an author of numerous designs complicit with Pinochet's vision. Intricacies like these reveal that the division between architectures endorsed by the State and architectures against the State proposed in this book is bound to be ambiguous. Projects such as Na Skarpie or North

DOI: 10.4324/9781003179467-6

120 Conclusion

Ursynów could be analyzed both in sections describing propagandistic and oppositional uses of postmodern architecture.

Essential to understanding projects like Na Skarpie or Santiago Poniente is acknowledging the oppositional intentions of the architects while keeping in mind their complicated relations with the State. Moreover, writing about the dissenting potential of Chilean and Polish postmodern architecture risks overblowing its actual transformative power, especially given that many of the progressive solutions proposed in these projects remained unrealized. Architects and urban planners did not overthrow Pinochet in Chile nor can they be credited with ending socialism in Poland. Nevertheless, they did play a role in changing their respective realities. To a degree, this question transcends the particularities of Chile and Poland in 1970s and 1980s and joins a broader conversation regarding the architect's role (or lack thereof) in social and political transformations. We can see a particularly skeptical view of the transformative possibilities of architecture in Manfredo Tafuri's *Architecture and Utopia Design and Capitalist Development*, in which he claims that architecture is incapable of generating meaningful changes in the social or political realm as, by default, it is always a part of power structures within which it was produced. For Tafuri, even if architects choose to take a political stance, their architecture cannot be politically critical in any true sense. Any fundamental changes in space need to be preceded by systemic transformations of the framework within which they emerge. Fredric Jameson, drawing upon Antonio Gramsci's enclave theory, responds to Tafuri's position, asserting that even though architects work within ideological frameworks that define the shape of their projects, they are nonetheless "able to form conceptions and utopian images" which are "as objective as material buildings: their possibilities – the possibility of conceiving such new space – have conditions of possibility as rigorous as any material artifact."[1]

Given Jameson's view on postmodernism it is perhaps ironic to use his theories to suggest the political validity of the design proposals analyzed in this book. However, the examples put forward in this book suggest that his thesis on postmodern architecture might be expanded after considerations of Eastern European and South American examples. Curiously, despite the fact that Jameson does not acknowledge postmodernism as a current that would offer any promise of challenging the status quo (he characterizes it as "vacuous of any utopian or protopolitical impulse" and as a "complacent free-play" from which "even the nostalgic memory of earlier commitments to radical change has vanished without a trace"[2]), he does note that "peripheral" locations can play a crucial role in imagining alternative political and social order through space:

> Those conditions of possibility can be found, first and foremost, in the uneven development of world history, and in the existence, elsewhere, in the Second and Third Worlds, of projects and constructions that are not possible in the First: this concrete existence of radically different spaces elsewhere (of whatever unequal realization) is what objectively opens the possibility for coming into being and development of "counterhegemonic values" here.[3]

Jameson does not elaborate on this speculation nor offer any in-depth analysis of particular case studies that would support this hypothesis, but the Chilean and Polish projects analyzed in this book present a response as to what such spaces could be and what they might teach us.

As with every example of urban design, these designs were embedded in the power structures on which they depended for their materializations,[4] but at the same time, they carried transformative potential ("open[ing] the possibility for coming into being and development of 'counterhegemonic' values," to use Jameson's words) that, combined with other instances of cultural dissent, eventually brought about real change. It is therefore possible to acknowledge the political role of the projects analyzed in this book without necessarily calling their architects "oppositional" (although, certain figures – like Bielecki – deserve this label more than others – like Boza) and while acknowledging their often problematic relationships with the power structures they wanted to contest.

In many ways, Chilean and Polish architecture in the 1970s and 1980s diverges from well-known examples of postmodernism. These differences vary from case to case with regards to the frameworks within which they emerged – from state (as opposed to commercial) patronage, through the utterly modern construction methods (prefabrication), to the lack of playful levity characteristic of postmodernism. Should we, then, call these works postmodern? Vladimir Kulić asks this question in his anthology of texts devoted to postmodern architecture in socialist countries: "Why, then, cling to an existing term that ultimately may be inadequate?" The reason, he writes, is "historiographic":

> to pry open a canonical historical formation in order to relativize its definition (however vague it may already be) as a way of destabilizing the established hegemonic narratives. If we were to invent a new term for the Second World phenomena described here, they could be easily relegated to their peripheral confines and continue to be ignored, as they have been for the past several decades. But by bringing them into the fold of a canonical concept and by demonstrating that they may have offered something dissonant and unexpected to its established definitions, we inevitably burst the very bubble of the canon.[5]

The reason to devote scholarly attention to locations neglected by mainstream architectural knowledge is not only to fill in our gaps in knowledge but also to undermine the very foundations of this knowledge as it rests upon West- and North-centered assumptions. In the same way, to discuss these examples as distinct phenomena would be to give in to claims as to their peripheral status, when they might instead be centrally folded into, thus destabilizing, canonical historical formulations.

Despite some critics' sense that "now is absolutely not the time to be indulging in postmodern revivalism,"[6] architectural practice and academic discourse in the last decade suggest that postmodern forms and theories still importantly inform working architects today. As this book has attempted to show, Chilean and Polish architecture offer different perspectives for understanding postmodernism, lessons quite different from those "learned from Las Vegas." Chilean and Polish architecture reveals that postmodern architecture was not necessarily focused solely "on aesthetics to the detriment of social content,"[7] it was not "the new corporate style," nor was it a movement characterized by "passivity vis-a-vis economic and political power."[8] Instead of formalist aestheticism and empty playfulness subjugated to commercial goals, architecture from these locations shows that postmodernism has the potential to function as a political and social project. Learning from the East and from the South, we can not only expand our sets of examples and definitions of postmodern architecture but also revise our understanding of the conventional architectural core and its historiography.

Notes

1 Jameson, "Architecture and the Critique of Ideology," 72.
2 Jameson, "Architecture and the Critique of Ideology," 83 and 87.
3 Jameson, "Architecture and the Critique of Ideology," 72–73.
4 This is true even in the case of unrealized design of Santiago Poniente as the architects still used institutional frameworks to make their project visible in the architectural discourse of that time: they responded to the call to revitalize Santiago Poniente issued by Pinochet-appointed mayor Patricio Mekis and they presented their project at the Bienal de Arquitectura, organized by Colegio de Arquitectos.
5 Kulić, *Second World Postmodernisms*, 3–4.
6 Griffiths, "Now Is Not the Time."
7 Cocotas, "Design for the One Percent."
8 McLeod, "Architecture and Politics in the Reagan Era," 29 and 38.

APPENDIX

Interviews

Interviews with Humberto Eliash, Pedro Murtinho, Pilar Garcia, Cristián Boza, and Fernando Pérez Oyarzún were conducted in Santiago de Chile; interviews with Marta Leśniakowska, Czesław Bielecki, Romuald Loegler, and Wojciech Szymborski & Ludwika Borawska Szymborska were conducted in Warsaw. Interviews with Chilean architects were conducted in English or in English in combination with Spanish. Interviews with Polish architects were conducted entirely in Polish. All translations into English are my own.

Interview with Humberto Eliash, August 23, 2016

(Chilean architect, founding member of the CEDLA group)

LK: What were the goals behind creating CEDLA?

HE: The story of CEDLA begins in London, 1975, when I met Cristián Boza, Fernando Castillo Velazco, and Fernando Montes. They were crucial for the creation of CEDLA two years later in Santiago. In London, we had a chance to visit the studios of Léon Krier and Rob Krier, as well as that of James Stirling. We knew with Cristián Boza that we wanted to go back to Chile. Fernando could not return to Chile, because he was in political exile, and he didn't know when he could come back. In London we made our first projects, taking advantage of the atmosphere of freedom which we couldn't find at the same time in Chile, because of the military regime and political infiltration of the universities there. When we decided to go back to Santiago, we realized that there would be no possibility for us to teach at the university so we created CEDLA.

LK: But eventually both Boza and yourself got to teach at the universities in Chile. When was that?

HE: It was in 1982 when I started teaching at Pontificia Universidad Católica de Chile – I graduated from Universidad de Chile and I wanted to teach there, but La Católica, which was a private Catholic university, was not as politically controlled as the national university. But eventually I got to teach at Universidad de Chile as well, starting in 1992.

124 Appendix: Interviews

LK: CEDLA published a magazine, *ARS*. How was it financed? I know that you got funding from construction companies, but how was it possible in the time of economic crisis when the construction industry slowed down significantly?

HE: I don't remember that it was a problem, ever. Nobody was worried about where the money came from. We not only sustained the magazine to express our ideas, but we also rented a house for our offices and gallery space, and every month we managed to pay the rent for it.

LK: Exactly, how did you manage to afford it, was anyone specific in charge of fundraising within CEDLA?

HE: Three people within the group had especially broad connections and many contacts – Cristián Boza, José Muzart, Pedro Murtinho – so they were mainly in charge of fundraising, but other members were doing this work too. We all had some projects, like every architect, so we were just asking the contractors and owners of the companies involved in our projects to contribute. Let's say we were designing a house with solar panels, so we would call them and said look, would you like to be advertised in our magazine? We needed money just to cover printing costs so it wasn't that much. [Eliash opens a copy of *ARS*.] For example, this company [points at advertisement], Cordillera, they paid the cost of the tiles that we used in the gallery. And everything was made like that with one exception – during the making of the third issue, we wanted to try out another way to finance it. We sent out a copy of the magazine with a letter asking for contributions, and we hoped that the people would simply pay us after they received the magazine. And – of course – nobody (or almost nobody) paid.

LK: But still, you managed to keep publishing the magazine.

HE: Yes, we never had problems with funds.

LK: I was wondering how you managed to criticize the government and its policies in the articles published in *ARS*. You even managed to have a very pro-government newspaper, *El Mercurio*, as one of your collaborators.[1]

HE: In Chile if you have contacts to the right people, you get what you want. That was true during the dictatorship as well. If you wanted to publish something in *El Mercurio* you just needed to find people you know and who work there and that's it.

LK: So they, *El Mercurio*, didn't back off from endorsing you even after your critical articles?

HE: No, I can't remember any problems really. They really didn't care what we are doing.

LK: How would you describe your relations with the Colegio de Arquitectos? The *CA* magazine published an official note welcoming CEDLA,[2] but I noticed that in the discussion sections of the magazine I rarely see CEDLA members as invited participants. Is that a coincidence, or were there some tensions?

HE: There were definitely tensions, but there is a difference between the Colegio de Arquitectos and the *CA* magazine published by it. The Colegio's head changed every four years, so naturally sometimes they agreed with us and sometimes not. But the magazine was always against our vision because its director, Jaime Marquez, was affiliated with the Pontificia Universidad Católica in Valparaíso and was very much critical of anything beyond the Valparaiso School.[3]

LK: CEDLA also organized meetings, for example the seminar in Caburga.[4] How was it possible to organize them, since meetings were forbidden by the government?

HE: The Caburga meeting was organized the same way we financed *ARS*. Two of us – Cristián Boza and Hernán Duval – had their houses there, so we just went there. The participants got there by train. We organized a seminar there and transcripts of our presentations and discussions were published in *ARS*. We also invited friends from Argentina, Colombia, and Peru. Argentinean contacts were especially important for us, because of the similar political situation of the dictatorship and a group of similarly minded architects with a group called La Escuelita. We tried to establish solid connections with La Escuelita, mainly with Tony Díaz and Justo Solsona, and other Latin American architects, like Juvenal Baracco.

LK: Since Caburga was an organized meeting, and you advertised it in *ARS*, I am still wondering, how was it possible to do it under dictatorship?[5]

HE: Well, in the 1980s the regime was more relaxed. Also, as for international contacts, in CEDLA we were inviting architects like Michael Graves or Aldo Rossi, and it was possible since La Escuelita was inviting them too. So, when they were already in Buenos Aires it was feasible for us to get them to Santiago, paying way less for tickets and simply hosting them in our houses.

LK: I also remember you saying that some people hesitated to come to Chile because of the regime.

HE: Yes, at the beginning nobody wanted to come, but in the second half of the 1980s it started to change. They wanted to support us as the opposition. Many of our guests made public declarations against the government or politicized universities, like Oriol Bohigas who came to Santiago on the occasion of the fourth Bienal de Arquitectura co-organized by CEDLA members.[6] It was the time when nobody wanted to come, but he said that he accepted the risk to come to the country ruled by the dictatorship because he suffered a similar isolation under Franco, so he understands us and wants to show his support. So yes, it was important for the architects that they were invited by an oppositional group. Same story with Aldo Rossi.

LK: But in *CA* these critical voices against the government voiced during Bienals weren't published, right?[7] Was there some internal censorship in *CA*?

HE: Yes. There wasn't explicit censorship of architectural publications or debates. But, for example, I remember that during a lot of the discussions during the Bienal de Arquitectura,[8] the public, especially the students, was voicing critical opinions against the government. Discussions which were part of the Bienal were then published in the *CA*, but excluding these voices. So there was a form of internal censorship within Colegio, and people were careful about what they were publishing.

LK: Who were your major theoretical inspirations?

HE: For me, Rossi, Krier brothers, Sterling, Jacobs, and Venturi were crucial for shaping an idea of what we want for the city and the society.

LK: What about Christopher Alexander?

HE: For me his philosophy of the city is central, yes.

LK: CEDLA emerged in a very particular time and in *ARS* you often criticize the neoliberal policies of the government. Did you treat architecture as a social and political project?

HE: Yes. CEDLA was a political project. We treated architecture as a social agent. Chilean society at that time was very divided and the neoliberal politics produced two things

126 Appendix: Interviews

that we were strongly opposing. The first was segregation, which pushed low-income people outside the city limits and welcomed only the middle and upper middle class in the city center. The second was that Pinochet's neoliberalism produced isolation, the society was becoming increasingly disintegrated and people were losing a sense of community. In this sense, CEDLA and Santiago Poniente were social and political statements, statements against that. At the same time, the group was also against the philosophy of the city embodied in San Borja, which also had alienating social effects.

LK: Would you say then that CEDLA's practice was an attempt to defend the city from two extremities – the late modernist approach to urban space (as in San Borja) on the one hand and the neoliberal approach to the city on the other?

HE: Yes. They were equally destructive for cities. I think that we trying to find a third way beyond these extremities.

LK: You were opposed to both late modern urban planning and the neoliberal approach to the city. Did CEDLA consider itself as an oppositional political project then, or was this thinking absent?

HE: It was oppositional, but not in terms of belonging to political parties, none of us were members of any parties, everyone was independent, but we tried to make politics through architecture.

LK: How different was your approach from that of Ciudad Abierta? They were also searching for the roots of Chilean architecture and its identity, also the social component and an emphasis on community building is present there as well, but in a different way than CEDLA. I was wondering if that was important to your discussions at all.

HE: We were really critical of this position. I had and have friends living and working there [Ciudad Abierta], but during the discussions we were on the opposite sites. We, CEDLA, believed that in order to be efficient, the city should be made in relation to the present reality, whether we like it or not, and they just isolated themselves. We criticized also the name – Ciudad Abierta – because it's not a "city," nor is it "open." It's rural (located on the beach) and not open, because it's gated, private.

LK: Are these debates between CEDLA and the members of the Ciudad Abierta community documented somewhere?

HE: No, they were private conversations, but I can tell you that they were extremely heated. With CEDLA, we wanted to do something very different than Ciudad Abierta, we didn't just separate ourselves but we tried to do something with the risk of contradictions. Just look at Boza's work, it's full of contradictions.

LK: Since you mentioned the work of Boza, did you discuss his works internally, within CEDLA? And did you – in CEDLA – identify any dangers in postmodernism?

HE: Yes, mostly we were critical of the understanding of postmodernism as simply the return of the historical forms. We were also very critical of caracoles designed by Boza, they are terrible for the city.

LK: Santiago Poniente is a manifestation of CEDLA's ideas and approach to the city. What other projects would you consider as especially important?

HE: The crossing of Amerigo Vespucio y Apoquindo streets and our social housing projects. We were very critical of social housing located on the peripheries, promoted by the State. Isolated little houses with no common public space, with limited infrastructure, and very far from urban connections, schools, etc. For my own practice, the work that

Appendix: Interviews **127**

were doing in CEDLA was very important and I incorporated some of the ideas that we worked on there in my later post-dictatorship housing projects.

Interview with Pedro Murtinho, August 30, 2016

(Chilean architect, founding member of the CEDLA group)

LK: How did CEDLA start?

PM: CEDLA was born as a reaction to the lack of possibility of architectural reflection under dictatorship. It was a reaction to an intellectual silence during dictatorship. We were inviting architects, like Peter Eisenman, organizing exhibitions, and designing projects. CEDLA was formed in 1977, and the first Bienal, where we presented Santiago Poniente, happened in the same year.[9]

LK: What was the relation between CEDLA and Colegio de Arquitectos de Chile?

PM: There was a tension. I was a director of the Bienal in 1983 and there was a tension obviously between *CA* and us, and specifically against me, because of Víctor Gubbins.[10]

LK: How did you manage to get funding for CEDLA?

PM: We are architects, so we had projects. And we had contractors. We fundraised among them and about 50% of the funding came from them and the other half was from us.

LK: How did you manage to get patronage from *El Mercurio* while being critical of the government politics?

PM: That wasn't a problem.

LK: But how, since you were critical toward the government?

PM: Architecture wasn't important for the government. Nobody cared.

LK: Did your position toward postmodernism change over the course of your time in CEDLA?

PM: It's hard to think about it in retrospect, but for us postmodernism meant the ideas like the importance of drawing, the human scale of the city and architecture, the importance of the street, typologies like the corner, the gallery, the courtyards, continuous façade. We were concerned with how the city works, not just the form itself.

LK: You don't use the word postmodernism often in *ARS*. Why not?

PM: We didn't care about declaring ourselves as postmodernists. But we were postmodernists. We were not like the Valparaiso school which always needed to stress that they are modern. For us, postmodernism was a cultural change. We thought that we were postmodern. We weren't interested in the form only but in the exploration of our roots, and of how the city functions. Postmodernism was a tool for us to look for other ways to think about the city. CEDLA was a critical movement concerned with architecture, but also with the state of the country. It brought strength and energy to criticize the current situation – the situation reduced to consumerism, mercantilism, and capitalism. I am not a communist. But the Chicago school that took over the country together with start of the dictatorship was terrible. We weren't political in the sense that we weren't linked to any political party, but CEDLA was a social project. It was a statement against the neoliberal treatment of the city as commodity, and it this sense it was oppositional. [interrupted by a phone call] … What were we talking about?

LK: You were saying that CEDLA was a statement against the neoliberal treatment of the city as commodity…

PM: Yes, exactly, and also against what projects like San Borja stood for. We were looking for something in-between. You know, we all went in different directions after CEDLA. Look at Boza for example, he went completely to the right.

LK: In *ARS* you introduced postmodernism as a functional, urban problem, not as a formal tendency or style, is that correct?

PM: Definitely. Postmodernism was important for us as a social problem, because the city is a social project. All architectural proposals must go together with social goals. I need to go, we can discuss something very quickly and meet again.

LK: Ok, let's start talking about the Santa Elvira project then.

PM: In this project we really fought hard with the investor. We fought because he didn't understand our principles of urbanism and social dwelling, and he was interested only in the commercial aspect. When we said that we wanted 30% of the project to be taken up by public space he simply said no way and insisted that it needed to be reduced to 5%. Let's continue another day, I'm already late.

Interview with Pedro Murtinho, September 1, 2016

LK: What readings were especially important for CEDLA?

PM: *Architecture of the City* by Rossi. Léon Krier, but we were interested more in his drawings than writing. [interrupted by a phone call] … Venturi, his *Complexity and Contradiction* especially. And Christopher Alexander.

LK: What was your (CEDLA's) attitude toward state agencies of urban planning, like CORMU?

PM: CORMU is a symbol of modernism, and its paradigm of the isolated tower. Like San Borja. San Borja and Santiago Poniente were symbols of CORMU's approach to the city based on the worst paradigms of modernism and Le Corbusier's urbanism of the isolated tower as a solution to urban problems. There was no reflection behind it and we were against it. It's not even that it was modernist, there was just no deeper thought behind it. We stood with CORMU's message of building for the people, working for the people, instead of subjecting architecture to market rules. But their approach to planning wasn't well thought through.

LK: What about CORMU as an institution, not its design philosophy, but its role for the country? I am asking because Humberto Eliash mentioned in the interview with me that it was important for CEDLA.

PM: Yes, I agree, it was very important for CEDLA and for me personally, even though I am not as socialist as Eliash, who especially in the times of CEDLA was very socialist or even communist. I think CEDLA was socialist but not communist, and Eliash was further left. This is why he has maybe more respect for CORMU than I do, as a state institution. Still, I am all for CORMU's ideals of social architecture.

LK: You mentioned Eliash's political beliefs. How would you describe your political position?

PM: I used to identify myself strongly with Democracia Cristiána.

LK: Humberto Eliash also said that for many of the foreign architects coming to Chile on CEDLA's invitation, their presence in Chile was like a statement of support of the opposition. Do you think that's an accurate statement?

PM: Yes. For example, Rogelio Salmona didn't want to come to Chile at all because of Pinochet. When I went to Argentina, I went to his lecture and I persuaded him to come.

Interview with Pilar Garcia, September 1, 2016

(Chilean architect, professor at the School of Architecture at the Pontificia Universidad Católica de Chile)

LK: In the 1980s, you were one of the initiators of a student journal, *Contrapropuesta* (*Counterproposal*) which was very much focused on postmodernism. Why did you decide to title the journal *Contrapropuesta*?

PG: It was a hard time for us in the school of architecture because of the context of the military government. Our school was closed for one year when the military government intervened. Before, during Allende´s government, the school was divided into three schools: architecture, urbanism, and public works.

LK: Could you say more about this division of the School in three parts?

PG: When I entered the school of architecture, it was already reunified by Hernán Riesco, the director of the school. Then in the early 1980s Gustavo Munizaga was named director of the school, he was an architect and urbanist, graduated from Harvard. He invited Cristián Boza, Manuel Moreno, and Hernán Duval to teach elective studios and I took them. This is how we, the students, learned all of these ideas of postmodernism. An important thing was that it wasn't a style, Cristián didn't speak of it as a style but he discussed postmodernism as an approach to the city. So *Contrapropuesta* was inspired by these ideas.

LK: So would you say that *Contrapropuesta* was a postmodern counterproposal to modernism?

PG: Yes, for us modernism destroyed the typology of our cities. It was a contrapropuesta, counterproposal, to the way of approaching the city and architectural design. Also, in modernist-oriented training there was no critical thinking beyond composition, we were just trained to operate by composition, there was no critical thinking behind that and this is something we really craved. We needed a platform to discuss, think.

LK: So, *Contrapropuesta* was a proposal against what was promoted by CORMU on the one hand and…

PG: Yes, it was funny, because my father was a director of CORMU. But when the military regime started he left CORMU, he met the CEDLA group and attended all of their meetings and events. I didn't know about that before I started my studies at the School of Architecture, I never heard about postmodernism from my father, I learned about it from Boza's and team seminars. Boza brought and make us read all these books, Rossi and others, and we didn't even have them in our school library. In these seminars we discussed postmodernism as an urban problem, a problem of how to design a city. We were finishing our studies, and we were taking part in CEDLA meetings, the one with Rossi for example. The architects involved in CEDLA taught us about people like Venturi or Graves and Europeans like Stirling, who was very important for Boza.

LK: Did you start *Contrapropuesta* in your 5th year?

PG: I don't remember, yes I think so… [showing photos]. This is the group, this is Hernán Duval, Juan Pablo Arrieta, Jorge Dominguez, Juan José Ugarte, and this is me, Jorge and Patricia Valenzuela. We were like a thinktank, or maybe it's an exaggeration, we were having meetings like once a week and discussing texts and projects, plus we also

130 Appendix: Interviews

run the magazine – the school of architecture lent us the photocopy machine so we could actually produce it.

LK: What elements of postmodernism did you consider relevant for Chilean architecture?

PG: Rossi, Krier, Colin Rowe …

LK: Was Venturi an inspiration as well?

PG: Yes very much, we had distance to his architecture, but his theory absolutely, yes. For us *Learning from Las Vegas* was like a big explosion, a revelation. But, we were aware of the dangers of postmodernism, that it can be treated like fashion, it's easy to treat it as a mere dress to change. Even though we did a lot of terrible things in our designs when we were young, and sometimes we are ashamed of it, we tried to be careful not to treat it as just another fashionable dress.

LK: You also mentioned that postmodernism was introduced as a problem of the city.

PG: Yes it wasn't about singular buildings, but about the city as a whole. Even though Boza's practice is a lot about individual buildings, many of the non-built projects were about the city. Because he is a very social guy, gained some jobs thanks to his social skills, but at the same time he was crucial for CEDLA's initiatives and very important for the popularization and dissemination of architecture in those days. He is a similar case to Cristián Undurraga who, thanks to his social skills, has always had good relations with the state, regardless of the political system. I don't know how he manages to do it. For example, he built Plaza de la Constitución and Barrio Civico as a result of winning competitions and maintaining good relations with Santiago's Town Hall in different political periods.

Interview with Cristián Boza, September 5, 2016

(Chilean architect, founding member of the CEDLA group)

LK: You worked at CORMU for two years. How did this experience influence your future career?

CB: I will tell you one story. One day in 1972, my director at CORMU asked me and my friend to go and buy wooden blocks. We had no idea why we were doing this, but we got the blocks and returned to the office. When we came back, we finally learned what they were needed for – they were used as models for buildings, he just took these blocks and arranged them evenly on the ground. I thought he must be joking! How can you build the city from wooden blocks like that? That moment made me start thinking about what "the city" is and what "city planning" is. Then I went to Edenborough, came back to Chile for a moment, and after that I worked with James Stirling in London. And then I came back to Chile, I wanted to teach here but due to the coup we weren't invited anymore to teach at the university. So I created CEDLA with Humberto Eliash, Pedro Murtinho, and a lot of other people. Since we couldn't teach at the university we thought, why don't we organize an institute to be able to freely discuss all the things that are important to us? Our ideas were rooted in postmodernism – Stirling, Léon Krier, Charles Jencks (whom I didn't like at all but his books on postmodernism were important), Aldo Rossi…. But it actually all started before, in London, when I met Humberto Eliash and we started to discuss about the city. When we returned to Chile all doors were closed to us so we decided to establish our own institute.

LK: Let's talk about CORMU for a minute, as from my previous conversations it looks like it was important for CEDLA. Did you share the social-oriented philosophy of CORMU?

CB: Absolutely. CEDLA shared with CORMU a pro-social idea of the city. This is visible in our project for Santiago Poniente. In this project, we focused on one part of the city and proposed our vision to recuperate this neighborhood. The key element was the central boulevard, La Rambla, and we wanted to keep the old, existing buildings, which were important for the community, such as the church, or places like the market square. Older architects couldn't understand this, and they were throwing shoes at us. Literally, when we presented Santiago Poniente for the first time, they were throwing shoes at us. It was like a fight between the old and young generations. It was very important for us to deal with the existing urban form, not deliberate on some abstract urban problems. We first wanted to analyze why places like Santiago Poniente weren't working, so we studied them following the method of, for example, *Learning from Las Vegas*. But the social component was crucial for us.

LK: Would you say that CEDLA was interested in postmodernism because of its social aspects?

CB: Yes, but it's very difficult to put it in words. Our position was: no to segregation, yes to the interchange of people. We tried to achieve this by creating public spaces based on traditional typologies, like street or square, and ensuring mixed-use spaces that encouraged people to interact. The design of Santiago Poniente was based on three typologies: the street, the square, and the boulevard, as places where people can meet, discuss, integrate and mingle. These elements were crucial. Our goal was to defend the old tissue and to foster integration of the people in the city, we were against the segregation and against the fact that low-income inhabitants were pushed to the peripheries of Santiago. We wanted to mix people with different incomes. And the students who came to see our project for Santiago Poniente were really enthusiastic about it all, so we thought we did our job.

LK: Can we go back for a moment to the origins of CEDLA? So, the idea of CEDLA was born between you and Humberto Eliash and then other people like Pedro Murtinho joined you in Chile. But what about Fernando Castillo Velazco? He couldn't join you as he was exiled, but did he take part in forming of CEDLA?

CB: Absolutely, he was crucial. He didn't join us in Chile as he was in exile in Cambridge, England. For us Fernando was sort of a statue, we respected him very much. He couldn't do CEDLA with us, but we went to conferences together, we discussed together. He agreed with us but couldn't act with us.

LK: How did you manage to find funding for CEDLA?

CB: We had very good connections with construction industries, they couldn't say no as we were their clients. Thanks to that we could bring the best architects to Chile – Aldo Rossi who stayed in my house, Álvaro Siza also in my house, Charles Moore, Tony Díaz and more…

LK: Yes, since you mentioned Díaz, was La Escuelita important for you?

CB: Yes, the idea of CEDLA was modeled on La Escuelita and we maintained close relations with this institute.

LK: What was your, CEDLA's, position toward the approach of Ciudad Abierta?

132 Appendix: Interviews

CB: Have you been there? Listen, the point is that the Valparaiso School of Architecture was a poetical act, and the actual, real, existing city wasn't important to them. The forms, and spatial craziness, the creative use of wood are all amazing, thirty years before architects like Benedetta Tagliabue were doing it. But this is not a city. A collection of very nice pieces of architecture, but not a city.

Interview with Fernando Pérez Oyarzún, September 6, 2016

(Chilean architect, critic and theorist, professor affiliated with Pontificia Universidad Católica de Chile, Director of Museo Nacional de Bellas Artes in Chile)

FP: Why are you interested in postmodernism in Chile?

LK: I am writing about how postmodernism was used both by Pinochet for propaganda purposes, and as part of oppositional agendas, as in the case of CEDLA.

FP: I am not sure about this, I think that this could be too simplistic. I feel that you are right in a certain way, but that you would need to be more precise to capture this correctly. It is true that in Chile postmodernism had a social agenda, but it also had a strong commercial agenda. Cristián Boza once compared postmodernism to the liberation brought by soft drugs, because it allowed the free use of forms. As a young professional he worked for CORMU in Allende's times, and then building "caracoles" in Pinochet times. This speaks a lot to changing trends.

LK: Yes, I am aware of this.

FP: A few years before assuming a very formalistic approach linked to postmodernism, Boza's work was characterized by a sensitivity close to that of James Stirling. It was very clear in his use of red tiles, which was common for the buildings he designed at that time; some of them are among his best projects. Postmodernism was one of the tendencies that informed his work.

LK: On the one hand, as you mentioned, postmodernism in Chile had this strong commercial component, but on the other hand, in what CEDLA was doing and publishing in *ARS* you can see how postmodernism was used to criticize the neoliberal policies of the government.

FP: In Chile, people with socialist beliefs mainly opposed postmodernism. They believed in rather traditional modern principles, at least in the form in which they evolved after World War 2. A good example of this were the architects involved in the *AUCA* magazine. CEDLA tried to link these new architectural ideas to some kind of social agenda, but I would say that the neoliberal agenda was stronger.

LK: What would you say about Santiago Poniente? Do you think that it was unsuccessful?

FP: It was completely unsuccessful and completely ignorant about the specific conditions of this historic traditional site. They were imposing something that was trendy at the moment. For instance, they were using the word "rambla," and you can never find a rambla in Chile. It is proper to use this term in relation to, for example, Havana, which has strong connections with nineteenth century Spanish culture, but not to Santiago de Chile. We don't have ramblas here!

LK: When I, for instance, talked to Humberto Eliash...

FP: He was always identified as left-wing man, which shows the complex nature of the relationship of politics and architecture in these times. But, again, if we look at Boza's career after the end of the dictatorship, it is clear that he was connected with people in power, like Sebastián Piñera, a right-wing business man and politician, who served two terms as the president of the country. I think that helped him get commissions. He was a very talented architect and he played a significant activist role in the architectural culture in the country, especially during the 80s and 90s, but his convictions about architecture weren't firm.

LK: Doesn't it boil down to a larger question of what dissent or opposition can mean in architecture? You always need to accept some external rules to remain practicing, unless you choose a path like Ciudad Abierta.

FP: Yes, Ciudad Abierta is an exception. I would say that if I was able to identify the most culturally important aspect of CEDLA, I would point to the recovery of a certain interest in architectural history, which was alien to most of modernist architects. More architects started to read historical texts again – Vitruvius, Palladio, eighteenth-century theoreticians. This renewed interest in history was very healthy for Chilean architects, and they learned about it, at least in part, through *ARS*. Secondly, this group was more sensitive to the urban fabric and to urban analysis, as well as to the understanding of urban morphology. Those tendencies had consequences for future generations, for people entering the practice in the 1990s – for instance, the famous generation of Chilean architects, like Alejandro Aravena or Smiljan Radic.

LK: Let's talk a bit more about complexities within CEDLA, particularly Boza's work.

FP: Those times were full of complexities. For example, Fernando Castillo Velasco, for a while, got embarrassed about the wonderful modernist work he had done as a partner of Bresciani, Valdés, Castillo, Huidobro (BVCH). This is surprising, especially if that work is compared with Boza's commercial buildings such as Eve or Lo Castillo, which, for me, are much less interesting architecturally and have no social agenda behind them.

LK: Absolutely, but in CEDLA there were very heated discussions at that point, and they – for example Humberto Eliash or Pedro Murtinho – were criticizing these projects very strongly.

FP: It is very complex, and also there are people who, when they looked back at their practice years after, were not happy with what they were doing at the time. For me, CEDLA is an interesting phenomenon worth studying but as a part of the recent history of Chilean architecture, as a symptom of the times.

Interview with Humberto Eliash, September 7, 2016

LK: I was thinking about figures like Nicolas Garcia, people who first worked with CORMU and then sympathized with CEDLA. Do you know about any similar stories?

HE: Yes, there were other people like Walter Bruce, for example, and there was an affinity in spirit between CEDLA and CORMU. CORMU promoted something we wanted as well – urban renewal – but they realized it in a fundamentally different, modernist, way. But we were supportive of the idea that the state take responsibility for planning and not give the city entirely to private hands as we saw under Pinochet.

LK: I recently talked to Fernando Pérez Oyarzún about Santiago Poniente and CEDLA, and we talked a bit about your use of typologies which for you were a way to regain the identity of the city threatened by neoliberal reforms. For him, they were artificial and imposed since you used typologies like La Rambla that aren't really Chilean.

HE: Well, Cristián Boza suggested the term La Rambla and maybe it wasn't the most appropriate term, but it's not about the name. The concept of the open promenade of mixed uses is present in many Chilean cities. In our projects, like in Santiago Poniente, everything happens on the street, activities are mixed, the society mixes, the architectural heritage is protected and intermingles with new buildings. We simply saw the city as integrated on many levels, in a formal and social sense. Maybe due to our lack of maturity we presented many things with inadequate language, but for us that was not the most important thing, terminology is only secondary.

LK: You said that one of the most important goals in Santiago Poniente was to act against segregation. How did you plan to achieve that mixing of people of different incomes?

HE: In our vision of the city, we wanted to mix uses, functions, and, most importantly, different economic strata of society. But we didn't have the actual tools to make it happen. It was mostly wishful thinking, given the market-driven reality of that time and the reality in which the military government was cutting the limbs of the state and giving more and more power to the private sector. Only years after the fall of the dictatorship did I manage to put these ambitions of social integration into practice.

LK: So the goal was to keep those people in the center instead of displacing them, but you didn't propose any specific solutions how to do it?

HE: Yes, we didn't have instruments to do it. But after the military government was over I managed to put it into practice, like in one of my housing projects I realized in la Reina.

LK: I also wanted to ask about La Escuelita as it seems like it was important for CEDLA. La Escuelita had a strong political and social component; for example, Avenida de Mayo could be interpreted as a political project.

HE: Yes of course! We knew the drawings of Avenida de Mayo, and yes, it was very important for us! In both countries we were living under dictatorships. And we were opponents of the military dictatorship. But also we thought in the same way about the role of architecture and the character of the city.

Interview with Fernando Pérez Oyarzún, September 12, 2016

FP: I think that in your research work you should put Chilean postmodernism against the broader background of what was happening in the country; I mean of course the political situation, but also other architects, mainly those linked to *AUCA*, who were opposing the dictatorship. You should probably also consider other South American countries, mainly Argentina and La Escuelita, which was very influential.

LK: Yes, I wanted to ask you about exactly those two things: 1. How other architects reacted to CEDLA, and 2. The relation with La Escuelita, which the members of CEDLA mention as their point of reference. With La Escuelita, I would like to talk about both similarities and differences between them and CEDLA.

FP: I think that that the main similarities, between La Escuelita and CEDLA were that they both emerged as independent organizations working under very difficult political conditions. Both shared a genuine cultural interest, in contrast to the economical and political agenda of dictatorships in Argentina and Chile. In both cases they contributed to the broadening of intellectual horizons for architects and brought some hope in very grim times.

LK: For Eliash, when I asked him, the political component of CEDLA and the fact that it emerged as a reaction to what was happening under the dictatorship was very important.

FP: For him it was that way. Both groups were outside of the system. But I am not sure if it's accurate to say that creating a statement against the regime was fundamental for CEDLA. There were people who strongly opposed the regime within CEDLA, but also people who did not worry about that.

LK: This was also my impression, that CEDLA wasn't homogeneous.

FP: I agree about that. Remember also about architects who were opposing both CEDLA and the government – like those associated with *AUCA*. *AUCA* defended the connection between socialism and modern architecture.

LK: CEDLA is not a monolith, I am aware of that. Boza – commercially oriented, then Eliash left-leaning and …

FP: Yes, because life and history are both complex. Boza was active in CEDLA but also taking part in the competition for the new Congreso Nacional de Chile building. The director of the competition was Horacio Borgheresi, an important character in the 1960s and 1970s. He was sympathetic to Democracia Cristiana, so against the regime, but he probably thought that it was better to get involved in the competition, in order to squeeze the best out of it.

LK: What were the reactions of other architects to the emergence of CEDLA?

FP: Architects were divided, some in favor of this new position, some against it. This was parallel to what was happening on the international scene – for example with Aldo van Eyck arguing against Rossi's ideas and defending the idea that there was a social project behind modern architecture that shouldn't be simply abandoned.

LK: I was wondering about the critical voices against CEDLA; for example, the *AUCA* circle was critical of CEDLA but the core of this criticism was CEDLA's postmodern sympathies. What about figures like yourself – people who weren't necessarily against postmodernism itself, but simply didn't think that CEDLA's approach was genuine?

FP: I was probably a rather isolated case.

LK: I also have an unrelated question: how did it happen that La Católica under Gustavo Munizaga decided to hire CEDLA members?

FP: I was in Spain between 1978 and 1981 when it happened. Gustavo Munizaga was a very complex character. He was mainly concentrated on urban studies and was considered a very charismatic teacher, interested in what new ideas could be brought into the school. His hiring policies were based both on academic merits and personal connections. Some CEDLA members joined during Munizaga's period but others had been hired before in a sort of open competition in 1974.

LK: Open?

FP: Well, yes, there was a call for academic hires when the school was reorganized under Hernán Riesco's direction. That's how Munizaga himself was elected. Montserrat Palmer from Universidad de Chile and Germán Bannen from the Valparaiso School were both engaged in the competition. Significant members of CEDLA like José Tuca, Max Nuñez, and Hernán Flaño, were already teaching at the school. Humberto Eliash had been Munizaga's teaching assistant at Universidad de Chile. Munizaga, who pursued graduate studies at Harvard under Sert's leadership, was very much connected to the young people. People like Eliash and Manuel Moreno got hired thanks to this connection. Gustavo was, of course, interested in what was happening in CEDLA, but at the same time criticized it. I should also mention that he was interested in social issues, mainly through urban design, and he didn't find that in CEDLA. Nevertheless, he was attracted to the intellectual value of CEDLA. His philosophy was to revamp the school with the help of young and active people and to hire new faces to make the school more attractive, but he didn't hire them because he agreed with CEDLA's ideas.

LK: Would you then say that during the time of Pinochet the Universidad de Chile was more free than Pontificia Universidad Católica de Chile?

FP: It's a difficult question. I would say that Universidad Católica was much luckier than Universidad de Chile under the dictatorship, in the sense that it was less politically controlled. Universidad Católica had a deputy rector, Hern**án** Larrain, who was, of course, right-wing, but was very intelligent, had an academic background, and could distinguish high-quality work from low-quality work. I think that this made Universidad Católica – despite that it was no doubt under political control – a more academically favorable environment. Within this system, there were of course parts totally under the control of the dominant ideology, like the Law School or Economics, but the School of Architecture was a rather different entity, one with more freedom. I think that Hern**án** Riesco was a man able to successfully mediate between different forces. Even some left-wing people were hired during his period, as he was genuinely interested in academic quality. Universidad de Chile suffered greatly from the continued changes of rectors designated by the regime, which made it difficult to take advantage of some academic developments, even those which were possible under such difficult political conditions.

Interview with Marta Leśniakowska, June 5, 2017

(Polish architecture historian and critic)

LK: When I sent you an email asking to meet and talk about postmodern architecture in Poland in the 1980s you responded that we should talk about "pleasant seminars during which we were saving the world, architecture and the homeland from the commies,"[11] organized by Czesław Bielecki. Could you elaborate on that?

ML: Czesław is the best person to talk about it.

LK: Who took part in these seminars? I assume that Jacek Zielonka and Marek Biskot were part of it (since they worked with Bielecki), who else?

ML: Yes, and also Wojtek Szymborski, Tomek Turczynowicz… These meetings were informal and they weren't regular. They were organized roughly every other month but sometimes once every two or three months. The participants were, on the most part, architects, but also for example scenographers or artists. Bielecki's book – "Gra w Miasto" which he published much later – is based on these seminars so it is a good source to study to get a sense of discussions happening there. The seminars took place in the 1980s, and very early 1990s. We were meeting at Wilcza street, in Bielecki's workshop.

LK: What readings did you discuss during these meetings?

ML: I really don't remember specific texts well, but generally speaking it was architecture theory, also some philosophy, but they were all centered around postmodernism. We were also reading a lot of Christopher Alexander because Zielonka was translating his book into Polish at that time. Jencks was an important author for sure…which I remember well because of intense discussions we had after reading him.

LK: What were the discussions about?

ML: I don't remember the details but in general, for us, in Poland, the interest in postmodernism was different than in the West. It was a chance to revive the traditions of Polish architecture instead of the universalist, international language of modernism. Postmodernism wasn't for us a matter of form, a matter of façade, we were interested in how the city works, we wanted to return to traditional urban forms such as streets, quarters or squares. We were interested in old traditional typologies. For us, the form was an expression of ideological and political attitudes. We understood postmodernism as a chance for the renewal of architectural vocabulary. We believed that the return to detail, to human and urban scales, traditional urban forms, to traditional thinking about urban fabric – very different from the oppressive character of late socialist architecture – would shape new kinds of social relations.

LK: Was postmodernism oppositional for you?

ML: Absolutely. The seminars at Wilcza street had a strong political dimension. The closer it was to the downfall of communism, the more chances we saw in creating new social forms with architecture and urbanism. It was strongly political, and of course Bielecki was the leader. Also, I should mention that his "Continuity in Architecture," which is a Polish manifesto of postmodernism, is a very political text.

LK: What else did you read?

ML: Venturi for sure…You know, the access to English-language publications at that time was very limited.

LK: I also wanted to ask about censorship in late socialist Poland. How would you describe censorship 1980s Poland in comparison to the 1950s or 1960s? I am asking mainly about architectural discourse of course.

ML: Everything needed to be approved by the censors. In the 1980s, I had a five-year long ban from publishing. In 1981 I wrote an essay for an exhibition catalogue, I don't even remember what it was about, but I refused to correct it and as a result I got the ban. In other words, censorship was gradually less intense with time, but it was still present in the 1980s.

Interview with Czesław Bielecki, June 9, 2017

(Polish architect and politician, founder of DiM group)

LK: I'd like to talk about your work in the 1980s, mainly about the Dom i Miasto (DiM) group that you established and its first presentation to the public at the International Congress organized by the International Union of Architects in 1981 in Warsaw during which the *DiM Charter* was presented.[12] When was DiM established?

CB: Our group was established during one of SARP's meetings in Gdańsk, in the Fall of 1980. This is when we started to formulate our views. We wanted to return to traditional forms of streets, to traditional urban fabrics, and as you can see from the condition of Polish architecture today, this postulate was never realized. But in short, we were an opposition, which is clear from the coda to our DiM Charter. As DiM, we felt

138 Appendix: Interviews

that the Congress would be a perfect occasion to voice our views on architecture. Our group included more than twenty members and it existed roughly until the martial law was introduced, on December 13th of 1981. After that I started to focus on underground activity completely. I tried to reactivate DiM in 1983 as a network of connected workshops gathered under this common name, DiM. It never came to fruition as there wasn't much enthusiasm for this idea.

LK: Did you interpret your activity in DiM politically?

CB: Everything was political in these times. We were a group of different personalities, but I definitely was a political animal.

LK: How was the DiM Charter presented?

CB: We printed the manifesto of the group on leaflets in Polish, French, English, German, and Spanish, and we distributed them among the visitors. I only have the French and Polish versions in my archive. We were endorsed by Solidarność.

LK: What was the character of this endorsement?

CB: We had close contacts with Solidarność, it was pretty simple; we explained our concept to them and they approved it, that's it.

LK: Was Solidarność interested in urban space and architecture?

CB: Not every member of course but some of them, for example Krystyna Zachwatowicz, did.

LK: What were the reactions to the DiM Charter among the public and critics?

CB: Foreign visitors, for example Charles Jencks, Joseph Rykwert and Paolo Portoghesi were very intrigued by our ideas and reacted very positively. Polish architects received DiM with mixed feelings, some of them were jealous of our connection with Solidarność, and that we managed to be endorsed by them.

LK: I would also like to ask you about the architectural seminars you organized on Wilcza street in your workshop. When did these meetings start and how long did they last?

CB: We started the seminars after I was released from prison in September 1986 and they were gradually losing intensity and frequency by the late 1980s. I was too busy with other activities and stopped organizing them; unfortunately nobody took over.

Interview with Romuald Loegler, July 1, 2017

(Polish architect, leader of the design team of Na Skarpie Estate in Kraków)

LK: You didn't design a lot of housing in socialist times. Why not?

RL: It was hard for me to work within the large concrete panel construction system. I had experiences from different countries where I studied and worked, and I knew that large panel construction methods could be used in great, creative ways, but in Poland it was just impossible. The list of prefabricates available in Poland was so limited, that you could build only very primitive, limited architecture, so it was a conscious decision. But for example in Prądnik Czerwony[13] we tried to squeeze as much as we could from this system.

LK: Was this realization a result of a competition?

RL: Yes, in this realization we tried to humanize late socialist architecture.

LK: Was it stated in the competition rules that it needs to be realized in prefabricated concrete panel technology?

RM: Yes.

LK: I'm asking because in the Nowa Huta competition, which you also won, it wasn't said that it needed to be realized in concrete panel construction, just that "all building materials and the construction technology needs to be generally available for realization in Cracow."[14]

RM: Yes, it is really interesting! I will tell you why. The competition was organized in a moment when the people knew that the system was fragile. The Party tried to resolve social tensions by showing its caring side and declared its attention to the people by the attempt to "humanize" architecture. They wanted architecture that would become a landmark in Poland. Zbigniew Zuziak[15] informed the organizer, the Cooperative Housing Association, that the entries should be postmodern proposals. But it wasn't official. It was stated unofficially and was not a part of official guidelines because everybody knew that postmodern architecture is expensive, for example due to its attention to detail and building materials. They organized this competition to show that the Party is going in a new direction. Prefabricated concrete was a symbol of the old, of everything bad in Polish architecture so they didn't want to mention it in the competition guidelines. The Nowa Huta competition was organized to appease unrest among the workers. They, the Party, wanted to show that they cared for the people in Nowa Huta, that's why the rules of the competition were different from most other competitions in late socialist times. The rules were defined by the Main Architect, Zuziak, a man who, simply by virtue of his position, was associated with the Party, and they were defined in a way that fit into the propaganda of humanizing architecture, about which I spoke before. For example, there was a recommendation to include pitched roofs, or that the buildings should have some architectural detail, like "historicizing" railing in the balconies.

LK: Would you see your projects as similar to what Budzyński was doing, as attempts to implement more progressive solutions within the possibilities of the time? From what you are writing and saying about your projects, it sounds like architecture was for you a medium for social change and an attempt to change social relations within the possibilities of late socialism.

RL: The intentions behind my projects, such as Centrum E or Prądnik Czerwony are parallel to Budzyński's intentions in Ursynów. This idea is analogical, no doubt. Of course, there are differences – like in Ursynów the greenery was one of the major elements to provoke social interactions. In our projects, we tried to create spatial remedies for social atomization and the anonymity of living in mass-produced, homogeneous housing estates by focusing on common spaces. Our goal was to create a bond between the people, and also identification of the inhabitants with the place they live in.

LK: With what technology was Nowa Huta built?

RL: "Wielki blok," which gave us more flexibility and allowed for some individualization.

LK: But it was more expensive than "wielka płyta," right?

RL: No! We managed to fit in the budget. Of course we struggled with material shortages, for example with aluminum.

LK: And, speaking of shortages, what is really amazing is that you decided to paint the external walls with poster colors as you didn't have access to proper color paint!

RL: Yes. I recently told this story at a conference in Berlin and the audience simply did not want to believe that it really happened, they thought that I was joking. Well, I wasn't joking, things like that were definitely possible in socialist Poland.

140 Appendix: Interviews

LK: Could you describe the function of the loggia?

RL: The intention was to create a new version of public spaces for interactions and gatherings known from historical cities – a nucleus of the urban. In our project, it was designed as an urban theater, a free and open platform for spontaneous activities, mainly for the local community, as well as a space for pre-planned shows or concerts. But the main point was to create a place where people could meet and talk without forcing them and without imposing anything, a place that simply invites everyone to be there. It was very different from socialist spaces. It was a symbolic way to give this space to the people and to encourage them to interact and cooperate without imposed regulations or rules, to free them from how people were taught to act in socialism, always on command, in a pre-programmed way.

LK: Why wasn't the loggia realized?

RL: Nobody wanted to invest in an empty space without a clear function assigned to it.

LK: I also wanted to ask you about the International Congress in 1981 which was a major event in the decade I am interested in. What was its role for Polish architectural discourse?

RL: It was very important, this is when Bielecki first presented DiM's [Dom i Miasto's] ideas. The congress was full of postmodern postulates, but not formalistic, they were mainly concerned with this attempt to humanize architecture, which I mentioned before, and which was so much needed in Poland.

LK: What was the reception of the DiM Charter?

RL: Bielecki interpreted postmodernism politically and for him it was clearly a critique of the regime. But also, in my opinion, this manifesto was superficial, it didn't help to solve any real problems. I know that many architects received it as superficial, and then when you see his realizations, and compare this theory with his later realizations, it is clear that he treated postmodernism in a superficial way.

Interview with Wojciech Szymborski (WS) and Ludwika Borawska Szymborska (LBS), July 26, 2021

(Polish architects, members of DiM [Dom i Miasto] group)

LK: I would like to talk about your engagement in Dom i Miasto, DiM. How did this group start?

WS: The leaders of the group were Czesław Bielecki, Jacek Cybis and Jacek Zielonka. We knew each other from the architecture school and we shared not only general beliefs, but also dissatisfaction with our work at state design offices which, at that time, was the only option to practice architecture and which forced us to work within a very rigid framework of prefabricated architecture. The way of thinking about urban planning practiced in these state design offices was abstract and theoretic, without respecting, analyzing or even considering particular urban conditions of a given site. The housing estates which were designed in these offices were complete negations of a traditional notion of the city. Long story short, DiM was in complete opposition to how we were taught to practice architecture in socialist Poland and what we needed to do in State Design offices. It was also an opposition against the government which dictated how we were taught architecture at universities and how state offices are operating. The break from traditional urban planning promoted at state design offices was a direct result of the politics of the government and it was designed to achieve political goals. State design offices were, of course, shaped not only by the socialist agenda of the government but also by Le Corbusier's ideas but his theories were then taken over by the communists. We had a strong sense that we live in times when we need to oppose the dominant discourse and this conviction informed our approach to architecture.

LK: Do you remember how the idea for DiM was born?

WS: This was Czesław Bielecki's idea, I also didn't work on the *DiM Charter* which was our manifesto.

LK: For Bielecki *DiM Charter* was a political manifesto. Did you think of it the same way?

LBS: Of course this was a political manifesto for us; we shared Czesław's beliefs and values.

LK: Bielecki said that DiM was supported by Solidarność. Can you say anything more about this?

WS: I don't know the details as it was all Czesław's agency. He was in touch with them, I remember that he was going to their headquarters on Mokotowska street and I remember that he even designed for them a very sturdy, brass sign that said "Solidarność" and that was screwed into the façade of their headquarters. I remember asking him why he made it so sturdy, and he said that something tells him that they (the government) will try to remove it so he didn't want to make it easy for them. And indeed, the sign was taken down around 1981 when martial law was introduced.

LK: Is it true to say that Solidarność was actively interested in architecture or it would be an exaggeration? Do you remember any particular figures in Solidarność interested in urban space?

WS: It's hard to say, I don't remember, but they had a culture department and I think that this is whom we contacted.

LK: Could we discuss the seminars on Wilcza street organized by Bielecki? What was their role?

WS: During these meetings on Wilcza we were discussing continuity in architecture; combining architectural alphabet from the past with contemporary font. We talked about the need to return to traditional, conservative urban planning that, we thought, doesn't get old. During these seminars we had discussions on urban planning, housing estates and how to design them, we were also talking a lot about designing urban squares and urban spaces and we thought that the government deliberately doesn't want architects to design them as they are gathering spaces, so spaces where connections and bonds between people are being formed which was dangerous to the regime. We talked mainly about this and that Warsaw should develop along the metro lines. We talked about the role of streets, we were also talking about Christopher Alexander's ideas (Zielonka was translating his book at this time) and about his canon of designing streets, about introducing elements that help people orient themselves in space. This is also when postmodernism was popular; when I look at this from distance, I think that it wasn't the best time for architecture but back then we were fascinated by postmodernism, by brothers Krier, by Stirling, Jencks, Venturi. We were in a way fascinated by postmodernism because of these links to traditional architecture.

LK: Marta Leśniakowska talked about this in an interesting way saying that for you the fascination in postmodernism wasn't formalistic but it was mainly about a different way of thinking about the city.

142 Appendix: Interviews

WS: Yes, postmodernism was aligned with our way of thinking about urban planning and the return to traditional thinking about the city.

LK: Were these meetings political in your opinion? Marta Leśniakowska described them as a way to "save the homeland from the commies." Did you, back then, felt this way too?

WS: Oh yes, I definitely agree.

LBS: Absolutely, this was natural for us back then. What is also important is that our parents and grandparents were always fighting with oppressive systems imposed on them so it was obvious for us, this was simply normal and natural.

LK: Were these postmodern ideas interesting for you also because you could use them in an oppositional way?

LBS: Yes, absolutely.

WS: Yes. We were desperate for change, change in both architecture and politics. We were surrounded by concrete prefabricate architecture and we wanted change. So yes, post-modernism was for us a way to achieve that. But pretty quickly we realized that this postmodernism is not real, that it won't work and that it is a passing fashion.

Notes

1 In the first issue of *ARS*, on the front page, *El Mercurio* is mentioned as one of the collaborators along with several construction companies.

2 "Saludamos a ARS," pages not numbered.

3 The Valparaíso School, or The Open City Group, is a group of the teachers and alumni at the Design and Architecture School in the Catholic University of Valparaíso. In 1971, they established an experimental housing colony – Ciudad Abierta (*Open City*) – which is a testing ground for their ideas of experimental architecture inspired by poetry and investigations of the material properties of the location.

4 A village 800 km away from Santiago. The meeting took place between April 6 and 8, 1984.

5 Free public meetings were prohibited by Pinochet's military government.

6 The Fourth Bienal de Arquitectura in Santiago (1983) was organized under the title *Patrimonio y Presente: La recuperación Crítica del pasado* (*Heritage and the Present: Critical Recuperation of the Past*) and was curated by Pedro Murtinho.

7 After each edition of the Bienal, *CA* published transcripts from discussions that took place within this event.

8 An architectural event (exhibitions, lectures, and discussions) organized from 1977 onwards in Santiago de Chile by the Colegio de Arquitectos.

9 The first Bienal de Arquitectura in Santiago (1977) was organized under the title *Patrimonio Nacional (National Heritage)* and was curated by Cristián Fernández Cox

10 Gubbins was the president of the Colegio de Arquitectos de Chile between 1982 and 1986.

11 Marta Leśniakowska, email message, July 8, 2016.

12 The Fourteenth International Congress of Architecture organized by the International Union of Architects under the title, "Architecture, Man, Environment," which took place between June 15, 1981, and June 21, 1981, in Warsaw.

13 Prądnik Czerwony housing estate, Kraków, 1987.

14 Loegler, "Konkurs SARP na rozwiązanie zespołu mieszkalnego," 53.

15 The Main Architect of Kraków, 1984–1991.

BIBLIOGRAPHY

Alexander, Christopher. *A Pattern Language: Towns, Buildings, Construction*. Oxford: Oxford University Press, 1977.

Allard, Pablo. "Traslademos el Congreso." *La Tercera* (April 9, 2012): 38.

Aman, Anders. *Architecture and Ideology in Eastern Europe during the Stalin Era: An Aspect of Cold War History*. Cambridge, MA: MIT Press, 1992.

"Architektów kłopoty z wolnością. Rozmowa z Cz. Bieleckim" (conversation between Tomasz Jastrun and Czesław Bielecki). *Architektura-Murator* 1 (1994): 26–28.

Arriola, Ricardo Contreras. "Editorial." *ARS* 7 (1986): 7.

"Bąbelki i socjalizm z ludzką twarzą: Pepsi-cola w PRL." *Polska Times*. August 18, 2010.

Barés, Enrique, Tomás Q. García, Santiago F. Bó, Roberto S. Germani, Emilio Sessa and Ivor Prinsloo. "Internacional Área de Remodelación en el Centro de Santiago Concurso Internacional." *AUCA* 24–25 (1973): 23–32.

"Bases y Fallo." *CA* 60 (1990): 28–30.

Basista, Andrzej. *Betonowe dziedzictwo*. Warszawa, Kraków: Wydawnictwo Naukowe PWN, 2001.

Bielecki, Czesław. "Ciągłość w architekturze." *Architektura* 3–4 (1978): 25–75.

———. *Gra w Miasto*. Warsaw: DOM Dostepny, 1996.

———. Interview by Lidia Klein. June 9, 2017 (published in Appendix).

Borawski, Ludwik, Jerzy Szczepanik-Dzikowski and Andrzej Szkop. "Dzielnica: młode miasto." *Życie i Nowoczesność: dodatek do Życia Warszawy* (July 6, 1971): 1–2.

Boza, Cristián. *Arquitectura, los dibujos previos*. Santiago, Chile: Corporación Cultural de Vitacura, 2015.

———. Interview by Joaquín Serrano in *Editar para transformar: publicaciones de arquitectura y diseño en Chile durante los años 60s y 70s, en el marco de la exposición Clip/Stamp/Fold*, edited by Pablo Brugnoli and Fernando Portal (Santiago: Capital Books, 2015): 158–167.

———. Interview by Lidia Klein. Santiago de Chile, Chile. September 05, 2016 (published in Appendix).

Boza, Cristián, Jorge Lührs, José Muzard, Hernán Duval, Teresa Lima-Campos, Eugenio Guzmán, Guillermo Hevia, Miguel Castillo, Pedro Murtinho, José Larraín, Luis González, Santiago Raby, Ricardo Contreras, Humberto Eliash, Ignacio Martínez, Carlos López, Pablo Astaburuaga, Roberto López and Eduardo Walker. "Tema II La ciudad de Santiago proposición para Santiago Metropolitano área Poniente anteproyecto Santiago Poniente Centro de Estudios de la arquitectura CEDLA." *AUCA* 34 (1978): 74–75.

144 Bibliography

Bristol, Katharine. "The Pruitt-Igoe Myth," *Journal of Architectural Education* 44.3 (May 1991): 163–171. http://www.pruitt-igoe.com/temp/1991-bristol-pruitt-igoemyth.pdf.

Brugnoli, Pablo and Fernando Portal (eds.). *Editar para transformar: publicaciones de arquitectura y diseño en Chile durante los años 60s y 70s, en el marco de la exposición Clip/Stamp/Fold*. Santiago: Capital Books, 2015.

Bruszewski, Andrzej. "Posłowie od redaktora." *Architektura* 3–4 (1978): 76–77.

———. "Od redaktora: Co dalej?" *Architektura* 379–380 (1979): 23.

Budzyński, Marek. "Architekt jako urbanista." Interview by Katarzyna Bilik and Karolina Matysiak. *Rzut* 6 (2015): 73–81.

———. "Betonowe Dziedzictwo." Marek Budzyński professional website. December 8, 2015. http://www.mbarch.pl/pl/teksty-i-idee/betonowe-dziedzictwo.html.

———. "Rozmowa z Markiem Budzyńskim" ["Interview with Marek Budzyński"] in *P2. Postmodernizm polski. Architektura i urbanistyka* [*Polish Postmodernism: Architecture and Urbanism, vol. 2: Interviews*], edited by Alicja Gzowska and Lidia Klein (Warszawa: 40000 Malarzy, 2013): 5–60.

———. "Ursynów Północny – uwarunkowania, zasady." *Architektura* 326–327 (1975): 25–26.

Budzyński, Marek, Ewa Przestaszewska-Porebska, Piotr Wicha and Anna Koziolkiewicz. "Pasaż Ursynowski – dyskusja." *Architektura* 417 (1984): 31–42.

Buszkiewicz, Jerzy. "Spotkanie konsultacyjne I Sekretarza KC PZPR towarzysza Edwarda Gierka z delegacja SARP przed VIII Plenum." *Architektura* 5–6 (1977): 7.

Cárdenas, Juan, José Covacevic and Raúl Farrú. "Primer Premio." *CA* 60 (1990): 30–38.

Carranza, Luis E. and Fernando Luiz Lara. *Modern Architecture in Latin America: Art, Technology, and Utopia*. Austin: The University of Texas Press, 2015.

Carvajal, Fernando. "Modernización autoritaria y cultura arquitectónica, Chile 1975–1992: una lectura crítica a partir del CEDLA." PhD diss., La Pontificia Universidad Católica de Chile, 2021. Repositorio, Tesis Doctoral, La Pontificia Universidad Católica de Chile. https://repositorio.uc.cl/handle/11534/48246.

De Castro, Sergio *El Ladrillo: bases de la política económica del gobierno militar chileno*. Santiago de Chile: Centro de Estudios Públicos, 1992.

Cichońska, Izabela, Karolina Popera and Kuba Snopek. *Day-VII Architecture: A Catalogue of Polish Churches Post 1945*. Berlin: DOM Publishers, 2019.

Christian, Shirley. "Chile's Handcuffed Press Can Still Jab at Pinochet." *The New York Times.* September 4, 1986. http://www.nytimes.com/1986/09/04/world/chile-s-handcuffed-press-can-still-jab-at-pinochet.html.

Cocotas, Alex. "Design for the One Percent." *Jacobin Magazine.* June 6, 2016. https://www.jacobinmag.com/2016/06/zaha-hadid-architecture-gentrification-design-housing-gehry-urbanism/.

Constitución de Chile de 1980. Barcelona: Linkgua, 2018.

Le Corbusier. *The Athens Charter*. New York: Grossman Publishers, 1973.

———. *Towards an Architecture*. Los Angeles: Getty Research Institute, 2007.

Cox, Cristián Fernandez. "Universalidad y peculiaridad en la dimension simbólica: un marco teórico." *ARS* 5 (1984): 13–16.

Dattwyler, Rodrigo Hidalgo. *La vivienda social en Chile y la construcción del espacio urbano en el Santiago del siglo XX*. Santiago de Chile: PUC, 2005.

Díaz, Francisco. "Los arquitectos y la falta de memoria." *Bifurcaciones: Revista de estudios culturales urbanos* (online journal). June 5, 2013. http://www.bifurcaciones.cl/2013/07/los-arquitectos-y-la-falta-de-memoria/. English version (unpublished): "Architects and the lack of memory: the project as alibi to forget. The José Domingo Gómez Rojas Park in Santiago and the Congress Building in Valparaíso, Chile." Essay, Columbia University Graduate School of Architecture, 2012.

———. "Complejidad y contradicción en la dictatura: Arquitectura y historia en el Chile de Pinochet" in *Santiago de Chile 1977–1990: Arquitectura, Ciudad y Política* (Santiago de Chile: Ediciones ARQ, 2021): 110–125.

Díaz, Francisco, et al. "Docoposmo: Documentacion y Conversaciones Sobre el Posmoderno." Leaflet independently produced and distributed. Santiago, 2008.

Dom i Miasto group. *Karta DiM*. Pamphlet. Warsaw, 1981.

———. *Drogi Rozwiązywania Kwestii Mieszkaniowej*. Pamphlet. Warsaw, c. 1981–1984.

Duval, Hernán. "Periferia metropolitana: algo mas que arquitectura." *ARS* 7 (1986): 9–10.

"Editorial." *ARS* 5 (1984): 7–9.

Edward Gierek na Ursynowie. Warsaw: TVP, January 8, 1977.

Eliash, Humberto. Interview by Lidia Klein. Santiago de Chile, Chile. August 23, 2016 (published in Appendix).

———. "La periferia dibujada." *ARS* 7 (1986): 11–21.

Fernandez, Julio. "2018 Dean's Roundtable," Center for Architecture, New York, November 3, 2018. https://vimeo.com/313237160.

Furman, Adam Nathaniel. "The Democratic Monument: Adam Nathaniel Furman's Manifesto for a New Type of Civic Center." *Archdaily*. July 3, 2017. https://www.archdaily.com/874860/the-democratic-monument-adam-nathaniel-furmans-manifesto-for-a-new-type-of-civic-center.

———. "Live interview with Adam Nathaniel Furman as part of Virtual Design Festival." *Dezeen*. May 22, 2020. https://www.dezeen.com/2020/05/22/adam-nathaniel-furman-screentime-vdf/.

Garcia, Pilar. Interview by Lidia Klein. Santiago de Chile, Chile, September 1 2016 (published in Appendix).

Gliński, Andrzej, and Zygmunt Skrzydlewski and Nina Smolarz. "Swiatowy Kongres Miedzynarodowej Unii Architektow." *Architektura* 326–327 (1975): 2–22.

Goldzamt, Edmund. *O polską architekturę socjalistyczną*. Warsaw: Stowarzyszenie Architektów Polskich, 1950.

Griffiths, Sean. "Now is not the time to be indulging in postmodern revivalism." *Dezeen*. October 30, 2017. https://www.dezeen.com/2017/10/30/sean-griffiths-fat-postmodern-revivalism-dangerous-times-opinion.

Groys, Boris. *The Total Art of Stalinism: Avant-Garde, Aesthetic Dictatorship, and Beyond*. Translated by Charles Rougle. London: Verso, 2011.

Gzowska, Alicja and Lidia Klein (eds.). *P2. Postmodernizm polski. Architektura i urbanistyka* [*Polish Postmodernism: Architecture and Urbanism, vol. 2: Interviews*]. Warszawa: 40000 Malarzy, 2013.

Habermas, Jürgen. "Modern and Postmodern Architecture" in *Critical Theory and Public Life*, edited by John Forester (Cambridge, MA: MIT Press, 1988): 317–331.

Harwood, Elain, and Geraint Franklin. *Post-Modern Buildings in Britain*. London: Batsford, 2017.

Hatherley, Owen. "Postmodernism will not be forgiven lightly for what it did to architectural culture from the 1970s onwards." *Dezeen Magazine*. August 20, 2015. http://www.dezeen.com/2015/08/20/postmodernism-not-forgiven-impact-architectural-culture-legacy-owen-hatherley-opinion/.

Hawthorne, Christopher. "Pritzker winner Alejandro Aravena on Pinochet, postmodernism, and building a house for $7,500" (interview with Alejandro Aravena). *Los Angeles Times*. January 13, 2016. http://www.latimes.com/entertainment/arts/culture/la-ca-cm-pritzker-winner-alejandro-aravena-hawthorne-interview-20160113-story.html.

Hearly, Derry. "Los arquitectos deben perder el tiempo." *ARS* 7 (1986): 26–30.

Herbst, Krzysztof. "Propozycje socjotechniczne." *Architektura* 326–327 (1975): 27.

Hernández, Pablo Fuentes. "La revista AUCA, 1965–1986: divulgación de la arquitectura y contribución disciplinar en el epílogo de la modernidad." *Arquiteturarevista* 7.2 (2011): 126–141. http://revistas.unisinos.br/index.php/arquitetura/article/view/arq.2011.72.04/638.

Hopkins, Owen. *Postmodern Architecture: Less Is a Bore*. London: Phaidon Press, 2020.

Ilori, Yinka. "Happy Street." Yinka Ilori professional website. May 17, 2022. https://yinkailori.com/work/happy-street.

Ioan, Augustin. "The History of Nothing: Contemporary Architecture and Public Space in Romania." *ARTMargins*. December 3, 2006. https://artmargins.com/the-history-of-nothing-contemporary-architecture-and-public-space-in-romania/.

Irving, Allan. "The Modern/Postmodern Divide and Urban Planning." *University of Toronto Quarterly* 62.4 (Summer 1993): 474–487.

Jacobs, Jane. *The Death and Life of Great American Cities*. New York: Vintage Books, 1992.

146 Bibliography

Jameson, Fredric. "Architecture and the Critique of Ideology" [1982] in *Architecture, Criticism, Ideology*, edited by Joan Ockman (Princeton, NJ: Princeton Architectural Press, 1985): 51–87.

———. *Postmodernism, or, The Cultural Logic of Late Capitalism.* Durham, NC: Duke University Press, 2003.

Jara Jara, Cristián. *Ciudad, sociedad y accion Gremial: los arquitectos de Chile en el siglo XX.* Santiago de Chile: LOM Ediciones, 2015.

Jencks, Charles. *The New Paradigm in Architecture: The Language of Post-Modernism.* New Haven: Yale University Press, 2002.

———. *The Story of Post-Modernism: Five Decades of the Ironic, Iconic and Critical in Architecture.* Chichester, West Sussex: Wiley, 2011.

———. *What Is Post-Modernism?* London: Academy Editions, 1986.

———. "What Then Is Post-Modernism?" in *The Post-Modern Reader* (2nd edition), edited by Charles Jencks (New York: Wiley, 2010): 14–37.

Klein, Lidia (ed.). *P1. Postmodernizm polski – architektura i urbanistyka* [*Polish Postmodernism: Architecture and Urbanism*]. Warsaw: Wydawnictwo 40000 Malarzy, 2013.

Klein, Naomi. "How Power Profits From Disaster." *The Guardian.* July 6 2017. https://www.theguardian.com/us-news/2017/jul/06/naomi-klein-how-power-profits-from-disaster.

———. *The Shock Doctrine: The Rise of Disaster Capitalism.* London: Penguin, 2008.

Klotz, Heinrich. *The History of Postmodern Architecture.* Cambridge, MA: MIT Press, 1990.

Kornai, János. *Economics of Shortage.* Amsterdam: North-Holland Publ. Co., 1980.

"Kościół na Ursynowie Północnym w Warszawie" (editors' discussion with Marek Budzyński and Piotr Wicha). *Architektura* 407 (1982): 61–69.

Krivý, Maroš. "Postmodernism or Socialist Realism? The Architecture of Housing Estates in Late Socialist Czechoslovakia." *Journal of the Society of Architectural Historians* 75.1 (2016): 74–101.

Kulić, Vladimir (ed.). *Second World Postmodernisms: Architecture and Society under Late Socialism.* London: Bloomsbury, 2019.

Lasota, Marek, Malgorzata Ptasinska and Zbigniew Solak. "Małopolska i Świętokrzyskie" in *Stan wojenny w Polsce 1981–1983*, edited by Antoni Dudek (Warsaw: Instytut Pamięci Narodowej, 2003): 217–285.

Lavin, Sylvia. "Architecture Itself and Other Postmodernist Myths." The Canadian Centre for Architecture website. May 17, 2022. https://www.cca.qc.ca/en/events/59012/architecture-itself-and-other-postmodernist-myths.

Leśniakowska, Marta. Interview by Lidia Klein. Warsaw, Poland. June 5, 2017 (published in Appendix).

Liernur, Jorge Francisco (ed.). *Portales del Laberinto. Arquitectura y ciudad en chile, 1977–2009.* Santiago: Universidad Nacional Andrés Bello, 2009.

Lipski, Zdzisław and Jakub Wujek. "Doświadczenia z projektowania i realizacji dużych zespołow mieszkaniowych na terenie Łodzi." *Architektura* 429 (January/February 1986): 18–40.

Loegler, Romuald. Interview by Lidia Klein. Warsaw, Poland. July 1, 2017 (published in Appendix).

———. "Rozmowa z Romualdem Loeglerem" ["Interview with Romuald Loegler"] in *P2. Postmodernizm polski. Architektura i urbanistyka* [*Polish Postmodernism: Architecture and Urbanism, vol. 2: Interviews*], edited by Alicja Gzowska and Lidia Klein (Warszawa: 40000 Malarzy, 2013): 154–201.

———. "Konkurs SARP na rozwiązanie zespołu mieszkalnego i koncepcji programowo-przestrzennej 'Skarpy' w Nowej Hucie. Dyskusja pokonkursowa." *Architektura* 429 (1986): 53–66.

McGurik, Justin. "Has postmodernist design eaten itself." *The Guardian.* September 12, 2011. https://www.theguardian.com/artanddesign/2011/sep/12/postmodernist-design-v-and-a-retrospective.

McLeod, Mary. "Architecture and Politics in the Reagan Era: From Postmodernism to Deconstructivism." *Assemblage* 8 (1989): 22–59.

Ministerio de Vivienda y Urbanismo, División de Desarrollo Urbano. "Política Nacional de Desarrollo Urbano." Publicación No. 114 (March 1979). http://politicaurbana.minvu.cl/wp-content/uploads/2012/10/Politica_19791.pdf.

Miranda, Carolina. "Rough, yet poetic: Chilean Architecture has its moment." *Los Angeles Times.* May 17, 2015. http://www.latimes.com/entertainment/arts/miranda/la-et-cam-chilean-architecture-goes-international-20150515-column.html.

Mouffe, Chantal. *On the Political*. New York: Routledge, 2005.

Murtinho, Pedro. Interview by Lidia Klein. Santiago de Chile, Chile. August 30, 2016 (published in Appendix).

———. Interview by Lidia Klein. Santiago de Chile, Chile. September 01, 2016 (published in Appendix).

Murtinho, Pedro, and Ricardo Contreras, Luis González, Humberto Eliash, and Santiago Raby. "Parque Santa Elvira." *ARS* 7 (1986): 54–57.

Myelnikov, Yevgeny. "Romantic Modernists." *Architektura* 379–380 (1979): 75–88.

Nadolny, Adam. "Postmodern architecture in the historical quarters of Poznan as a shaping element of the city's cultural environment." *Architectus* 2.32 (2012): 49–53. Accessed January 25, 2018. http://www.architectus.arch.pwr.wroc.pl/32/32_08.pdf.

"Nadzwyczajny Walny Zjazd SARP w stulecie organizacji polskich architektow 13–15 maja 77, Kraków." *Architektura* 5–6 (1977): 7–8.

"Najbardziej ludzka sypialnia" (discussion between Krzysztof Herbst, Jan Dziubecki, Marta Bieniasz, Dominik Dobrzański, Jerzy Szczepanik-Dzikowski, Marek Budzyński, and Stanisław Chrzanowski). *Architektura Murator* 6 (2005): 64–75.

Ockman, Joan. "Review: *Complexity and Contradiction in Architecture* by Robert Venturi." *Journal of the Society of Architectural Historians* 74.4 (December 2016): 490–492. http://jsah.ucpress.edu/content/75/4/490.

Ogólnopolska Narada architektów. Materiały do dyskusji. Zeszyt 3. Warszawa: ZG SARP, 1956.

Oyarzún, Fernando Pérez. Interview by Lidia Klein. Santiago de Chile, Chile. September 6 2016 (published in Appendix).

Palmer, Monserrat. "Urbanismo, ideologias y dependencia." *CA* 22 (1978): pages not numbered.

Pańków, Lidia. *Bloki w słońcu. Mała historia Ursynowa Północnego.* Wołowiec: Czarne, 2016.

Paperny, Vladimir. "An Interview with Denise Scott Brown and Robert Venturi." *Architectural Digest* (Russia) (July 2006): 36–41. http://www.paperny.com/venturi.html.

Pérez de Arce, Rodrigo. "The Garden of Intersecting Paths: The Remodelación San Borja and the Schools of Architecture." *ARQ* 92 (2016): 50–67.

Petit, Emmanuel. *Irony; or, The Self-Critical Opacity of Postmodern Architecture.* New Haven, CT: Yale University Press, 2013.

Portoghesi, Paolo. *Postmodern: The Architecture of the Post-Industrial Society.* New York: Rizzoli, 1982.

Preston, David A. *Latin American Development: Geographical Perspectives.* New York: Routledge, 1996.

Rabascall, Julia Talarn. "Chile's presidential palace basement was Pinochet's torture chamber." *Agencia EFE.* October 16, 2016. https://www.efe.com/efe/english/world/chile-s-presidential-palace-basement-was-pinochet-torture-chamber/50000262-3069436.

Ravenscroft, Tom. "Yinka Ilori covers adult playground in Pinterest's most pinned colours at Cannes Lions." *Dezeen.* June 21, 2019. https://www.dezeen.com/2019/06/21/yinka-ilori-playground-pinterest-cannes-lions/.

Rebolledo, Mauricio Becerra. "Las olvidadas erradicaciones de la dictadura" (interview with Cristián Palacios and César Leyton). *El Ciudadano.* December 17, 2012. https://www.elciudadano.cl/entrevistas/las-olvidadas-erradicaciones-de-la-dictadura/12/17/.

"Remodelación Santiago Poniente." *ARS* 1 (1978): 15–28.

Reyes, María Isabel Pavez. *Diseño urbano inclusivo para Santiago Centro: Concurso internacional 1972 Santiago de Chile.* Santiago: Universidad de Chile, Facultad de Arquitectura y Urbanismo, 2015.

"Rezolucja Krajowej Partyjnej Narady Architektow w dniu 20–21 czerwca 1949 r. w Warszawie." *Architektura* 6–8 (1949): 162.

Rigotti, Ana Maria. "El otro cruce de los Andes: Megaformas proyectadas en Argentina para Santiago" in *Sudamérica moderna: objetos, edificios, territorios,* edited by Hugo Mondragón and Catalina Mejía (Santiago: Ediciones Arq, 2015): 206–226.

Rose, Margaret A. *The Post-Modern and the Post-Industrial: A Critical Analysis.* Cambridge: Cambridge University Press, 1991.

Rossi, Aldo. *The Architecture of the City.* Cambridge, MA: MIT Press, 2007.

"Saludamos a ARS." *CA* 22 (1978): pages not numbered.

Shapira, Abraham. "Renovación Urbana: en busca de Consenso." *AUCA* 50/51 (1986): 15–18.

148 Bibliography

De Simone, Liliana. "*Caracoles* comerciales y otras especies en vías de extinción: La evolución del proto-mall en Santiago de Chile y su vigencia actual." *Bifurcaciones: Revista de estudios culturales urbanos* (online journal). September 24, 2012. http //www.bifurcaciones.cl/2012/11/caracoles-comerciales/.

Stanek, Łukasz. "Mobilities of Architecture in the Global Cold War: From Socialist Poland to Kuwait and Back." *International Journal of Islamic Architecture* 4.2 (October 2015): 365–398.

———. *Postmodernizm jest prawie w porzadku: polska architektura po socjalistycznej globalizacji* [*Postmodernism Is Almost All Right: Polish Architecture after Socialist Globalization*]. Warsaw: Fundacja Narodowej Kultury Bęc Zmiana, 2012.

Stepan, Alfred. "The Last Days of Pinochet?" *The New York Review.* June 2, 1988. http://www.nybooks.com/articles/1988/06/02/the-last-days-of-pinochet/.

Stern, Steve J. *Battling for Hearts and Minds: Memory Struggles in Pinochet's Chile, 1973–1988.* Durham, NC: Duke University Press, 2006.

———. *Reckoning with Pinochet: The Memory Question in Democratic Chile, 1989–2006.* Durham, NC: Duke University Press, 2010.

"Stonka w płynie " *Newsweek Polska.* July 29, 2007.

Szkop, Andrzej. "Rehabilitacja Ulicy." *Architektura* 326–327 (1975): 41.

Talesnik, Daniel. "Fue el posmodernismo la arquitectura del pinochetismo? Arquitecturas en el centro de Santiago en la década de 1980" in *Santiago de Chile 1977–1990: Arquitectura, Ciudad y Política* (Santiago de Chile: Ediciones ARQ, 2021): 96–109.

Tafuri, Manfredo. *Architecture and Utopia: Design and Capitalist Development.* Cambridge, MA: The MIT Press, 1973.

Undurraga, Cristián, and Ana Luisa Devés. ", Remodelación Plaza de la Constitución." *CA* 29 (1981): 8.

Urban, Florian. *Postmodern Architecture in Socialist Poland: Transformation, Symbolic Form and National Identity.* New York: Routledge, 2021.

"Vanguardia y Post Modernismo en Chile." *ARS* 4 (1981): 24–31.

Venturi, Robert. *Complexity and Contradiction in Architecture.* New York: Museum of Modern Art, 2011.

Venturi, Robert, and Denise Scott Brown and Robert Izenour,. *Learning from Las Vegas.* Cambridge, MA: MIT Press, 1972.

Weisman, Alberto Gurovich. "La Pintana: la ciudad interminable." *Revista INVI* 9 (1990): 5–19.

Walala, Camille. "Profile." Camille Walala professional website. May 17, 2022. https://www.camillewalala.com/profile.

———. "Walala Play." Camille Walala professional website. May 17, 2022. https://www.camillewalala.com/architectureinteriors/2019/1/15/now-gallery-walala-x-play

Weizman, Ines. "Citizenship. Mobilizing Dissent: The Possible Architecture of the Governed" in *The SAGE Handbook of Architectural Theory*, edited by C. Greig Crysler, Stephen Cairns and Hilde Heynen (London; Thousand Oaks, CA: SAGE Publications, 2012): 107–120.

Winn, Peter (ed.). *Victims of the Chilean Miracle: Workers and Neoliberalism in the Pinochet Era, 1973–2002.* Durham, NC: Duke University Press, 2004.

Woś, Rafał. "Gra w miasto." *Dziennik Gazeta Prawna.* October 10, 2013.

Wujek, Jakub. "Rozmowa z Jakubem Wujkiem" [Interview with Jakub Wujek] in *P2. Postmodernizm polski. Architektura i urbanistyka* [*Polish Postmodernism: Architecture and Urbanism, vol. 2: Interviews*], edited by Alicja Gzowska and Lidia Klein (Warszawa: 40000 Malarzy, 2013): 114–153.

Yurchak, Alexei. *Everything Was Forever, Until It Was No More: The Last Soviet Generation.* Princeton, NJ: Princeton University Press, 2006.

Zdhanov, Andrei A. "Soviet Literature – The Richest in Ideas, the Most Advanced Literature." Speech, Soviet Writers' Congress, August, 1934. Marxists Internet Archive. https://www.marxists.org/subject/art/lit_crit/sovietwritercongress/zdhanov.htm.

Zholtovski, Ivan V. and Yevgeny Myelnikov. "The Classics of the Soviet Architecture." *Architektura* 375–388 (1979): 82–85.

Zwoliński, Zygmunt. "Biuro Projektów Budownictwa Ogólnego 'Budopol' w Warszawie." *Architektura* 383–384 (1979): 4–18.

INDEX

Note: *Italic* page numbers refer to figures and page numbers followed by "n" denote endnotes.

Alexander, Christopher 7, 16, 64, 95, 104
Allard, Pablo 44
Allende, Salvador 29–38
apolitical legacy of postmodernism 12–15
Aravena, Alejandro 21
Arce, Rodrigo Pérez de 32
"Architecture and Politics in the Reagan Era: From Postmodernism to Deconstructivism" (McLeod) 12
Architecture of the 7th Day (Snopek, Cichońska, and Popera) 22
The Architecture of the City (Rossi) 6, 7
Architecture's Desire: Reading the Late Avant-Garde (Hays) 20
Architektura 74–79, 100–101, 109, 114
ARS 54, 55, 64–66
Ascension Church 106–109, *107, 108*
AUCA 37–38

Bajerska, Irena 106
Bergson, Henri 64
Berman, Ila 2
Bielecki, Czesław 17, 75, 77, 78, 90–95, 115, 116n5, 137–138
Borawski, Ludwik 100
Boza, Cristián 17–18, 23, 49, 50, 53, 56, 57, 69, 119, 130–132
Brown, Denise Scott 7
Bruszewski, Jerzy 77, 78
Budzyński, Marek 24, 90, 96–102, 104, 106, 109, 111, 114, 115
Bujas, Piotr 22
Buszkiewicz, Jerzy 101, 114

CA 37–38
capitalism 12, 21, 70, 72, 73, 94, 96, 97, 99, 114, 116
caracoles 50–53
Cárdenas, Juan 23, 42, 45
Carranza, Luis E. 27n89
Casa Republicii 18, 19
Carvajal, Fernando 22
CEDLA (Centro de Estudios de la Arquitectura, Center for Architectural Studies) 17, 18, 22, 23, 48–50, 53, 54, 56, 57, 60–66, 69; emergence, Santiago 49–56; origins 49–56; Santiago Poniente 56–62
censorship in Pinochet's Chile 37–38
censorship in socialist Poland 74–75
Chicago Boys 34, 35
Chilean National Congress 41, 44
catholic churches in late socialist Poland 108–109
The City Game (Bielecki) 95
Cocotas, Alex 2
Colegio de Arquitectos de Chile 37
Collage City (Koetter and Rowe) 5
community building 17, 49, 50, 57, 59–61, 88, 115
Complexity and Contradiction in Architecture (Venturi) 5
Congreso Nacional de Chile 38–46, 51
CORMU (Corporación de Mejoramiento Urbano, Corporation of Urban Improvement) 31–32, 35, 36, 38, 50, 56, 62
Covacevic, José 42, 45, 47n36
Cox, Cristián Fernandez 55

150 Index

The Death and Life of the Great American Cities
  (Jacobs) 4, 61
Del Sol, Germán 52
The Democratic Monument 14, 15
Devés, Ana Luisa 39, 40, 71n45
Dezeen 1
Díaz, Francisco 22, 41, 42, 44
Díaz, Tony 19
DiM Charter 91, 92–94
"Docoposmo" 22
Dom i Miasto (DiM) group 90–95, *91, 92, 93,*
  114–115
Duval, Hernán 71n39

Editar para transformar 22
Eliash, Humberto 17, 38, 49, 50, 53, 54, 56, 61,
  123–127, 133–134
Elser, Oliver 20
Exhibiting the Postmodern: The 1980 Venice
  Architecture Biennale (Szacka) 20

Farrú, Raúl 42, 45
Fernandez, Julio 2
Fitch, Robert 71n27
Foster, Hal 27n90
Frampton, Kenneth 27n90
Furman, Adam Nathaniel 13–15

Galigniana, Carlos Buchholtz 31
Garcia, Nicolas 62
Garcia, Pilar 129–130
Gierek, Edward 3, 101, 102, 108
Goldzamt, Edmund 97, 98, 117n38
Gomułka, Władysław 101
Griffiths, Sean 1, 2, 12, 13, 40
Gubbins, Victor 44
GUKPPiW 73, 74
Gzowska, Alicja 22

Habermas, Jürgen 11, 70
Hatherley, Owen 40
Hays, K. Michael 20
Herbst, Krzysztof 105, 114
Hopkins, Owen 1

I Am a Monument: On Learning from Las Vegas
  (Vinegar) 20
Ilori, Yinka 13, 14
Ioan, Augustin 18
Irony; or, The Self-Critical Opacity of Postmodern
  Architecture (Petit) 20

Jacobin magazine 2
Jacobs, Jane 4, 5, 16, 61, 104
Jameson, Fredric 11, 26n59, 27n90, 70
Jencks, Charles 8, 10, 16, 93

Katzenstein, Ernesto 19

kitchen architects 18
Klotz, Heinrich 26n55
The Klotz Tapes (Elser) 20
Koetter, Fred 5
Krivý, Maroš 99
Kuroń, Jacek 117n24

La Escuelita 19–20
La Pirámide del Sol 51
Lara, Fernando Luiz 27n89
Las Vegas 5, 6
Las Vegas in Rear View Mirror (Strieli) 20
late capitalism, logic of 20
late socialist architecture 17, 22, 94, 95,
  99, 107
Lawner, Miguel 31
Learning from Las Vegas (Venturi, Brown and
  Izenour) 5, 25n19
Le Corbusier 4
Leśniakowska, Marta 17, 95, 136–137
Leyton, César 36
Lipski, Zdzisław 114
Loegler, Romuald 16, 18, 78, 79, 81, 85, 90, 91,
  115, 138–140

Martin, Reinhold 20
McGuirk, Justin 12
McLeod, Mary 12, 27n90, 70
Mekis, Patricio 56
military government 17, 41, 48, 55, 56,
  61, 62
modern architecture 4, 8, 11, 12, 23, 77, 93
Modern Architecture in Latin America (Carranza and
  Lara) 27n89
modernism 5, 7–11, 16, 17, 50, 75, 76, 93, 95
Modzelewski, Karol 117n24
Montalva, Eduardo Frei 29–38
Moore, Charles 65, 75
Mouffe, Chantal 15
Muranów neighborhood 98, 99; view of *98*
Murtinho, Pedro 17, 49, 53, 66, 68, 127–129
Myelnikov, Yevgeny 76

Nadolny, Adam 28n98
Na Skarpie Estate (Centrum E) 79–89, *84,*
  85, 115
neoliberalism 12, 20, 22, 34, 48–49, 54, 56, 96
Neue Staatsgalerie 9
"New London Fabulous" 13, 15
The New Paradigm in Architecture: The Language of
  Post-Modernism (Jencks) 8
North Ursynów 100–114, *113*; architects of *112*;
  housing estate, plan *103*; spatial and functional
  analysis of *110*
Nowa Huta 80, 81, 86, 88

Ockman, Joan 5
Oyarzún, Fernando Pérez 44, 132–136

Palacios, Cristián 36
Palmer, Monserrat 62
Parque Santa Elvira housing complex *66–68*
A Pattern Language (Alexander) 7, 92
Petit, Emmanuel 20, 21, 45
Pinochet, Augusto 2, 3, 16, 18, 20, 21, 23,
    27–28n95, 29–47, 95, 126, 129, 132, 133, 136;
    dictatorship 48–71
Playland 3
Plaza de la Constitución (Constitution Square)
    38–46, *39, 51*
Polish People's Republic 72–89; *Architektura*
    74–79; postmodern architecture and
    propaganda 72–74
Polska Kronika Filmowa (Polish Film
    Chronicle) 101
*Portales del Laberinto. Arquitectura y ciudad en
    Chile, 1977–2009* (Liernur) 22
Portoghesi, Paolo 9, 10, 93
*Postmodern Architecture in Socialist Poland:
    Transformation, Symbolic Form and National
    Identity* (Urban) 22
postmodern revivalism 1–4, 12, 15, 16, 40, 119;
    apolitical legacy 12–15
*Postmodern: The Architecture of The Post-Industrial
    Society* (Portoghesi) 9
post-politics 15
The Presence of the Past 11

Radić, Smiljan 21
"Rehabilitacja Ulicy" ["The Rehabilitation of the
    Street"] 103
Riesco, Germán 30
Rodriguez, Sergio Miranda 31
Rohe, Mies van der 5
Rosende, Eugenio Salvi 31
Rossi, Aldo 6, 7, 16, 20
Rowe, Colin 5

San Borja housing complex *31,* 31–32
San Louis housing project 31
*Santiago de Chile 1977–1990: Arquitectura, Ciudad
    y Política* (Talesnik) 22
Santiago Poniente 32, 50, 54, 56–62, 68, 69;
    model of *58;* plan for *59;* sketches for *59, 60;*
    typological study *58*
Schinkel, Karl Friedrich 9
The Self-Critical Opacity of Postmodern Architecture
    (Petit) 45
SERVIU 62, 63, 66, 68

Siemiński, Waldemar 105
Simone, Liliana de 30
social housing 31, 62–68
socialist postmodernism 72–89
socialist realism 24, 72–73, 96–99, 103, 115–116;
    legacy of 96–99
Solidarność (Solidarity) movement 91–93, 96,
    116n6
Solsona, Justo 19
Stanek, Łukasz 22
Stern, Robert 26n63
Stern, Steve J. 37, 38
The Story of Post-Modernism (Jencks) 93
Stowarzyszenie Architektow Polskich (SARP) 73,
    74, 79, 101
Strieli, Martino 20
Szacka, Léa-Catherine 20
Szkop, Andrzej 106
Szymborska, Ludwika Borawska 140–142
Szymborski, Wojciech 140–142

Tafuri, Manfredo 27n90
Talesnik, Daniel 22, 30
The Timeless Way of Building (Alexander) 7
Trump, Donald 1, 2

Undurraga, Cristián 39, 40, 71n45
*Utopia's Ghost: Architecture and Postmodernism,
    Again* (Martin) 20

Velazco, Fernando Castillo 49
Venturi, Robert 5, 7, 64
Vesnin brothers 76
Videla, Jorge Rafael 19
Vinegar, Aaron 20
Viñoly, Rafael 19

Walala, Camille 13, 14
Walala x Play 13
Weizman, Inez 18
Western capitalism 96, 109
What Is Post-Modernism? (Jencks) 9
Wicha, Piotr 112
Wojtyła, Karol 109
Wujek, Jakub 114

Yamasaki, Minoru 8
Yurchak, Alexei 78

Zuziak, Zbigniew 80, 81, 139

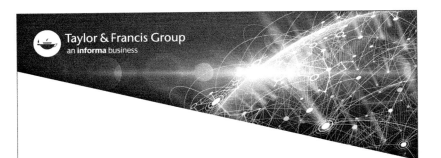